AQA French
Foundation

Marie-Thérèse Bougard

Jean-Claude Gilles

Oliver Gray

Steve Harrison

Ginny March

Nelson Thornes

Published in 2009 by:
Nelson Thornes Ltd
Delta Place
27 Bath Road
CHELTENHAM
GL53 7TH
United Kingdom

09 10 11 12 13 / 10 9 8 7 6 5 4 3 2 1

A catalogue record for this book is available from the British Library

ISBN 978 1 4085 0426 0

Cover photograph courtesy of Photolibrary
Page make-up by eMC Design, www.emcdesign.org

Printed and bound in Spain by GraphyCems

Contents

Nelson Thornes has worked in partnership with AQA to ensure this book and the accompanying online resources offer you the best support for your GCSE course.

All resources have been approved by senior AQA examiners so you can feel assured that they closely match the specification for this subject and provide you with everything you need to prepare successfully for your exams.

These print and online resources together **unlock blended learning**; this means that the links between the activities in the book and the activities online blend together to maximise your understanding of a topic and help you achieve your potential.

These online resources are available on **kerboodle!** which can be accessed via the internet at **www.kerboodle.com/live**, anytime, anywhere. If your school or college subscribes to **kerboodle!** you will be provided with your own personal login details. Once logged in, access your course and locate the required activity.

For more information and help on how to use **kerboodle!** visit **www.kerboodle.com**

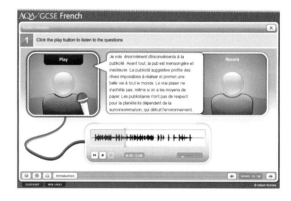

How to use this book

Objectifs

Look for the list of **Objectifs** based on the requirements of this course so you can ensure you are covering everything you need to know for the exam.

AQA Examiner's tip

Don't forget to read the **Examiner's Tips** which accompany the Controlled Assessment sample tasks, to help you prepare for the Speaking and Writing assessments. Listening and Reading **Examination-style questions** are available online so you can practise and prepare for the exam papers.

Visit **www.nelsonthornes.com/aqagcse** for more information.

AQA GCSE French – foundation

■ How to use this book

This book is arranged in a sequence approved by AQA which matches precisely the structure of the GCSE specification.

- The book is split into four sections, one for each Context of the specification.
- Each Context is split into two Topics.
- The Topics are divided into sub-topics which fit the Purposes of the specification.

At the beginning of each Context you will find the sub-topics, grammar and communication strategies listed, so you can see precisely how the content you are learning matches the GCSE specifications and be sure you are covering everything you need to know for your exams.

The features in this book include:

📖 Reading icon – you can listen to the reading texts in your book on *kerboodle!*, so you can hear the language spoken by native speakers as you read it. Interactive reading activities are also available.

🎧 Listening icon – audio material for listening and/or reading activities is online. Interactive listening activities are available on *kerboodle!*.

📹 Video icon – videos can be found online to support listening activities, with further interactive activities also available on *kerboodle!*.

🗨 Speaking icon – an activity designed to practise speaking skills. Worksheets for further practice are also available on *kerboodle!*.

✎ Writing icon – an activity designed to practise writing skills. Worksheets for further practice are available on *kerboodle!*.

Stratégie – outlines different strategies you can employ to help you communicate effectively. The strategy box includes the icon of the activity it supports: Listening, Reading; Speaking or Writing.

🌐 Strategy icon – When this icon appears next to an activity, you should use the communication strategy introduced in the strategy box on that page to complete the task.

Astuce – provides handy hints which you can use to help you with your language learning.

Grammaire – provides a summary of the main grammar point. Further grammar points are also provided here. Go to the pages listed to find activities to practise them.

G Grammar icon – an activity designed to help you practise the grammar point introduced on the page. You will also find interactive grammar practice on *kerboodle!*.

V Vocabulary icon – a vocabulary learning activity. The essential vocabulary used within each Topic is listed on Vocabulary pages. Here you can learn key words for each Topic. You can also go to *kerboodle!* to hear how they sound. Some words are in light grey. This is to indicate that you do not need to learn them for your Listening and Reading exams, but you may still want to use them in your Speaking and Writing Controlled Assessments.

> **Language structure** – boxes show you how to construct key sentences designed to help you carry out the Speaking and Writing tasks.

Controlled Assessment – Controlled Assessment tasks are designed to help you learn language which is relevant to the GCSE Topics and Purposes.

These tasks are not designed to test you and you cannot use them as your own Controlled Assessment tasks and submit them to AQA. Although the tasks you complete and submit to AQA may look similar to the tasks in this book, your teacher will not be able to give you as much help with them as we have given with the tasks in this book.

Go to *kerboodle!* to see sample answers. Look at them carefully and read the AQA Examiner's Tips to see how you can improve your answers.

AQA Examiner's tip

> These provide hints from AQA examiners to help you with your study and prepare for your exams.

Résumé – a summary quiz at the end of each Context tests key language and grammar learnt in that Context. This is also available as a multiple-choice quiz, with feedback, on *kerboodle!*.

Le sais-tu? – an anecdotal insight into facts/figures relating to the Context.

Numbers 1–20, ages and days of the week

1a 📖🎧 Read the bubbles and select the matching Post-it note: A, B or C?

Tu as quel âge?

J'ai quinze ans.

Tu as des frères et sœurs?

J'ai deux frères et une sœur: Lucas a quatre ans, Léo a douze ans et Marie a dix-neuf ans.

A
14 ans – 2 sœurs (4 ans et 24 ans)

B
15 ans – 3 frères (2 ans, 14 ans et 19 ans)

C
15 ans – 2 frères (4 ans et 12 ans), 1 sœur (19 ans)

1b ✏️ Complete the text below to match the other two Post-it notes. Look at *Grammaire* to help you.

1 J'ai _____ ans. J'ai _____ sœurs. Nadia _____ _____ ans et Anissa _____ _____ ans.

2 J'_____ _____ ans. J'ai _____ frères. Mehdi _____ _____ ans, Karim _____ _____ _____ et Adel _____ _____ _____.

1c 🗨️ Work in pairs. Partner A calls five numbers between 1 and 20. Partner B notes them down, and uses them in sentences. Then swap parts.

Exemple: **A** Deux, sept, treize, dix-neuf, vingt.
B J'ai 2 frères: Tom a 7 ans et Sam a 13 ans. Ma sœur a 19 ans … ah non, 20 ans!

2 ✏️ Solve the anagrams to find the correct days of the week.

1 dinlu
2 madichen
3 diuje
4 drinvede

Grammaire page 169

Saying your age
Remember you need to use *avoir* when saying how old you are.

Tu as quel âge? How old are you?
J'ai quinze ans. I am fifteen.
Elle a seize ans. She is sixteen.
Il a dix-huit ans. He is eighteen.

Vocabulaire

lundi	Monday
mardi	Tuesday
mercredi	Wednesday
jeudi	Thursday
vendredi	Friday
samedi	Saturday
dimanche	Sunday

Months, birthdays and time

1

Marion:	Mon anniversaire, c'est au mois de décembre.
Pierre:	Le vingt-cinq décembre?
Marion:	Non, le quinze décembre. Et toi?
Pierre:	Moi, c'est le dix janvier.

2

Charles:	Mon anniversaire, c'est le quatorze avril. Et toi?
Chloé:	Euh ... Moi, c'est le premier octobre.
Charles:	Le premier octobre? C'est aujourd'hui! Bon anniversaire!

1a 📖🎧 Look at the two conversations above and write the four dates digitally, for example 25/12, in the order they occur.

1b 🗨 Read the conversations in pairs. Then have a similar conversation about your own birthdays.

2 📖🎧 Match each sentence to the corresponding clock.

1 Il est cinq heures.
2 Il est midi moins cinq.
3 Il est huit heures vingt.
4 Il est une heure et demie.
5 Il est trois heures et quart.
6 Il est onze heures moins le quart.

a
b

c  d  e  f

3a 📖🎧 Reorganise the sentences below into chronological order, and write the times digitally (1–6).

Exemple: 1 07h15 (6)

1 Le soir, nous mangeons vers dix-neuf heures quarante-cinq.
2 Les cours finissent généralement à dix-sept heures.
3 Je prends mon petit déjeuner à sept heures vingt.
4 En général à vingt-deux heures trente, je dors.
5 J'arrive au collège à huit heures trente.
6 Je me lève à sept heures quinze.

3b 🖊 Adapt the sentences above to describe your own typical school day.

Vocabulaire

janvier	January
février	February
mars	March
avril	April
mai	May
juin	June
juillet	July
août	August
septembre	September
octobre	October
novembre	November
décembre	December
Bon anniversaire!	Happy birthday!

Dates in French *Grammaire page 172*

To say dates in French, use:
le + number + month.

le six janvier
(literally) the six January

The only exception is for the first day of each month:

le premier avril
(literally) the first April

Vocabulaire

et quart	quarter past
et demi(e)	half past
heures	o'clock, hours
midi	midday
minuit	midnight
moins le quart	quarter to

Time *Grammaire page 172*

■ To ask the time, you can say:
Quelle heure est-il? (formal)
Il est quelle heure?
Quelle heure il est?

■ A typical reply is:
Il est midi / deux heures et demie.

■ To say when something happens / is happening, use *à* to introduce the time:
Je me lève à sept heures.

Weather and seasons

Vocabulaire

il fait beau	the weather's nice
il fait chaud	it's hot
il fait froid	it's cold
il fait mauvais	the weather's bad
il pleut	it rains, it's raining
il neige	it snows, it's snowing
il y a …	its …
du soleil	sunny
du brouillard	foggy
du vent	windy
des nuages	cloudy
l'automne (m)	autumn
l'été (m)	summer
l'hiver (m)	winter
le printemps	spring

1 📖🎧 Read the weather report for today and forecast for tomorrow. Copy the grid and complete it.

La météo

Aujourd'hui, il y a du brouillard en montagne, mais il y a du soleil sur la côte et il fait assez chaud. Demain, il va continuer à faire beau avec beaucoup de soleil sur la côte, mais il va neiger en montagne. Dans la vallée, il ne pleut pas en ce moment, mais il y a des nuages. Il va probablement pleuvoir demain.

Region	Today	Tomorrow
in the mountains		
on the coast		
in the valley		

2a 📖🎧 Read the text and answer the questions.

Vous pouvez venir à Châtel en été si vous aimez le VTT. Si vous préférez le ski, venez en hiver. Il y a généralement assez de neige pour skier de décembre à avril. Les remontées mécaniques sont ouvertes pour les skieurs en hiver et pour les cyclistes en été. Évitez octobre et novembre, parce qu'il pleut beaucoup en automne. Il y a souvent du soleil au printemps, mais il fait assez froid. Si vous aimez les fleurs, venez en mai ou juin.

1 Which months have enough snow for skiing at Châtel?
2 Which season is best for mountain biking?
3 Are the ski lifts open in summer?
4 Which season is not recommended for a visit to Châtel?
5 What is the weather like in spring?
6 When would you go to look at flowers?

2b 💬 Work in pairs. Partner A describes the weather. Partner B guesses the season in question.

Exemple: **A** Il fait froid et il neige.
B C'est en hiver.

2c ✏️ Adapt the text of 2a to describe the different seasons in your region.

Grammaire — page 169

Describing weather

1 *il fait* + adjective: *Il fait beau.*

2 *il y a* + noun: *Il y a du vent.*

3 *il* + verb: *Il pleut.*

▪ Use *il va* + infinitive to talk about what the weather will be like:
Il va pleuvoir.

▪ To say 'in summer / in autumn / in winter':
en été / en automne / en hiver

▪ To say 'in spring':
au printemps

kerboodle!

Classroom equipment and colours

description	prix	coloris
Stylo GEL	2,50 € (les 2)	bleu, rouge, vert, violet, noir
crayon à papier	2 € (les 6)	noir
gomme	0,45 €	rose, orange, jaune
calculatrice SOLAIRE	15 €	gris, noir
règle plastique souple	1,20 €	rouge, jaune
cahier papier recyclé	3 €	blanc

SPÉCIAL RENTRÉE

Vocabulaire

blanc(he)	white
bleu(e)	blue
un cahier	notebook
un crayon	pencil
une calculatrice	calculator
un dictionnaire	dictionary
une gomme	eraser
gris(e)	grey
jaune	yellow
un livre	book
noir(e)	black
une règle	ruler
rose	pink
rouge	red
un stylo	pen
une trousse	pencil case
vert(e)	green
violet(te)	purple

1a 🎧 📖 Can these items be bought from the catalogue above?

1
2
3
4
5
6

1b 💬 Work in pairs. Partner A chooses from the items above and describes what she / he is looking for. Partner B guesses the correct number. Then swap parts.

Exemple:　A Je voudrais un crayon jaune et un stylo gris.
　　　　　　B C'est le numéro 3.

2a ✏ Complete with *un*, *une* or *des*, and make the adjectives agree when necessary.

Je voudrais _____ calculatrice gris___ , _____ cahier et _____ dictionnaire. Je vais aussi commander _____ stylos (_____ stylo bleu___ et _____ stylo rouge ___), _____ trousse jaune___ , _____ règle vert___ , _____ crayons et _____ gommes.

2b ✏ Adapt the text above to say what <u>you</u> would like to order.

Saying 'an' or 'some'

- How to say 'a(n)'/'some':
  un stylo　　a pen
  une gomme　an eraser
  des crayons　(some) pencils
  Although you can leave out 'some' in English, you have to include *des* in French.

- When using adjectives, make them agree with the nouns when necessary.
  un stylo vert　　a green pen
  une gomme verte　a green eraser

Grammaire page 160

Parts of the body and useful words

A *'Portrait du père de l'artiste' par Paul Cézanne*

B *'Picasso et les pains' par Robert Doisneau*

Vocabulaire

la bouche	mouth
le bras	arm
les cheveux (m)	hair
la jambe	leg
la main	hand
le nez	nose
l'œil / les yeux (m)	eye(s)
l'oreille (f)	ear
le pied	foot
la tête	head

1 📖🎧 Choose the correct words to complete each sentence. In each case, say which of the two portraits is being described.

1 On voit   la   les   jambes.
2 On ne voit pas   le   les   mains.
3 Il porte un bonnet sur   la   le   tête.
4 Il tient un journal dans   la   les   mains.
5 On voit seulement   la   l'   oreille droite.
6 On voit   le   la   nez, mais pas   l'   les   pieds.

How to say 'the'

- masculine: *le nez*
- feminine: *la tête*
- before a vowel: *l'oreille*
- plural: *les mains*

Grammaire *page 160*

2 🗨 Work in pairs. Partner A says one thing about one of the portraits above. Partner B guesses which one it is.

Exemple:

On voit les pieds.

C'est le père de Cézanne.

3 📖🎧 Complete the description using words from the vocabulary list.

La photo en noir _____ blanc est un portrait de Picasso _____ Robert Doisneau. Sur la photo, Picasso a 60 _____ 61 ans, _____ il n'a pas _____ de cheveux! Il ne regarde pas le photographe, _____ on voit qu'il a les yeux _____ noirs. On ne voit pas les jambes, _____ il _____ assis à table. On voit la tête, les épaules et le haut des bras. Pour remplacer les mains, _____ des pains sur la table. C'est _____ amusant!

Vocabulaire

alors	so
assez	quite
beaucoup	a lot
car	because
est	is
et	and
il y a	there is / there are
mais	but
ou	or
par	by
très	very

kerboodle!

Numbers and dates

1a 📖🎧 Replace the following digits with words from the vocabulary list.

> Mon père a 53 ans.
> J'ai économisé 99 euros …
> Ma grand-mère a 84 ans!
> Il y a 27 élèves dans ma classe.
> Mon nouveau jean a coûté 68 euros.
> Mon frère a regardé 75 matchs de foot.

1b 💬 Work in pairs. Partner A reads one of the numbers from the posts above. Partner B reads the corresponding sentence. Then swap parts.

Exemple: **A** Vingt-sept.
            B Il y a 27 élèves dans ma classe.

2 📖🎧 Read the text in the bubble, then complete the quantities required for each ingredient – using digits.

> Pour ce gâteau, il faut cinq cents grammes de pommes, deux cent cinquante grammes de farine, cent vingt-cinq grammes de beurre et cent grammes de sucre.

3a ✏️ Rewrite the following years using digits.

1   deux mille sept
2   mille neuf cent soixante-huit
3   mille neuf cent quarante-cinq
4   mille sept cent quatre-vingt-neuf
5   mille neuf cent quatre-vingt-seize

3b 💬 Work out how to say the year you were born in French.

> Je suis né en _____.

> Je suis née en _____.

Vocabulaire

27	vingt-sept
30	trente
40	quarante
50	cinquante
53	cinquante-trois
60	soixante
68	soixante-huit
70	soixante-dix
71	soixante et onze
75	soixante-quinze
80	quatre-vingts
81	quatre-vingt-un
84	quatre-vingt-quatre
90	quatre-vingt-dix
91	quatre-vingt-onze
99	quatre-vingt-dix-neuf
100	cent
999	neuf cent quatre-vingt-dix-neuf
1000	mille
2000	deux mille

Grammaire   *page 172*

Numbers

70 is literally 60, 10 (*soixante-dix*)

71 is literally 60 and 11 (*soixante et onze*)

72 is literally 60, 12 (*soixante-douze*)

And so on.

80 is literally 4, 20 (*quatre-vingts*)

81 is literally 4, 20, 1 (*quatre-vingt-un*)

And so on.

Use *mille* (the word for 1000) when saying years in French.

1995: *mille neuf cent quatre-vingt-quinze*

2010: *deux mille dix*

French Pronunciation

🎧 It is not hard to produce the correct sounds for a good French accent.

Remember that vowel sounds in French are not all exactly like English, and can change if they have an accent. You also need to know how some combinations of vowels sound. Vowels may have more than one sound depending on the word. Where this occurs below we have given examples.

a	*chat, grand*
e	*sept, le, entrer*
é	*café*
è	*crème*
ê	*fête*
i	*dix*
î	*gîte*
ie	*bien, géographie*
o	*dommage, poser*
ô	*drôle*
oi	*toi*
u	*tu*
au or eau	*beau*
eu	*deux*
ou	*rouge*
œu	*sœur*
ui	*puis*

Vowels followed by *n* have a nasal sound, e.g. *sans, gens, fin, bon, train, bien*.

🎧 Then there are some patterns of letters which make these sounds:

ç or ce or ci (soft c)	*garçon, morceau, cinéma*
ch (like English 'sh')	*chaussure*
ge or gi (the g is soft)	*géographie, gîte*
gn (sounds like 'nyuh')	*espagnol*
h (silent)	*hôtel, huit, thé*
ill (sounds like 'y')	*billet, bouteille*
qu (sounds like 'k')	*quel*

r / rr	growled slightly in the back of your throat, e.g. *Robert, marron*
s or t	at the end of a word these are usually silent, e.g. *gris, petit, mais*
ail (at the end of a word)	*travail*
ain (at the end of a word)	*demain*
ais or ait (at the end of a word)	*mais, fait*
an or am; en or em	*grand, chambre; sens, temps*
im or in	*impossible, international*

1 Now try saying these well known French-speaking places with the correct accent.

Paris   Bordeaux   Marseille   Belgique   Avignon

🎧 **The alphabet sounds**

A	ah	B	beh	C	seh
D	deh	E	euh	F	eff
G	zheh	H	ash	I	ee
J	zhee	K	kah	L	ell
M	emm	N	enn	O	oh
P	peh	Q	koo*	R	err
S	ess	T	teh	U	oo*
V	veh	W	doobluh veh	X	eeks
Y	eegrek	Z	zed		

* *oo* pronounced with your lips pushed forward

Typing French accents and punctuation

One way to type letters with accents is to click on: Insert > symbol > then find the letter and accent you want.

Alternatively you can hold down the ALT key and type these numbers. Make sure that the Number Lock is on. It may be different for laptops.

131 = â	133 = à	135 = ç	130 = é	136 = ê	0156 = œ
138 = è	140 = î	147 = ô	150 = û	151 = ù	0128 = €

Using a dictionary

French > English

- Make sure that you find the meaning that makes sense for the particular sentence you are translating. Many French words have more than one meaning, e.g. *le temps* = 'time' or 'weather'.
- If you are trying to work out the meaning of a verb, you will have to find the infinitive in the dictionary (ending in *-er, -re* or *-ir*) and then look at the verb ending to work out the person and tense of the verb, e.g. *mangez > manger* = 'to eat'.

English > French

- Make sure you know if the word you need is a noun (a person, place or thing), a verb (usually an action) or an adjective (describes a noun).
- Sometimes the word in English can be the same when written, even though you pronounce it differently.

Example of dictionary layout

Ignore the words in [ ]. They are there to show French speakers how to pronounce the English word.

light [laÎt] n. *lumière* **f.**

| English word | n. = noun | the French noun meaning 'light' | f. = feminine (you will need *la lumière* for 'the light' and *une lumière* for 'a light') |

light [laÎt] adj. *léger* **(not heavy);** *clair* **(colour)**

| adj. = adjective | the French adjectives for 'light' (two meanings) |

light [laÎt] vt. *allumer*

| vt. / vi. = verb | the French verb 'to light' (i.e. 'to light a candle') |

It is very important to understand that a dictionary will help you to find individual words, but you have to use your knowledge of how the French language works in order to put a sentence together. Very often the way a phrase is said is completely different from the English, e.g. *le chien de Paul* literally means 'the dog of Paul', but we would say 'Paul's dog'.

The most common mistake people make when using a dictionary is thinking that they can translate something literally word for word, without realising if the French they have looked up is a noun, verb or adjective. The result can be quite funny for an English speaker who knows French, but a French speaker won't understand anything.

Try to find the correct translations for these words.

1 a match (to light a candle)
2 a case (for clothes)
3 fair (as in fair hair)
4 move (as in move house)
5 fly (as in fly in a plane)
6 left (as in the past tense of leave)

1 Lifestyle

Food and drink; family members and pets

1 📖🎧 Find the correct label for each item.

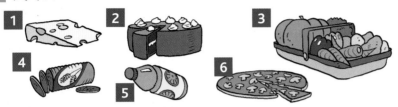

a beaucoup de légumes	d une bouteille de jus d'orange
b un paquet de biscuits	e un peu de fromage
c un gâteau au chocolat	f une pizza aux champignons

Vocabulaire

beaucoup de	a lot of
la boîte	box / tin
la bouteille	bottle
le champignon	mushroom
le citron	lemon
l'eau (f)	water
le fromage	cheese
le légume	vegetable
le paquet	packet
un peu de	a little

2 📖🎧 Use the words below to complete the Internet chat.

Clara Géniale, la photo de l'anniversaire de ta **1** _____ avec le chat, le chien et le **2** _____ rouge ! Elle a quel âge?

Théo Elle a 80 ans!

Clara Ton **3** _____ est où?

Théo Il est mort.

Clara Pardon … Il y a aussi ta **4** _____ et ton père?

Théo C'est mon beau-père. Mes **5** _____ sont divorcés.

Clara Et ta sœur?

Théo Je n'ai pas de **6** _____ . C'est Nadia, la petite amie de mon **7** _____ avec Tintin, le **8** _____ de ma grand-mère!

Contents and quantities

- Words expressing contents and quantities are followed by *de* (*d'* before a vowel):

  un litre d'eau
  une boîte de tomates

- Flavours and ingredients are introduced with *au, à la, à l'* or *aux*, and come at the end:

une tarte au citron	a lemon tart
une glace à la fraise	a strawberry ice cream

Grammaire pages 160, 170

Vocabulaire

le beau-père	stepfather
la belle-mère	stepmother
le chat	cat
le chien	dog
divorcé	divorced
la grand-mère	grandmother
le grand-père	grandfather
la mère	mother
mort(e)	dead
le père	father
le petit ami	boyfriend
la petite amie	girlfriend
le poisson rouge	goldfish

frère	mère	parents	grand-mère	grand-père	poisson	sœur	chat

Ailments and solutions

1a 📖🎧 Match each complaint with the correct picture.

1 Ouille! J'ai mal aux oreilles.
2 Aïe, aïe, aïe! J'ai mal aux dents. Oh, là, là!
3 J'ai mal au ventre, j'ai mal au cœur, j'ai envie de vomir.
4 J'ai un gros rhume et j'ai mal à la gorge. Ça ne va pas très bien.
5 J'ai mal au genou et j'ai mal au bras. Je suis tombé de vélo hier!
6 J'ai mal à la tête et au dos. J'ai de la fièvre. J'ai la grippe.

a  **b**  **c**

d  **e**   **f**

1b 💬 Work in pairs. Partner A says what's wrong. Partner B says which picture it relates to. Then swap parts.

Exemple: **A** Aïe! J'ai mal aux oreilles.
              B C'est "f".

2a 📖🎧 Use the words below to complete the following advice.

1 Tu as mal aux dents? Va chez le _____.
2 Tu es tombé de vélo? _____ de l'arnica.
3 Tu as mal aux oreilles? _____ chez le médecin.
4 Vous avez mal à la tête? Prenez de _____ et allez au lit.
5 Vous avez un rhume et mal à la gorge? Prenez ces _____ et ce sirop.
6 Vous avez mal au ventre? _____ ces comprimés et buvez beaucoup d'eau.

| dentiste | l'aspirine | pastilles | prends | prenez | va |

2b 📖✏️ Reply to this message. Then compare your advice with your partner's.

> Je suis tombé de vélo. J'ai mal au dos et à la jambe.
> Qu'est-ce que je fais? Merci d'avance.

Grammaire *page 169*

Describing ailments

J'ai mal is followed with *au, à la, à l'* or *aux* + part of the body.

J'ai mal au pied.	My foot hurts.
J'ai mal à la tête.	I have a headache.
J'ai mal à l'œil.	I have a pain in my eye.
J'ai mal aux oreilles.	I have earache.

Vocabulaire

le cœur	heart
les dents (f)	teeth
le dos	back
le genou	knee
la gorge	throat
la grippe	'flu
l'oreille (f)	ear
le rhume	cold
le ventre	stomach

Vocabulaire

bois / buvez	drink (command)
le comprimé	tablet
mets / mettez	put (command)
la pastille	pastille, lozenge
prends / prenez	take (command)
le sirop	(cough) syrup
va / allez	go (command)

Grammaire *page 168*

The imperative

Use the imperative to give advice.

Informal singular (the *tu* form):
Va chez le dentiste.
Prends de l'aspirine.

Formal or plural (the *vous* form):
Allez chez le médecin.
Prenez un comprimé.

1 ⓥ Sort these items of food into two categories: *bon pour la santé, mauvais pour la santé.*

| les chips | le chocolat | un chou-fleur | des fraises | du sucre | du jambon |

| de la limonade | du porc gras | une tomate | la soupe aux légumes | le yaourt |

| une glace à la vanille | le poulet | des frites | du beurre |

Des jeunes parlent de la nourriture

1 Je suis végétarienne depuis deux ans parce que je pense que manger de la viande est cruel. Je mange beaucoup de fruits et de salades.
Floriane, 15 ans

2 Mes copains aiment manger des hamburgers, mais moi je ne vais pas au McDo. Je pense que le fast-food est mauvais pour la santé.   *Christian, 14 ans*

3 Je mange beaucoup de chocolat. J'ai vu des émissions sur l'obésité et je sais que c'est un grand problème de notre société, mais j'adore le chocolat!   *Amélie, 17 ans*

Je fais attention à ce que je mange parce que je ne veux pas devenir grosse. Je ne mange pas de biscuits, de chocolat ou de gâteaux. En général je préfère la cuisine italienne, surtout les pâtes et les pizzas. **Patrice, 16 ans**

Je ne mange jamais de porc parce que c'est interdit aux musulmans. J'aime beaucoup le poulet et les légumes, surtout les haricots verts et les petits pois.
Halima, 14 ans

2a 📖 🎧 🌐 Read texts 1–3 and match them with pictures A–C. Which one of the three do you think has the least healthy diet?

2b 📖 🎧 🌐 Read all five texts and match the names above to the statements below.

1 I am aware of the obesity problem.
2 I can't eat certain things because of my religion.
3 I never eat meat.
4 I am fond of pasta.
5 I like eating fruit and salad.
6 I don't eat fast-food.

📖 When reading, look out for clues to help you understand the main messages, such as the layout, the title, the typeface and any photos or drawings. Pick out words you know already, then look at words that are similar in English, e.g. *végétarienne, pizzas*

Stratégie

3 🄶 Choose the correct form of the verb.

1 Elle   bois   boit   boire   souvent du jus d'orange.
2 Vous   aime   aimes   aimez   le fast-food?
3 Tous les soirs, ils   mange   manges   mangent   de la viande.
4 J'   adore   adores   adorer   manger des fruits.
5 Ils   boire   boit   boivent   trop de vin.
6 Nous   déteste   détestons   détestez   les légumes.

4a 🎧 Listen to Section A and choose the two correct statements.

1 Hamidou lives in America.
2 The people in his country eat a lot of fish.
3 Hamidou eats a lot of meat.
4 Most families in his country can't afford much meat.

4b 🎧 Listen to Section B and choose the two correct statements.

1 Sauces tend to be very mild.
2 Doussa is made with fish, lemon and onions.
3 Bread is eaten more often than potatoes.
4 Hamidou and his family often eat outside.

5 🗨 Work with a partner and ask and answer these questions.

1 Est-ce que tu aimes le fast-food? Pourquoi?
2 Tu aimes manger des fruits et des légumes?
3 Tu manges souvent des choses sucrées?
4 Tu es végétarien(ne)? Pourquoi / pourquoi pas?
5 Quel est ton plat préféré?
6 Tu prends toujours un petit déjeuner?

	parce que	
J'aime manger des fruits		c'est bon pour la santé.
Je n'aime pas les légumes		le goût est horrible.
J'aime beaucoup le chocolat et les bonbons		mais c'est mauvais pour les dents.
Je suis végétarien(ne)		j'adore les animaux.
Je ne suis pas végétarien(ne)		j'adore manger de la viande.
Je préfère le poisson-frites / le rosblf / les pizzas	parce que	c'est délicieux / pratique / équilibré.
Je prends toujours un petit déjeuner		c'est un repas important.
Je ne prends jamais de petit déjeuner		je n'ai pas le temps.

Grammaire page 174

-*er* verbs and *boire*

Most French verbs are -*er* verbs and follow the same pattern as *aimer*.

aimer = to like

singular	plural
j'aime	nous aimons
tu aimes	vous aimez
il / elle / on aime	ils / elles aiment

Boire (to drink) is an irregular verb and does not follow this pattern. Look it up in the verb tables on page 175 and make a table similar to the one above.

Also revise how to say 'some' in French.   *See page 28* ➡️

Est-ce que tu aimes le fast-food?

Pourquoi?

Oui, j'aime les hamburgers mais je n'en mange pas trop.

C'est mauvais pour la santé.

Astuce

Try to vary your language so as not to overuse certain words. There are, for example, alternatives to *manger* and *boire* such as *essayer, consommer.*

J'aime manger des yaourts, je ne consomme pas trop de sucre.

1.2 Le bien-être

Avez-vous la forme?

1

Deux semaines au Centre Blairot pour 20 euros. Offre spéciale d'introduction.

Deux visites par semaine à notre gymnase c'est exactement ce qu'il vous faut pour vous aider à garder la forme. Ici, pendant une visite d'une heure vous pouvez faire du cyclisme, comme sur la photo, et aussi courir sur place.

2

3 paquets de sachets "Relax" pour le prix de 2 paquets. Offre spéciale jusqu'à vendredi.

Vous ne dormez pas très bien? Vous avez peut-être une vie stressante? Chaque nuit, avant de vous coucher, il faut boire une tasse de notre infusion. Pour garder la forme, nous recommandons huit heures de sommeil par nuit. Notre boisson va vous aider à dormir, et à vous réveiller le matin plein d'énergie.

3

L'auteur va signer cette nouvelle bible anti-stress, venez dans notre magasin entre 10 et 11 heures samedi!

Voilà sept idées pour éliminer le stress:

- Pour me relaxer je joue de la guitare ou de la flûte.
- De temps en temps, je lis un bon livre.
- Le week-end, je fais souvent des promenades à la campagne.
- Je fais la grasse matinée de temps en temps.
- Tous les jours je me lève à la même heure, parce que la routine est importante pour moi.
- Je mange équilibré et j'évite les matières grasses et les sucreries.
- Moi, je cours dans le parc, comme ça je reste en forme.

Achetez le livre *Mille idées pour éliminer le stress* et trouvez des possibilités qui vont transformer votre vie et vous aider à vous relaxer.

1a 📖🎧 Read the adverts 1–3 and match them to the photos A–C.

1b 📖🎧 Read the adverts again and decide which of the statements below are true (T), which are false (F) and which are not mentioned in the text (?).

1 A two-hour visit to the gym is needed to fit in some cycling and running.
2 You shouldn't miss out the stepper machine in the gym.
3 Most people should have eight hours of sleep per night.
4 To get your anti-stress book signed, you need to go to the shop on Saturday morning.
5 One recommendation for relaxing is listening to music.
6 One person has a lie-in from time to time.
7 One person keeps fit by running round the race track.

2a 🎧 🔊 Listen to Section A of Docteur Bernard's advice, and fill in the gaps in the sentences below.

1 C'est une bonne idée de faire du sport _____.
2 Si vous n'aimez pas le sport, vous pouvez faire des _____.
3 Le sport vous aide à éviter les _____ cardiaques.
4 Pour combattre le stress, il est important de bien _____.
5 Il ne faut pas se _____ trop tard.

promenades   coucher   maladies

régulièrement   dormir   copains

Refer to the vocabulary (pages 30–31) to help with new words. The lists of words on those pages are the ones that are likely to be in the reading and listening exams, so you need to learn them! You might like to download the audio file to help you with the pronunciation. Try covering the English words and testing yourself, or asking a friend to test you.

Stratégie

2b 🎧 🔊 Listen to Section B, and fill in the gaps below.

1 Les jeunes ne doivent pas passer trop de temps devant l' _____ .
2 Beaucoup d'aspects de la vie peuvent avoir un mauvais effet sur le _____ - _____.
3 Il ne faut pas négliger l'_____ – manger bien c'est important!
4 Il ne faut pas manger trop de _____ - _____ .
5 C'est une bonne idée de boire de l'_____ regulièrement.

3 🄖 Work with a partner. First decide whether the gap should be filled with *faire* or *dormir*. Then decide what the ending should be and write down the missing word.

1 Il est sportif. Il _____ du sport tous les jours.
2 Je me couche à dix heures et je _____ à huit heures.
3 De temps en temps elles vont au centre commercial où elles _____ du shopping.
4 Vous êtes fatigué! Est-ce que vous _____ bien?
5 Ma sœur et moi, nous _____ dans la même chambre.
6 Tu _____ ton lit le matin?

Faire and *dormir*
Faire is an irregular verb.

faire = to make or do

singular	plural
je fais	nous faisons
tu fais	vous faites
il / elle / on fait	ils / elles font

Dormir is also irregular. Find it in the verb tables on page 176 and draw a table like the one above to help you learn it.

Also learn about adverbs of frequency.   *See page 29* ➡

Grammaire *page 169*

4 ✎ How healthy is your lifestyle? Write a few paragraphs about your own lifestyle.

- What do you eat and how often?
- How often do you do physical exercise?
- What time do you go to bed / get up?
- How do you relax?
- Do you think you are healthy?

To develop your writing, you can use negative forms. In other words, you can say what you don't eat and so on, e.g. *Je ne mange pas de viande, je ne dors pas bien, je ne me couche pas de bonne heure.*

Astuce

Je mange	souvent / rarement /	des frites / de la viande.
Je fais	quelquefois / régulièrement	de la natation / du sport.
Je me couche Je me lève	assez / très	tôt / tard.
Pour me relaxer, je	lis / fais du sport / regarde la télé.	
À mon avis je suis en bonne forme / je ne suis pas en bonne forme	parce que je mange / dors bien. parce que je ne fais jamais de sport.	

1.3 On parle de l'alcool et de la drogue

Objectifs

Discussing smoking, alcohol, drugs

Making negative sentences

Giving opinions

Les opinions des jeunes

Georges, 17 ans

On commence avec des cigarettes et de la bière. Plus tard on essaie le whisky, la vodka et les drogues dures. L'alcool et les drogues sont dangereux parce que c'est trop facile de devenir dépendant

Fatima, 17 ans

Je ne bois pas d'alcool parce que c'est contre ma religion. J'ai essayé les cigarettes mais je n'ai pas aimé le goût. Ça ne me dit rien.

Pauline, 16 ans

L'alcool est une drogue mais c'est une drogue légale et il est facile d'acheter du cidre dans les supermarchés. Je bois avec mes copines pour être sociable. Il est plus facile de parler aux garçons quand on a bu, on est moins timide.

Victor, 16 ans

Je bois pour oublier mes problèmes au lycée. Je me sens très stressé en ce moment à cause des examens. Quand je bois de la bière je me relaxe et je me sens bien. Je sais que c'est mauvais pour la santé mais je ne peux pas résister à l'alcool, surtout le samedi soir quand je suis avec mes amis.

1a 📖🎧 Read Georges and Fatima's opinions and complete these sentences.

1 According to Georges, young people start with _____.
2 They then move on to _____.
3 He thinks it's too easy to become_____.
4 Fatima does not drink because _____.
5 She doesn't like _____.

1b 📖🎧 Read Pauline and Victor's opinions and complete these sentences.

1 Pauline thinks it's easy to get hold of _____.
2 She drinks with her _____.
3 After drinking, she finds that she becomes less _____.
4 Victor drinks to forget his problems at _____.
5 When he drinks he feels _____.

2 🎧 Choose the correct English sentence for each speaker. Listen to Section A for Coralie and Félix and Section B for Maika and Olivier.

1 **Coralie**
   a I am a heavy smoker.
   b Cigarettes calm my nerves.
   c My parents don't know I smoke.

2 **Félix**
   a I still smoke from time to time.
   b I think my friends smoke to appear more grown-up.
   c I think cigarettes are very expensive.

3 **Maika**
   a Je ne fume pas parce que c'est trop cher.
   b Je suis contente, on ne peut plus fumer dans les restaurants.
   c Ma mère est en bonne santé.

4 **Olivier**
   a Certaines jeunes fument pour faire comme leurs amis.
   b Il est facile pour les jeunes d'arrêter de fumer.
   c Personne ne fume dans mon école.

3 **G** Work with a partner. Partner A reads out the sentence and Partner B makes it negative. Try to use *jamais* and *plus* at least twice each.

1 Il fume des cigarettes.
2 Je suis végétarien.
3 Ils se droguent.
4 Il prend un petit déjeuner.
5 Il va arrêter de fumer.
6 Je vais commencer à boire de l'alcool.

Making negative sentences

Put *ne* (or *n'*) before the verb and a negative word after.

Je ne fume pas.	I don't smoke.
Je ne fume plus.	I don't smoke any more.
Les fumeurs ne respectent personne.	Smokers don't respect anyone.
Je ne fume jamais.	I never smoke.
Ça ne me dit rien.	That does not interest me.

Also learn about using *avoir* and *être*. *See page 29* ➡

Grammaire page 168

4 🗨 🌐 Read these opinions and, with your partner, say whether you think they are true or not. Try to also give some extra information, e.g. why you think it's true / not true, and an example.

- Fumer cinq cigarettes par jour, ce n'est pas trop grave.
- Il est facile d'arrêter de fumer.
- Les jeunes boivent de l'alcool parce que ça fait adulte.
- Boire avec des amis, c'est sociable.
- L'odeur du tabac est désagréable.
- Le cannabis est dangereux.
- C'est bien, on ne peut plus fumer dans les restaurants.
- Après les drogues douces, on essaie les drogues dures.

🗨 Don't just say 'it's true' (*c'est vrai*) or 'it's false' (*c'est faux*), justify your opinion. If you agree, use a connective such as *parce que* (because). If you disagree, you can say that you think (*je pense que …*) or use *à mon avis* (in my opinion).

Stratégie

If you don't completely agree, you can qualify your opinion using terms such as *toujours* (always), *tout à fait* (completely), e.g. *Ce n'est pas tout à fait vrai.*

Astuce

Fumer cinq cigarettes par jour, ce n'est pas trop grave.

C'est faux, parce que les cigarettes sont mauvaises pour les poumons.

Je pense / crois / trouve que c'est	vrai / faux / ridicule / stupide / choquant / difficile à croire	parce que / car	il est difficile d'arrêter de fumer / si on ne fume pas, on n'aime pas l'odeur du tabac.
Je trouve ça			les jeunes boivent pour être sociables / pour se relaxer / pour s'amuser / faire comme les autres.
À mon avis c'est			toutes les drogues sont dangereuses / il est très facile de devenir dépendant.

Health

1 Look at the speech bubbles surrounding a panicky Pauline. Sort the advice into three groups.

1 Organisation   2 Leisure   3 Diet

Faire, dormir and *prendre*

This text contains examples of forms of the verbs *faire* and *dormir* which you have practised recently. You will also see forms of the verb *prendre* (to take), which you have probably met before, but not worked on recently. Can you pick them out?

See also page 28 ➡

Grammaire *page 174*

Tu peux être bien préparé pour les examens si ...

La veille de l'examen:

Tu ne révises pas à la dernière minute, mais …

a) Tu continues à faire des activités que tu aimes (sport, loisirs ...).

b) Tu limites les visites chez les copains: le stress se communique, et les copains vont parler de l'examen!

c) Le soir, tu manges léger, par exemple: assiette de pâtes, poulet, yaourt, fruit.

d) Tu prépares ton sac et tu penses à emporter le matériel nécessaire (stylos, calculatrice) et les documents importants.

Le jour de l'examen:

e) Tu manges bien avant de quitter la maison: du pain, des biscottes, ou des céréales, un fruit, du lait ou un yaourt, et une boisson (thé, café, chocolat ...).

f) Tu ne quittes pas la maison au dernier moment. Comme ça tu vas arriver calme.

g) Tu manges quelque chose pendant la matinée (barre de céréales, carrés de chocolat, biscuits ...).

h) Tu ne paniques pas pendant l'examen: tu vas avoir le temps de lire ta copie avant la fin de l'examen. À l'oral: parle calmement, articule bien.

2 📖 🎧 Read the advice for the day before and the day of an exam. Decide which piece of advice fits with each of the categories below and write the letter.

1 Preparing equipment.
2 Having a good breakfast.
3 Preventing friends from making you worry more.
4 Allowing enough time to get to school.
5 Staying calm during the exam.
6 Making time for leisure.
7 Eating sensibly the night before.
8 Eating an energy-boosting snack during the morning.

3a 🎧 Listen to Section A, the introduction to the interview with Thomas, a young sportsman. Which of the following sports does he NOT mention?

football   rugby   badminton   basketball
tennis   swimming   athletics   judo

3b 🎧 Listen to Section B. In what order does he mention the things represented in the pictures?

Vocabulaire

la veille	the day before
emporter	to take
s'entraîner	to train
le gymnase	the gym
les pâtes (f)	pasta
le poulet	chicken
le yaourt	yogurt

3c 🎧 Listen again and note the time at which each of the pictured activities occurred.

Exemple: **A** 07h30

(G) Health

How to say 'some'; Two irregular verbs

1 ✏ For each of the items pictured, write a sentence starting with *Je voudrais* (I would like) followed by one of the following expressions: *du, de la, de l'* or *des* and then the name of the item. Use the word snake at the bottom to help you.

Exemple:

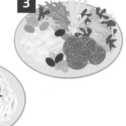

Je voudrais de la soupe.

Grammaire page 161

> **How to say 'some'**
>
> The French words for 'some' or 'any' are *du* (masculine), *de la* (feminine), *de l'* (before vowels) and *des* (plural). Note that most food nouns ending in -*e* are feminine, and that pasta is always plural.

 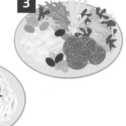  

eaufraisesgâteaupâtespouletsaladesoupe

2a 📖 ✏ Copy the verb table in the grammar box and make a similar one for *dormir*. You will find the verbs in the verb tables on page 174.

2b 📖 Choose the word that fits in the gap each time.

1 Qu'est-ce que vous `fait` `faites` `dormons` pour être en forme?

2 Je `dors` `fais` `font` de la musculation et l'été, avec ma copine, nous `dormons` `faisons` `font` beaucoup de randonnées en montagne.

3 Vous `dort` `dormez` `faites` bien?

4 Oui, je `dors` `dormez` `fais` environ huit heures par nuit. Par contre, mes frères `dormez` `dorment` `font` mal, parce qu'ils se couchent trop tard.

5 Ils `dorment` `dort` `font` souvent la grasse matinée?

6 Mon grand frère `dors` `dort` `fait` souvent la grasse matinée, mais mon petit frère ne `dort` `dormez` `fait` pas beaucoup.

Grammaire page 174

> **Two irregular verbs**
>
> Below is a table for the present tense of the irregular verb *faire*.
>
> *faire* = to make or do
>
> | singular | plural |
> |---|---|
> | *je fais* | *nous faisons* |
> | *tu fais* | *vous faites* |
> | *il / elle / on fait* | *ils / elles font* |
>
> To find the present tense of *dormir* look at the verb tables on page 174.

Adverbs of frequency; Negative sentences; Expressions with *avoir*

3 ✏ Put the sentences (a–f) in order from the least to the most frequent and copy down the expressions of frequency in each case.

a Je fais la grasse matinée de temps en temps.
b Je mange des légumes tous les jours.
c Je mange rarement des gâteaux.
d J'écoute toujours mes parents.
e Je fais souvent du sport.
f Je ne fume jamais.

Adverbs of frequency *Grammaire page 164*

The most common adverbs of frequency are:

de temps en temps	from time to time
ne … jamais	never
rarement	rarely
souvent	often
toujours	always
tous les jours	everyday

4 📖 Match the French and the English.

1 Il ne prend jamais de petit déjeuner.
2 Il ne mange rien au petit déjeuner.
3 Je ne mange jamais de viande.
4 Nous ne nous droguons pas.
5 Je ne mange plus de viande.
6 Il n'écoute personne.

a I never eat meat.
b We do not take drugs.
c He never has breakfast.
d I don't eat meat any more.
e He doesn't listen to anybody.
f He doesn't eat anything for breakfast.

Negative sentences *Grammaire page 168*

Look at the grammar box on page 25 where negative verbs were introduced.

5a ✏ Draw tables similar to the one for *faire* (on page 28) for the verbs *avoir* and *être*.

5b 📖 Choose the correct form of *avoir* or *être* each time.

1 Je n' ai est a pas d'alcool chez moi, car je ai suis est musulman.
2 Tu n' as es et pas d'énergie, parce que tu ai es est fatigué.
3 Elle a ai est très malade, elle a est ont un cancer du poumon.
4 Nous avons ont sommes trop de travail et nous avons êtes sommes très stressés.
5 Vous n' avez est êtes pas en bonne santé et vous a avez êtes mal au cœur.
6 Elles avons ont sont envie de prendre des drogues qui est ont sont dangereuses.

Expressions with *avoir* *Grammaire page 169*

Avoir normally means 'to have', e.g. *J'ai beaucoup d'énergie* / 'I have lots of energy', but in certain expressions it can mean 'to be', e.g. *J'ai faim* / 'I am hungry'. Learn the expressions below:

avoir … ans	to be … years old
avoir froid / chaud	to be cold / hot
avoir faim	to be hungry
avoir soif	to be thirsty
avoir raison	to be right / correct
avoir envie de	to want (to do something)

Health

Ce que je mange ➡ *pages 20–21*

le	beurre	butter
le	bifteck	steak
les	chips (f)	crisps
le	chou-fleur	cauliflower
	épicé(e)	spicy
	équilibré(e)	well-balanced
	essayer	to try
la	fraise	strawberry
les	frites (f)	chips
	gros(se)	fat
les	haricots verts (m)	green beans
	interdit(e)	forbidden
le	jambon	ham
les	musulmans	Muslims
la	nourriture	food
l'	obésité (f)	obesity
la	pêche	fishing
les	petits pois (m)	peas
le	plat (m)	dish
le	poisson	fish
la	pomme de terre	potato
le	porc	pork
le	régime	diet
la	santé	health
	sucré(e)	sweet
la	tomate	tomato
	végétarien(ne)	vegetarian
la	viande	meat

Le bien-être ➡ *pages 22–23*

l'	activité physique (f)	physical activity
une	alimentation saine (f)	healthy eating
le	bien-être	well-being
la	boisson	drink
se	coucher	to go to bed
	courir	to run
se	détendre	to relax, calm down
	dormir	to sleep
en	bonne forme	in good shape
	faire des promenades	to go for walks
	faire des randonnées	to go hiking
	garder la forme	to keep in shape
se	lever	to get up
les	maladies cardiaques (f)	heart disease
	manger équilibré	to eat a well-balanced diet
	prévenir	to prevent, warn
se	réveiller	to wake up
se	sentir bien	to feel well
le	sommeil	sleep
	stressant(e)	stressful

1 Ⓥ *L'activité physique, la relaxation ou une alimentation saine?* With a partner, decide which of these categories each of the following activities falls into:

courir régulièrement   lire des magazines

bien dormir   se coucher tôt

éviter le chocolat   écouter de la musique

manger des légumes   faire du cyclisme

boire assez d'eau

On parle de l'alcool et de la drogue

➡ *pages 24–25*

	arrêter	to stop
	dangereux(-euse)	dangerous
se	*droguer*	to take drugs
les	*drogues douces (f)*	soft drugs
les	*drogues dures (f)*	hard drugs
	fort(e)	strong
	fumer	to smoke
le	*fumeur*	smoker (m)
le	*goût*	taste
l'	*habitude (f)*	habit
	malade	ill, sick, unwell
le	*non-fumeur*	non-smoker (m)
l'	*odeur (f)*	odour
	oublier	to forget
les	*poumons (m)*	the lungs
la	*pression*	pressure
se	*relaxer*	to relax
	respirer	to breathe
le	*tabac*	tobacco
	tousser	to cough
	vivre	to live

2 🇻 Sort the following into three groups: A for words to do with smoking; B for words to do with alcohol; C for words to do with drugs.

boire	fumer	se droguer
un dealer		arrêter de fumer
le tabac	le cannabis	tousser
le vin	un comprimé	
non-fumeur	la bière	
les poumons	la cocaïne	

Quantity and measurement

	assez	enough
	beaucoup	lots
la	*boîte*	box, tin
la	*bouteille*	bottle
un	*centimètre*	centimetre
	demi(e)	half
	encore de	more (of)
un	*gramme*	gramme
	grand(e)	big, tall
	gros(se)	big, fat
un	*kilo*	kilo
	large	wide
un	*litre*	litre
	maigre	thin
un	*mètre*	metre
	mince	thin
le	*morceau*	piece
le	*moyen*	average
le	*paquet*	packet
	pas mal de	quite a lot of
	petit(e)	small, little
	peu de	a little of
	plein de	lots of, full of
la	*pointure*	size
	rien	nothing
la	*tranche*	slice
	suffisamment	plenty
la	*taille*	size
	très	very
	trop	too (much)

🇻 Various words to do with quantities and measurement have been summarised for you here. They will be useful with this and many other topics that you are going to study for your exam.

Stratégie

1.4 La famille

Objectifs

Talking about your family

How to say 'my', 'your' etc.

Working out the meaning of words

Une famille camerounaise

Aminata habite à Yaoundé, la capitale du Cameroun, en Afrique. Elle habite avec sa belle-mère, la deuxième femme de son père. Elle a deux frères, trois demi-frères et trois demi-sœurs. Avec Aminata, ça fait neuf enfants dans la petite maison! Si on compte le père et les deux mères, ça fait douze personnes en tout!

Aminata pense que la situation est tout à fait normale, parce qu'au Cameroun beaucoup de maris ont deux ou même trois femmes. Sa mère et sa belle-mère travaillent ensemble à la maison, et le soir, tout le monde mange ensemble. Son père ne veut pas de divisions entre les deux parties de la famille.

Ce système a des problèmes, mais aussi des avantages. En France le divorce est de plus en plus commun, et beaucoup d'enfants sont tristes parce que leurs parents sont séparés. Beaucoup de pères ne voient plus leurs enfants, et de nombreuses mères sont seules avec les enfants, et elles n'ont pas assez d'argent pour acheter les choses de première nécessité. Au Cameroun on pense que le mariage est très important, et le divorce n'est pas commun. Aminata trouve qu'au Cameroun la famille est plus stable qu'en France.

1a 📖🎧 ⓦ Read the first two paragraphs and answer the questions in English.

1 What is unusual about Aminata's family situation (from a European point of view)?
2 How many people live in Aminata's house?
3 Who does the housework?
4 What are the arrangements for meal times in Aminata's house?

1b 📖🎧 ⓦ Read the third paragraph and answer the questions in English.

1 What three consequences of divorce does she mention?
2 What does she think about French marriages compared to Cameroonian ones?

> 📖 Remember that sometimes written words are exactly the same in English and French, e.g. *parents*. Sometimes they are nearly the same and so still easy to work out, e.g. *enfants* > 'infants', *famille* > 'family'.
>
> *Stratégie*

2 ⓥ Match the adjectives below with their translations. Decide whether each one is in its masculine form (m) or its feminine form (f). If it does not change, write (m or f).

casse-pieds	gentil	shy	kind
compréhensive	sympa	lazy	sad
mignonne	timide	annoying	older
jaloux	aînée	nice	numerous
triste	paresseux	alone, lonely	funny
seule	drôle	jealous	understanding
nombreux		sweet	

3 Ⓖ Fill in the gaps with the correct words.

1   J'ai des problèmes avec _____ parents. (my)

2   _____ amis sont tout le temps ici. (your)

3   _____ chambre est en désordre. (your)

4   _____ mère et _____ père vont divorcer. (her)

5   _____ enfants ne sont pas très aimables. (her)

6   Je veux sortir avec _____ petit ami. (my)

Grammaire — page 163

How to say 'my', 'your' etc.

	masculine singular	feminine singular	plural (m and f)
my	*mon*	*ma*	*mes*
your	*ton*	*ta*	*tes*
his / her	*son*	*sa*	*ses*

If the word is masculine and singular (e.g. *frère*) and you want to say 'my', the word you need is *mon* (*mon frère* = my brother).

Also revise the position and agreement of adjectives.

See page 42 ➡

4a 🎥🎧 Listen to and / or watch Section A of the video and decide which sentences are true.

1   **Florence**

a   Florence aime bien son frère.

b   Ses parents sont trop sévères.

c   Son père est drôle.

2   **Jean-Jacques**

a   Jean-Jacques n'a pas de frère.

b   Il habite avec sa mère.

c   Son père est drôle.

4b 🎥🎧 Listen to and / or watch Section B and decide which sentences are true.

1   **Abdul**

a   Abdul a des rapports difficiles avec ses parents.

b   Il a des difficultés à l'école.

c   Abdul voudrait aller à l'université.

2   **Liliane**

a   La mère de Liliane s'est remariée.

b   Liliane a de bons rapports avec sa belle-mère.

c   Elle trouve son demi-frère très sympa.

5 ✏ You are working as part of the scriptwriting team for a TV soap and you are describing a new family. In a group, decide who is in the family. Then, each person should describe one member of the family.

■   Who is in the new family?

■   What are they like?

■   How do they get on with each other and why?

■   What do they argue about?

Astuce

When writing French, always try to include adjectives in your work in order to make it more individual and interesting. Remember that most adjectives in French follow the noun and you need to check you have put on the correct ending (Is it masculine or feminine? Is it singular or plural?).

Dans la famille, il y a	une mère célibataire et trois enfants / les parents et un fils unique.	
Le père / la mère est		grand(e) / amusant(e), généreux(-euse).
xxxxx a de bons rapports avec sa sœur parce qu'elle est	très / assez	gentille / aimable / sympa / compréhensive.
xxxxx n'aime pas sa sœur /son frère parce qu'elle / il est		méchant(e) / désagréable / casse-pieds / sérieux(-euse).
Ils / Elles se disputent au sujet		du travail à l'école / du travail à la maison / de l'argent / de l'heure de se coucher.

Les rapports avec les autres

L'amitié

Bernard

J'ai beaucoup de copains, et mon meilleur ami s'appelle Cédric. On s'amuse ensemble. Nous avons beaucoup de choses en commun et nous aimons la même musique et les mêmes émissions de télé. Cédric est toujours très tranquille et bien organisé, je m'entends bien avec lui.

Pierre

Je n'ai pas de meilleur ami, mais je suis toujours avec le même groupe de garçons. Je m'entends bien avec eux parce qu'on s'intéresse aux mêmes choses: le football, jouer de la guitare, voir des films d'horreur. On sort toujours ensemble le samedi soir. On boit quelques bières ensemble, mais jamais trop.

Aurélie

Je n'ai pas beaucoup d'amis, car je suis assez timide. J'ai des problèmes en ce moment parce que ma meilleure amie, Stéphanie, est déprimée. Elle est toujours de mauvaise humeur. Elle a des problèmes à la maison; elle se dispute avec ses parents. Elle a aussi des difficultés au lycée. Les profs ne la comprennent pas, et moi, je ne sais pas quoi faire.

Hortense

En ce moment je ne m'entends pas bien avec ma meilleure amie. Elle s'appelle Claire. Normalement on est toujours ensemble et elle me fait rire, mais en ce moment il y a un problème. J'aime bien un garçon de ma classe, mais je suis trop timide pour lui parler. Claire l'a invité à aller au cinéma avec elle, et il a accepté! Ce n'est pas très loyal, ça. En plus, elle achète toujours les mêmes vêtements que moi. Elle m'énerve!

1a Read the first two entries by Bernard and Pierre and link the two halves of the sentences together.

1	Bernard and Cédric like …	a	… go out for a few beers.
2	Bernard thinks Cédric is always …	b	… a best friend.
3	Pierre does not have …	c	… the same TV programmes.
4	Pierre likes to …	d	… calm and well organised.

1b Read the last two entries by Aurélie and Hortense. Link the two halves of each sentence together and write A (Aurélie) or H (Hortense) next to each one.

1	xxxxx does not have many friends …	a	… because she is quite shy.
2	xxxxx's friend is always …	b	… makes her laugh.
3	xxxxx is not getting on with …	c	… in a bad mood.
4	Normally xxxxx's best friend …	d	… her best friend.

2 **G** Work with a partner. Partner A says the sentence filling in the missing reflexive pronoun, and Partner B translates the sentence into English. Swap over for each sentence.

1 Ma meilleure amie _____ appelle Morgane.
2 Je _____ entends bien avec mon frère.
3 On _____ dispute tout le temps.
4 Mon beau-frère _____ appelle Jean-Claude.
5 On _____ intéresse aux mêmes choses.
6 Tu ne _____ entends pas bien avec tes parents.

Grammaire *page 166*

Reflexive verbs

These verbs always have **reflexive pronouns** (*me, te, se*) before them. If the verb begins with a vowel, shorten these to *m'*, *t'* and *s'*. Here are two examples: *se disputer avec* (to argue with) and *s'entendre bien avec* (to get on well with).

Use *elle* and *lui* at the end of a sentence, e.g. *Je m'entends bien avec elle* (I get on well with her). *Tu te disputes avec lui* (You are arguing with him).

Find out more about *elle*, *lui* and other disjunctive pronouns. *See page 165* ➡

3a 🎧 Pick an adjective from the list below to describe each of these people.

1 François 2 Georges 3 Caroline 4 Delphine

réservé(e) · triste ne pense pas aux autres

sportif(-ve)   amusant(e)   barbant(e)   calme

Stratégie

Remember that many endings in French are silent.

Pay particular attention to verbs. *Tu aimes*, *ils aiment*: these endings are silent and sound exactly the same as (*il*) *aime*.

Watch also the plural form of nouns: *j'ai un frère* and *j'ai trois frères*. The words *frère* / *frères* sound exactly the same.

3b 🎧 Listen again and complete these sentences.

1 Georges doesn't want to listen to _____.
2 Caroline is not interested in _____.
3 Delphine has a good _____.
4 Anne can tell Fatima _____.
5 Fatima has listened to Anne's _____.
6 Benoît's main feeling for Thomas is _____.

Astuce

To talk about your own qualities, you might like to mention what others say about you. You can use the expression: *On dit que je suis …* (People say that I am …).

4 Work with a partner (not your best friend) and interview them about their own and their friends' qualities.

- Quelles sont tes qualités?
- Comment s'appelle ton meilleur ami / ta meilleure amie?
- Tu t'entends bien avec lui / elle tout le temps?
- Qu'est-ce que tu as fait le week-end dernier avec tes copains / copines?
- Tu as un petit ami / une petite amie?

Quelles sont tes qualités?

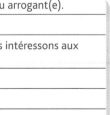

On dit que je suis assez amusant, mais parfois je suis un peu timide.

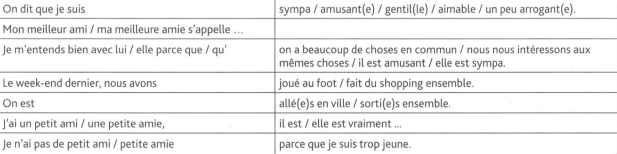

On dit que je suis	sympa / amusant(e) / gentil(le) / aimable / un peu arrogant(e).
Mon meilleur ami / ma meilleure amie s'appelle …	
Je m'entends bien avec lui / elle parce que / qu'	on a beaucoup de choses en commun / nous nous intéressons aux mêmes choses / il est amusant / elle est sympa.
Le week-end dernier, nous avons	joué au foot / fait du shopping ensemble.
On est	allé(e)s en ville / sorti(e)s ensemble.
J'ai un petit ami / une petite amie,	il est / elle est vraiment …
Je n'ai pas de petit ami / petite amie	parce que je suis trop jeune.

On parle de la vie familiale

1 **Maintenant**: J'apprécie la solitude. Je passe beaucoup de temps dans ma chambre devant mon ordinateur, mais je fais du babysitting quelquefois et ça me plaît. J'aime aussi faire des promenades tout seul. Je n'ai pas beaucoup d'amis de mon âge, mais j'aime les enfants.

a **Le futur**: Je vais trouver un partenaire très sympa et loyal, et on va vivre ensemble. On va tous les deux avoir un bon travail, donc on va avoir assez d'argent pour acheter une belle maison. Je voudrais avoir deux enfants, mais je ne vais pas rester à la maison, je vais payer quelqu'un pour les garder.

A

2 **Maintenant**: Mes parents sont divorcés. J'habite avec ma mère et mes sœurs. Ma mère trouve que le mariage n'est pas nécessaire, et je suis d'accord avec elle. À mon avis il n'est pas important de se marier pour avoir une famille. Je pense que la famille idéale, c'est une mère, un père, une fille et un garçon.

b **Le futur**: Je vais me marier à l'église, peut-être dans trois ou quatre ans. Je trouve que la cérémonie du mariage est très romantique. Ça va être une journée très spéciale pour nous deux, et un bon souvenir pour toute la vie. Nous n'allons pas avoir d'enfants.

B

3 **Maintenant**: Pour moi la religion est importante. J'ai une petite amie, et on sort ensemble depuis un an. Elle habite chez ses parents. Je ne veux pas vivre avec elle sans être marié. Je n'aime pas les enfants – ils m'énervent!

c **Le futur**: Je vais acheter un appartement en ville. Je vais inviter mes amis de temps en temps, mais généralement je vais être seule. Je ne vais pas me marier, mais je vais peut-être avoir un enfant. À mon avis, une famille monoparentale n'est pas une mauvaise idée.

C

1a 📖🎧 Match the different views on family life (1–3) with plans for the future (a–c) and the correct pictures (A–C).

1b 📖🎧 Read the views on family life and plans for the future again. Who says the following? Write the correct combination (1–3, a–c, A–C).

1 I intend to live with my partner without getting married.

2 I want to live alone.

3 I want to get married quite young.

4 I don't want children.

5 It's not important to get married before having children.

6 I like the idea of being a single parent.

2a 🎧 Choose three qualities that each person would like in his / her ideal partner.

Chloé   **Vincent**   **Patricia**

a musical	c honest	e strict	g shy	i generous	k fond of children
b unselfish	d clever	f funny	h faithful	j rich	l good sense of humour

2b 🎧 Answer these questions in English.

1 What does Chloé say about her marriage ceremony?

2 Why does Vincent know so many details about his ideal partner?

3 Why doesn't he want any children?

4 What reason does Patricia give for not wanting to get married soon?

5 What does she want to do after her marriage?

3 🄖 Transform the following sentences into the immediate future tense using *aller*.

Exemple: Il voyage en Australie. > Il va voyager en Australie.

1 Elle trouve l'amour!

2 Je me marie à l'âge de 25 ans.

3 Elle sort avec son petit ami.

4 J'ai deux enfants.

5 Tu es riche et célèbre?

6 J'adore ma femme.

Aller + infinitive

Use the verb *aller* (to go) in the present tense followed by an infinitive (e.g. *travailler*) to express future plans.

Je vais travailler.   I am going to work.

Elle va se marier.   She is going to get married.

If you have forgotten the present tense of *avoir*, look it up in the verb tables (page 175).

Also revise phrases such as *je voudrais, j'aimerais, j'ai l'intention de* + infinitive to express future intentions.

See page 42 ➡

Grammaire *page 167*

4 ✏️ 🌐 Conduct a survey to find out what qualities people would like in their future ideal partner. Use the following questions, or invent more of your own.

- Comment sera-t-elle (sa personnalité)?
- Qu'est-ce qu'il / elle aime faire pendant son temps libre?
- Est-ce qu'il / elle aime les enfants?
- Que fait-il / elle dans la vie (comme métier)?
- Tu veux te marier avec lui / elle?
- Si tu réponds oui à cette question, où et quand?
- Si tu réponds non à cette question, pourquoi pas?

Ask the questions and write down the answers for each person in your group.

Stratégie

✏️ To ask questions in French:

- use the normal word order but make sure your voice rises at the end of the question, e.g. *Tu veux te marier?*
- swap the subject and verb over, e.g. *Veux-tu te marier?*
- use *est-ce que*, e.g. *Est-ce que tu veux te marier? Quand est-ce que tu veux te marier?*

Astuce

When speaking or writing, try to include opinions as often as you can. In the present tense, of course, you can use *c'est* followed by an adjective to give a simple opinion. In the future, you can use *ce sera* (it will be).

Mon / Ma partenaire idéale sera	gentil(le) / sympa / généreux(-euse).
Il / Elle va / aimera	faire du sport / aller au ciné / écouter de la musique / danser / faire du cyclisme.
Il / Elle va avoir d'enfants Il / Elle ne va pas avoir des enfants	parce qu'ils sont (souvent) adorables / mignons / casse-pieds / méchants.
On va se marier	à l'âge de … ans. à l'église / dans un château.
Je vais vivre avec mon / ma partenaire sans me marier	parce que (pour moi) le mariage n'est pas important / essentiel.

kerboodle!

Qu'est-ce qu'on peut faire pour aider les personnes défavorisées?

Léon habite à Paris, où il y a environ 5 000 hommes et femmes sans domicile fixe dans les rues. Il travaille pour une organisation qui s'occupe des personnes qui n'ont pas de maison. Ces personnes sont presque toujours sans travail, elles ont faim et elles n'ont pas de logement. Voici ce que dit Léon: «Mon travail c'est d'offrir de la soupe et une tranche de pain à chaque personne malheureuse qui arrive au centre».

Thomas travaille pour une organisation caritative. Il remplit des cartons de toutes sortes de choses pour les SDF, par exemple des sacs de couchage, du shampooing et du savon. Comme ils sont au chômage, ils n'ont pas assez d'argent pour acheter les choses indispensables de la vie. Thomas dit «Ces pauvres gens attendent avec impatience notre arrivée.»

Jules est volontaire dans un groupe sportif qui aide les jeunes des quartiers défavorisés. Il passe cinq heures par semaine à faire du sport dans les centres de loisirs d'un quartier de Paris où il y a beaucoup de familles pauvres. Grâce au sport, ces adolescents ont la chance d'avoir une vie meilleure. «La première fois, il n'y avait que cinq garçons et trois filles, mais ils ont parlé à leurs voisins et maintenant on a trente jeunes dans notre groupe. On est très populaire!» explique Jules.

1a 📖🎧 Write the name of the appropriate person for each picture (1–3).

1b 📖🎧 Which four of the following sentences are true?

1 The people who come to Léon are usually unemployed.
2 Léon helps by giving the people money to buy soup and bread.
3 Thomas's charity helps by providing basic necessities for the homeless.
4 The homeless are always happy to see the volunteers.
5 Jules earns money by working for his charity.
6 Sport gives hope to these young people.

2 🎧 Listen to Sections A and B and answer the questions in English.

1 When is the programme starting?
2 Why is the programme necessary?
3 What has destroyed the farmers' plants?
4 What has caused many children to have no parents?
5 What is the first long-term aim of the programme?
6 Why do some families not have a home?
7 What improvement does the doctor want to see in schools?

Médecins sans frontières is a charity created in 1971 by a group of French doctors. The organisation provides medical care by volunteer doctors and nurses to victims of war and disaster whatever their race, religion or politics.

3a **G** Complete the grid by following the pattern, for the verbs *remplir* (to fill) and *attendre* (to wait for).

remplir = to fill

singular	plural
je _____	nous _____
tu _____	vous remplissez
il /elle / on remplit	ils / elles _____

attendre = _____

singular	plural
j' _____	nous _____
_____ attends	vous _____
il /elle / on _____	_____

Grammaire | page 166

-ir and -re verbs

For *-ir* verbs, take off the *-ir* and add the endings given below.

finir = to finish

singular	plural
je finis	nous finissons
tu finis	vous finissez
il /elle / on finit	ils / elles finissent

Find the pattern for *-re* verbs (e.g. *vendre*) in the verb tables (page 174) and make a similar table to help you learn it.

Also learn about the modal verbs: *pouvoir, devoir, vouloir*. *See page 43* ➡

3b **G** Fill in the missing words. First decide which verb you need from the list below, then choose the correct ending.

1 Je _____ des cartons de toutes sortes de choses à manger et à boire.

2 Les gens du village _____ l'arrivée du docteur de Médecins sans frontières et de son équipe.

3 Nous _____ des cartes d'anniversaire au marché pour collecter de l'argent pour une école au Congo.

4 Nathalie commence son travail avec les SDF à huit heures du soir, et elle _____ à minuit.

5 On ne _____ pas d'être sans domicile fixe: ça peut arriver parce qu'on n'a pas de travail.

vendre   attendre   choisir   remplir   finir

Stratégie

🖋 Check written work, using a dictionary and the grammar section (page 158) as needed.

■ Masculine words need *le, un* or *du*, feminine words *la, une* or *de la*.

■ With feminine or plural words, adjectives with the nouns will also have to change.

■ Check also verb endings, using the verb tables (page 174).

4 🖋 🌐 Imagine that you do some voluntary work for a charity on a regular basis. Write a short magazine article giving some information about your work.

■ What kind of organisation do you work for?

■ What hours do you work each week?

■ What do you do?

■ What do you think of the work?

■ Who benefits from your work?

■ What are the plans of the organisation for the near future?

Astuce

Each time you answer a question, try to give an extra detail such as an example or an opinion.

Je travaille pour une organisation qui	aide les enfants / s'occupe des animaux.
Chaque semaine je consacre / passe	deux heures à ce travail.
Je vends	des magazines / des vêtements.
J'organise	des jeux / des événements spéciaux.
Je trouve le travail	satisfaisant / enrichissant.
Notre organisation est utile aux SDF (etc.)	parce qu'ils reçoivent des conseils / de l'aide / de l'argent / de quoi manger.
À l'avenir on voudrait créer	un nouveau centre d'accueil.

kerboodle!

Relationships and choices

Pavel – bon fils, bon frère

Une petite famille et de grandes B responsabilités

Je m'appelle Pavel. J'habite avec ma mère et ma sœur, Sonia. Elle a six ans et elle est handicapée. Pour ma mère la vie est difficile, car elle travaille dans un hôpital, mais elle fait aussi beaucoup pour ma sœur. Moi, je m'entends bien avec ma mère et ma sœur.

Du travail au collège et à la maison C

Comme ma mère travaille, je passe beaucoup de temps avec Sonia. Le matin, je me lève et j'aide ma sœur quand elle se lave et s'habille. Normalement, elle passe la journée à l'école primaire et moi je vais au collège. À trois heures et demie, je vais chercher Sonia, et je reste avec elle jusqu'à l'arrivée de maman.

Les promenades – agréables malgré les difficultés A

S'il fait beau, nous allons au parc. Elle adore donner du pain aux oiseaux sur le lac. Le chemin du parc à la maison peut être difficile, car dans notre ville les trottoirs ne sont pas bien adaptés aux fauteuils roulants, et souvent les automobilistes ne sont pas très patients quand nous traversons la rue.

Le soir à la maison E

À la maison, je prends le goûter avec Sonia, et puis je fais mes devoirs et elle regarde la télé. Maman est toujours très fatiguée et stressée quand elle rentre à six heures. Le soir, c'est moi qui joue avec Sonia et maman prépare le dîner. Quand Sonia se couche, je vais dans le salon avec maman, et nous discutons de nos activités ou bien nous regardons la télé.

Un samedi sportif D

Pour moi, il est difficile de sortir avec mes copains ou de faire du sport en semaine à cause de ma sœur, mais le samedi ma grand-mère passe la journée chez nous. Elle reste avec ma sœur et fait le ménage. Ma mère va faire du shopping en ville, et je vais au centre sportif. Je joue au basket et j'aime nager. J'adore ma sœur, mais j'aime aussi beaucoup le samedi, car je suis avec mes copains.

1a 📖🎧 Look at the paragraph headings in the article. From what they tell you about the contents, put the pictures into the correct order (1–5).

1b 📖🎧 Look at the article in detail. Which person does each of the following: Pavel (P), his mother (M), his grandmother (G)?

1 Spends the day in a hospital.
2 Helps Sonia get ready for school.
3 Takes Sonia to the park.
4 Looks after Sonia while she watches television.
5 Looks after Sonia on Saturdays.
6 Does the shopping.
7 Goes swimming.
8 Cleans the house.

> **AQA** *Examiner's tip*
>
> Although activity 1b refers to the whole article, the sentences will roughly follow the order of the text. This is usually the case in this type of task. You are not likely to need to read the whole passage eight times to find the answers.

2a 🎧 Match each of the people in the list below to one of the speakers (1–5).

a a wheelchair user
b a Muslim girl
c a female car mechanic
d a girl who wants to work as an electrician
e a vegetarian

> **Reflexive verbs** — *Grammaire page 166*
>
> Several reflexive verbs are used in the article. Can you find three examples when Pavel is talking about himself, and three when he is talking about his sister? To remind yourself how they are used, see page 166.

2b 🎧 Listen again. Choose the correct version of the statements about each of the people in the list above.

1 The wheelchair user will:
   a write a letter to the council.
   b write a letter to the newspaper.
   c write a letter to the shopkeepers.

2 The Muslim girl will:
   a leave her scarf at home.
   b stop going to school.
   c wear her scarf on her way to school.

3 The car mechanic will:
   a ask her boss for more money.
   b leave her job.
   c ask her boss for more work.

4 The girl who wants to be an electrician will:
   a train with her father.
   b look for a different career.
   c train at a technical college.

5 The vegetarian will:
   a go home for lunch.
   b take a packed lunch.
   c have a school lunch.

> **Vocabulaire**
>
> | | |
> |---|---|
> | l'école primaire (f) | primary school |
> | l'électricien (m) | electrician |
> | le fauteuil roulant | wheelchair |
> | le foulard | headscarf |
> | le lycée technique | technical college |
> | traverser | to cross |

> **The immediate future** — *Grammaire page 167*
>
> Each speaker uses *je vais* + an infinitive to say what they are going to do. Can you pick out the infinitive used by each? For more information on this form of the future tense see page 167.

(G) Relationships and choices

Adjective agreement; *Je voudrais ...* and *J'ai l'intention de ...*

1 📖 Choose the correct adjectives to complete the following sentences.

1 Sa mère est bavard bavarde , mais elle n'est pas méchant méchante .

2 Ta grand-mère est triste tristes parce qu'elle est seul seule .

3 Il a des parents riche riches et célèbre célèbres .

4 J'ai une copine très gentil gentille mais timide timides .

5 Mon grand grands frère est paresseux paresseuses .

6 Ses petits petites sœurs sont pénible pénibles .

7 Mon frère aîné aînée est très égoïste égoïstes .

8 Elle a des grands-parents pauvre pauvres mais gentils gentilles .

Grammaire page 161

> ### Adjective agreement
> Adjectives have different endings depending on whether they describe masculine, feminine, singular or plural nouns. Add *-e* if the noun is feminine, and add *-s* if it is plural. They usually go after the noun:
>
> *une fille intelligente*   a clever girl
>
> If the adjective already ends in *-e*, there is no need to add another one:
>
> *un garçon timide* a shy boy
>
> *une fille timide*   a shy girl
>
> Some adjectives, including *petit*, *grand* and *joli* usually go before the noun:
>
> *ma grande sœur*   my big sister

2 ✏️ Complete each caption using the words below, then translate the sentences into English.

1 J'_____ l'intention de me marier.

2 Je _____ remercier mes parents...

3 Je _____ avoir beaucoup d'enfants.

4 Je ne _____ pas _____ sans voisins.

5 Elle _____ _____ un gâteau.

6 Ce couple n'_____ pas l'intention de _____!

Grammaire page 170

> ### *Je voudrais ...* and *J'ai l'intention de ...*
> When *je voudrais* or *j'ai l'intention de* is followed by another verb, that verb is in the infinitive.
>
> *Je voudrais acheter un chien.*   I would like to buy a dog.
>
> *Elle voudrait avoir deux enfants.*   She would like to have two children.
>
> *Il a l'intention d'écrire à son père.*   He intends to write to his father.

ai   divorcer   être   manger

a   voudrais   voudrais

voudrais   voudrait

Pronouns after prepositions; *Devoir*, *pouvoir* and *vouloir*; Question words

3 📝 Follow the English prompts to complete these sentences.

1 Tu te disputes souvent (with her) _____?
2 Tu ne peux pas vivre (without me) _____!
3 Le chat est (for you) _____.
4 J'ai l'intention d'aller (to his house) _____.
5 Ils sont toujours sympas (with us) _____.
6 Je ne m'entends pas bien (with her) _____.

> **Pronouns after prepositions** *Grammaire page 165*
>
> Use these pronouns after prepositions (*avec, sans, chez, pour*):
>
> | *moi* | me | *lui* | him | *nous* | us |
> | *toi* | you | *elle* | her | | |
>
> *Il s'entend bien avec moi.* He gets on well with me.
> *Tu es triste sans lui.* You are sad without him.
> *Je vais venir chez toi.* I am going to come to your house.
> *Il y a un cadeau pour nous.* There is a present for us.

4 📖📝 Choose the correct form of *devoir, pouvoir* and *vouloir* each time. Then find the correct translation and complete it.

1 Je ne veux / voulons pas me marier avec lui.
2 Tu ne dois / doit pas être méchant avec ton copain.
3 Il ne devez / doit pas bavarder avec ses copains.
4 Elle ne veut / veux pas habiter chez sa mère.
5 Nous ne veulent / voulons pas divorcer.
6 Vous ne peut / pouvez pas vous entendre.
7 Ils ne peuvent / pouvons pas avoir d'enfants.
8 Elles ne devons / doivent pas critiquer mes parents.

a _____ can't get on.
b _____ can't have children.
c _____ don't want a divorce.
d _____ don't want to marry him.
e _____ doesn't want to live with her mother.
f _____ mustn't be mean to your friend.
g _____ mustn't gossip with his friends.
h _____ mustn't criticise my parents.

> **Devoir, pouvoir and vouloir: present tense** *Grammaire page 169*
>
> *devoir* = to have to
>
> | singular | plural |
> |---|---|
> | je dois | nous devons |
> | tu dois | vous devez |
> | il /elle / on doit | ils / elles doivent |
>
> *pouvoir* = to be able to
>
> | singular | plural |
> |---|---|
> | je peux | nous pouvons |
> | tu peux | vous pouvez |
> | il /elle / on peut | ils / elles peuvent |
>
> *vouloir* = to want (to)
>
> | singular | plural |
> |---|---|
> | je veux | nous voulons |
> | tu veux | vous voulez |
> | il /elle / on veut | ils / elles veulent |

5 📖📝 Match the French and the English, and complete the French sentences using the words below

1 _____ chien préfères-tu?
2 _____ de frères ont-elles?
3 _____ n'a pas le sens de l'humour?
4 _____ bavardez-vous avec mes voisins?
5 _____ attend-elle ses grands-parents?
6 _____ vas-tu écrire à ton oncle?
7 _____ pomme prend-il?

a Which apple is he taking?
b Who doesn't have a sense of humour?
c When are you going to write to your uncle?
d Where is she waiting for her grandparents?
e Why are you chatting with my neighbours?
f How many brothers do they have?
g Which dog do you prefer?

> **Question words** *Grammaire page 169*
>
> Make sure you know the following words and use them to introduce questions.
>
> | *combien?* | how much / how many? |
> | *où?* | where? |
> | *pourquoi?* | why? |
> | *quand?* | when? |
> | *quel (quelle)?* | which / what? |
> | *qui?* | who? |

combien   où   pourquoi   quand   quel   quelle   qui

Relationships and choices

La famille ➡ pages 32–33

	avoir de la chance	to be lucky
	casse-pieds	annoying
	compréhensif(-ive)	understanding
	critiquer	to criticise
le	demi-frère	stepbrother / half-brother
le	divorce	divorce
	divorcer	to divorce
	drôle	funny
	ensemble	together
la	femme	woman / wife
le	frère aîné	older brother
	gentil(le)	kind / nice
	jaloux(-ouse)	jealous
le	mari	husband
le	mariage	marriage
	méchant(e)	nasty, wicked
	mignon(ne)	sweet, cute, pretty
	paresseux(-euse)	lazy
les	rapports (m)	relationships
se	remarier	to remarry
le	sens de l'humour	sense of humour
la	séparation	separation
	sévère	strict, severe
	timide	timid
	vivre en concubinage	to co-habit

Les rapports avec les autres ➡ pages 34–35

	barbant(e)	boring
les	choses en commun (f)	things in common
le	copain	friend (m)
la	copine	friend (f)
	déprimé(e)	depressed
se	disputer	to quarrel, argue
	égoïste	selfish

	ennuyeux(-euse)	boring
s'	entendre bien avec …	to get on well with …
	fâché(e)	angry, cross
	fidèle	faithful, loyal
s'	intéresser à	to be interested in
la	meilleure amie	best friend (f)
le	meilleur ami	best friend (m)
	rire	to laugh
la	vérité	truth

1 Ⓥ Match the following adjectives to the correct definition.

égoïste   drôle   tranquille

ennuyeuse   déprimée

timide   sportif

1 une fille réservée
2 une femme triste
3 un garçon qui ne pense pas aux autres
4 un homme amusant
5 une personne barbante
6 un copain actif
7 une sœur calme

L'avenir ➡ pages 36–37

à l'	avenir (m)	in the future
l'	amour (m)	love
les	cheveux (m)	hair
l'	église (f)	church
une	famille monoparentale	single-parent family
au	futur	in the future
	maintenant	now
la	mairie	town hall
le	mariage	marriage
	marié(e)	married
se	marier	to get married

	méchant(e)	spiteful, nasty
un / une	*partenaire*	partner
	séparé(e)	separated
	vivre	to live
les	*yeux (m)*	eyes

2 **V** Match each term with its English translation.

1 des parents divorcés	a a single-parent family
2 se marier à l'église	b separated parents
3 vivre avec un / une partenaire	c a married couple
4 des parents séparés	d to have children
	e to get married in church
5 une famille monoparentale	f to get married at the town hall
6 avoir des enfants	g divorced parents
7 vivre seul(e)	h to live on your own
8 un couple marié	i to live with a partner
9 se marier à la mairie	

La pauvreté ➡ *pages 38–39*

	attendre	to wait
une	*bonne cause*	good cause
	caritative	charitable
	choisir	to choose
le	*chômage*	unemployment
	construire	to build, construct
l'	*éducation (f)*	education
	finir	to finish
	grave	serious
la	*guerre*	war
le	*logement*	housing
	loger	to live
la	*maladie*	illness
	malheureux(-euse)	unfortunately
la	*mort*	death

la	*nourriture*	food
	pauvre	poor
la	*pluie*	rain
le	*quartier*	district, area
	remplir	to fill
la	*responsabilité*	responsibility
	riche	rich
un	*sac de couchage*	sleeping bag
	SDF (sans domicile fixe)	homeless
	sans travail	without work, unemployed
la	*santé*	health
le	*savon*	soap
le	*shampooing*	shampoo
	vendre	to sell
le	*voisin*	neighbour

3 **V** Link the person's ambitions to the correct phrase.

1 Je voudrais aider les SDF au centre-ville.	a help the young in urban areas
2 J'ai l'intention de travailler dans un pays où il y a des personnes pauvres.	b help AIDS sufferers
	c help the homeless
	d raise money for poor children
3 Je veux faire découvrir le sport aux jeunes d'un quartier pauvre.	e work in a country where there are people affected by poverty
4 Mon ambition est d'aider les victimes du sida en Afrique.	
5 Je vais collecter de l'argent pour les enfants pauvres.	

1 🗨 Une vie saine

You are talking to your French friend Adrien about your lifestyle. He wants to know:

1 if you are in good health
2 if you eat healthily
3 if you exercise regularly
4 if you have a stressful lifestyle
5 if you smoke
6 if you drink alcohol
7 !

! Remember you will have to respond to something that you have not yet prepared.

1 If you are in good health
- say that you are usually in good health
- mention the last time you weren't well
- say what you did about it
- say that generally you have a healthy lifestyle

2 If you eat healthily
- say what you like to eat and drink
- say what you don't eat or drink and why
- say if you think that you have a healthy diet
- say what you think is an ideal diet

3 If you exercise regularly
- say which sports you play
- say when, where and with whom
- say whether you usually walk or cycle to various places
- say what you intend to do to get fitter

> **AQA Examiner's tips**
>
> Start off with *Oui, ça va bien*.
> Use the perfect tense for the second and third bullet points, e.g. *j'ai eu la grippe*.
> Use *mode de vie* for 'lifestyle'.

> **AQA Examiner's tips**
>
> Now, start your plan. Write a maximum of six words for each of the seven sections that make up the task. Here are some suggested words for the first section: *aller, grippe, médecin, pharmacie, médicaments, sain* Although *aller* does not by itself indicate that you are in good health, it reminds you that it is the correct verb to use to say that you are well. Use words in your plan that will help you to remember what to say next and will also help you speak accurate French.

> **AQA Examiner's tips**
>
> Give details about what you eat and drink for breakfast, lunch and evening meal. Use different verbs to avoid repetition of *manger* and *boire*, e.g. *je prends, il y a, j'aime, je n'aime pas*.
> Use *Pour être en bonne santé, il faut manger / boire / prendre …* to describe a healthy diet.
> Use different words in your plan. The repetition of *manger*, for example, might confuse you on the day you take the task.

> **AQA Examiner's tips**
>
> If you can use the word 'play' a sport in English, use *jouer au* + sport, e.g. *Je joue au basket*. If you can't, use *faire du / de la / de l'* + sport, e.g. *Je fais de l'athlétisme*.
> Use *je vais … à pied / à vélo* to say that you walk or cycle to a place.
> You can give yourself grammatical markers in your plan, e.g. *avenir* given the question 'Do you exercise regularly?', which suggests that you should talk about what you intend to do in the future in terms of exercise.

4 If you have a stressful lifestyle

- ■ say whether you work too hard
- ■ say whether you sleep well
- ■ say what stresses you out
- ■ say what you do to avoid stress

Use *de ... heures à ... heures* to say that you work / sleep 'from ... to ...' .

Start the last bullet point with *Pour ne pas être stressé, je ...*

Use fewer than six words if possible in your plan. Here, four words are probably enough to remind you of what you should be talking about. You may appreciate the luxury of more than six words when dealing with another question!

5 If you smoke

- ■ say whether you smoke
- ■ say whether you have friends who smoke
- ■ say why you think young people start smoking
- ■ say why it is foolish to start smoking

Use different ways of expressing your opinion, e.g. *À mon avis ... / Je pense que ... / Je trouve que ...*

To explain the problem with young people and alcohol, start with *Quelquefois, les jeunes boivent ...*

If you cannot recreate what is in the bullet points by looking at your plan only, you need to rethink what is in your plan. Selecting words that will allow you to remember everything is difficult. Take your time and choose well.

6 If you drink alcohol

- ■ say whether you drink alcohol
- ■ say what you think of the price of alcohol
- ■ say whether you think people aged under 18 should be allowed to drink alcohol
- ■ say what you think is the problem with young people and alcohol

Use *commencer à* + infinitive to say 'start to' + verb.

Use *il est bête de ...* to say 'it is foolish to ...'.

7 ❗ At this point you may be asked

- ■ if you take drugs
- ■ what you have done recently to improve your fitness
- ■ how you intend to change your lifestyle in order to improve your health
- ■ about the importance of peer group pressure in trying to have a healthy lifestyle

Choose which **two** options you think are the most likely, and for each of these, note down **three** different ideas. In your plan, write three words that illustrate each of the two most likely options. For the second bullet point you might choose: *vélo, fruits, dormir*. Learn these two options using your reminder words.

Remember to check the total number of words you have used. It should be 40 or fewer.

You should now have completed your plan and prepared your answers. Give your plan to your teacher for feedback. Compare your answers to the online sample version – you might find some useful hints to make yours even better.

kerboodle!

1 ✏️ Les rapports avec les autres

You are writing to your French friend about relationships with family and friends and also about your choices for the future. You could include:

1 how you get on with your family
2 details of the person you get on best with
3 what you like to do with that person
4 what happened last time you went out as a family
5 details about your friends
6 where you intend to live in the future
7 what you plan to do when you leave home

AQA Examiner's tips

Start off with *dans ma famille, il y a …*
Use *je m'entends bien avec …* to say that you get on with someone.
If you prefer talk about someone you don't get on with, use *je ne m'entends pas bien avec …*

1 How you get on with your family

- say who is in your family
- say who you get on with (or don't get on with) and why
- say who you have arguments with and why
- ask your friend how he / she gets on with his / her family

AQA Examiner's tips

Now, start your plan. Write a maximum of six words for each of the seven sections that make up the task, remembering that the total maximum is 40, so two sections will need to have only five words. Here are some suggested words for the first section:
famille-membres, s'entendre avec, disputes, question
Remember that verbs can only be used in the infinitive or the past participle on your plan.

2 Details of the person you get on best with

- say who he / she is, his / her name and age
- say what he / she looks like
- say what his / her personality is like
- say why you get on well

AQA Examiner's tips

Remember that if you describe a girl or a woman using adjectives, the adjectives have to be made feminine. See grammar section (page 161).
Use the correct form of *avoir* to say his / her age, i.e. *il / elle a … ans.*
You may find it useful to use cognates or semi-cognates on your plan (French words that look like English words), e.g. *personnalité, disputes.*

3 What you like to do with that person

- say what activities you do together
- talk about your favourite activity
- say what you like but he / she doesn't like and vice versa
- say how often you go out together

AQA Examiner's tips

You can use *on* or *nous* to mean 'we', e.g. *on va* means the same as *nous allons.*
Use *fois par semaine / mois* to express frequency and *le lundi* to mean 'on Mondays'.
Remember you have the option to use visuals as well as words on your plan.

4 What happened last time you went out as a family
- say when you went and how you travelled
- say where you went
- say what you did
- say what you thought of it

Check how to use the perfect tense. See grammar section (page 167). With *être* verbs, start with *nous sommes,* with *avoir* verbs, start with *nous avons.*
Use *j'ai aimé* and *je n'ai pas aimé* to introduce what you enjoyed and didn't enjoy.
Add up to six words to your plan.

5 Details about your friends
- say who they are
- say what you like doing with them
- give details about your best friend
- give details of an outing with your best friend

Use *mon meilleur ami* or *ma meilleure amie* to introduce your best friend.
You could deal with the last bullet point in two ways – either recounting an outing that has already taken place, e.g. *samedi, nous sommes allés …* or looking forward to an outing that has not yet happened, e.g. *samedi, nous allons aller …*
In order for you to be clear about the timing of the event for the last bullet point, include the words *dernière sortie* or *prochaine sortie* on your plan.

6 Where you intend to live in the future
- say when you intend to leave home
- say where you intend to live
- say how you will keep in touch with your family
- say how often you will visit them

Use *à l'âge de … ans, je …* to say at what age you intend to leave home.
Use various ways of referring to a future event, e.g. *je voudrais / j'aimerais / j'espère/ j'ai l'intention de …*
Remember only to use words that you know the meaning of on your plan.

7 What you plan to do when you leave home
- say whether you would like to take a gap year
- say whether you intend to get married
- say whether you would like to have children
- conclude by saying how important family and friends are to you

Use *une année sabbatique* for 'a gap year'.
Use *se marier* for 'to get married'. Take care! With reflexive verbs, if you use *je,* you also have to use *me.*
Remember to check the total number of words you have used in your plan. It must be 40 or fewer.

You should now have completed your plan and prepared your answers. Give your plan to your teacher for feedback. As this is a practice task, your teacher might also choose to give you feedback on your first draft. However, when it comes to a task that is part of your GCSE French, you will get feedback on your plan but **not** on any draft you may have produced. Now compare your answers with the online sample version – you might find some useful hints to make yours even better.

kerboodle!

Résumé

1 Choose the correct ending of this sentence:

Chaque nuit il est recommandé de dormir pendant …

a une heure   b quatre heures

c huit heures   d douze heures

2 Choose the form of the verb to complete this sentence:

Ils ne _____ pas assez de sport.

a faire   b fait

c font   d fais

3 Which of the following is the healthiest?

a les frites   b le poisson

c un gâteau à la crème   d le chocolat

4 Which of the following is the unhealthiest?

a les frites   b les haricots verts

c le riz   d les céréales

5 Find the correct French translation for the following sentence:

I'm going to get married at the age of 25.

a Je vais me marier à l'âge de vingt-cinq ans.

b Il va se marier à l'âge de vingt-cinq ans.

c Je vais me marier à l'âge de vingt-sept ans.

d Je vais me reposer à l'âge de vingt-cinq ans.

6 Find the correct English translation for the following sentence:

Je veux aider les pauvres en Afrique.

a I want to help the war victims in Africa.

b I want to travel to Africa.

c I want to work with people in Africa.

d I want to help the poor in Africa.

Le sais-tu? ???????

Les Français achètent beaucoup de médicaments. Chaque Français dépense en moyenne 480€ par an pour les médicaments. De quelle couleur est la croix que l'on voit sur les pharmacies en France?

Le sais-tu? ??????

En France il faut se marier à la mairie. On peut aussi avoir un mariage religieux, mais on doit d'abord se marier devant le maire. Pour organiser une réception en France, il faut payer environ 12 000€!

2 Leisure

Sport and leisure; clothes

1a 📖🎧 Read about each person's activities and find the correct symbols for each one.

«Je fais de l'athlétisme et je joue au foot.»
Nadia

«Je joue de la guitare. L'été, je fais de la voile.»
Théo

«Je joue du piano et de la flûte.»
Alice

«Je ne joue pas d'un instrument de musique. Je fais du judo et du skate.»
Mehdi

a **b** **c** **d** **e**

f **g** **h** **i** **j**

1b 💬 **G** Work in pairs. Partner A chooses one of the symbols from Activity 1a. Partner B asks questions to find which one it is. Then swap parts.

Exemple: **A** Tu fais du judo? **B** Non. **A** Tu joues du piano?

Talking about pastimes

- When talking about games, use *jouer + au / à la / à l' / aux*:
  Je joue au tennis / à la pétanque / aux cartes.

- When talking about other sports or pastimes, use *faire + du / de la / de l' / des*:
  Je fais du karaté / de la natation / de l'équitation

- When talking about musical instruments, use *jouer + du / de la / de l' / des*:
  Je joue du violon / de la batterie / des percussions.

Grammaire page 169

2a 📖🎧 Find the correct clothes to match the speech bubbles.

a  **b** **c** **d** **e**

f  **g**

1 Quand je joue dans mon orchestre, je porte une robe violette et des chaussures marron.

2 Quand je fais du sport, je porte un short bleu et des baskets blanches.

3 Quand je fais du skate, je porte un pantalon gris et un sweat rouge.

2b ✏️ Complete these two descriptions.

1 Quand je _____ au basket, je porte un _____ vert, un sweat et des _____ noires.

2 Quand je joue _____, _____ …

Transport; places in town; simple directions

1 📖🎧 Read how each person travels to school, and find the correct pie chart for the group of ten students.

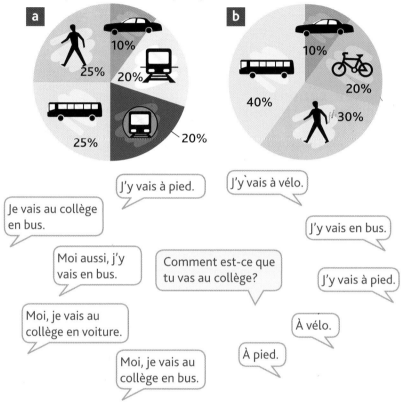

a 10% 25% 20% 25% 20%

b 10% 20% 40% 30%

Je vais au collège en bus.

J'y vais à pied.

J'y vais à vélo.

J'y vais en bus.

Moi aussi, j'y vais en bus.

Comment est-ce que tu vas au collège?

J'y vais à pied.

Moi, je vais au collège en voiture.

À vélo.

À pied.

Moi, je vais au collège en bus.

Vocabulaire

à pied	on foot
à vélo	by bike
en avion	by aeroplane
en bateau	by boat
en bus	by bus
en car	by coach
en métro	by underground
en TGV	by high-speed train
en train	by train
en voiture	by car

2 📖🎧 Find the correct sketch map for each dialogue.

1

– Pour aller à l'hôtel de ville, s'il vous plaît?

– Allez jusqu'au rond-point, puis continuez tout droit.

2

– Où est le stade, s'il vous plaît?

– Tournez à droite aux feux.

3

– Où est le marché, s'il vous plaît?

– Prenez la première rue à gauche.

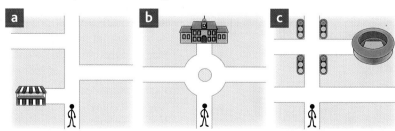

Vocabulaire

à droite	right
à gauche	left
le cinéma	cinema
les feux (m)	traffic lights
la gare	the station
le lycée	upper secondary school
l'hôtel de ville (m)	town hall
le marché	market
la patinoire	skating rink
la piscine	swimming pool
la première / deuxième rue	the first / second street
le rond-point	roundabout
le stade	stadium
le théâtre	theatre
tout droit	straight on

Saying where you are going

Use au / à l' / à la / aux to introduce the names of the place you are going to:

Je vais au cinéma.

Tu vas à la patinoire.

Elle va à l'hôtel de ville.

Grammaire page 170

Ce que j'ai fait chez moi

1 ❶ Sort these activities into three categories – those you like, those you don't like and those you've never tried.

jouer de la clarinette	faire les devoirs	promener le chien	surfer
regarder des DVD	faire du jardinage	faire la cuisine	chanter
chatter sur MSN	faire de la lecture	écouter de la musique	danser

Trois jeunes nous parlent de leur samedi

Marine

Le matin j'ai promené le chien. L'après-midi, j'ai écouté de la musique sur mon lecteur mp3, et j'ai joué de la clarinette. La musique, c'est ma passion. Le soir ma sœur et moi, nous avons préparé le dîner pour toute la famille.

Alexis

Mes parents m'ont défendu de sortir avec mes copains parce que les profs m'ont donné de mauvaises notes au lycée. Mon père m'a demandé de faire du travail pour l'école dans ma chambre. En réalité, j'ai passé des heures à surfer sur le net. J'ai chatté avec mes amis et j'ai regardé des DVD, et j'ai lu un peu. J'aime beaucoup lire les bandes dessinées.

Charlotte

Dimanche, j'ai rangé ma chambre et j'ai travaillé dans le jardin pour mes parents. L'après-midi, j'ai joué aux cartes avec ma sœur et j'ai gagné cinq parties. Elle a pleuré, elle était très vexée. Après, j'ai regardé mon feuilleton favori et les actualités. Après le dîner, j'ai fini mes devoirs de maths, quelle barbe! Et enfin j'ai bavardé avec ma meilleure copine au téléphone. Nous avons parlé des vedettes de cinéma qu'on aime bien.

2a 📖🎧 ⟳ Write the names of the people who carried out the activities pictured.

2b 📖🎧 ⟳ Who says the following?

1 I didn't do any school work.
2 I did some tidying.
3 I cooked a meal.
4 I chatted online.
5 My sister was fed up with me.
6 I really like music.

🎧 Stratégie

🎧 You can often work out whether a sentence is in the past or present tense by the time expressions used.

Present: *aujourd'hui* (today), *en ce moment* (at the moment), *le matin* (in the mornings), *d'habitude* (usually), *normalement* (normally).

Past: *l'année dernière* (last year), *hier* (yesterday), *il y a quatre jours* (four days ago).

3a 🎧 Listen to Maxime and Sandra. Decide whether their attitudes to the activities pictured are positive or negative.

3b 🎧 ⊛ Listen to Valentin and Lucie. Decide whether their attitudes to the following are positive, negative or mixed.

1 **Valentin**
  a gardening
  b playing the guitar
  c the cake
  d badminton

2 **Lucie**
  a TV
  b the newspaper
  c the soup
  d the sandwich

  e boardgame
  f music
  g chatting online

4a 🅖 Work with a partner. First decide which verb belongs with which sentence from the list of infinitives below. Then put the correct ending on (é or i). Read the sentence out in French then in English.

1 J'ai _____ le travail.
2 Est-ce que tu as _____ la télé?
3 Elle a _____ aux cartes.
4 Est-ce que vous avez _____ dans le jardin?

    finir   travailler   choisir   écouter

       jouer   regarder

4b 🅖 One partner adds the correct form of *avoir* to the following sentences to make the perfect tense, the other translates the sentence.

1 J'_____ choisi la clarinette.
2 Nous _____ dansé ensemble.
3 Elle _____ fait la cuisine.
4 Ils _____ écouté la radio.

5 🗨 With a partner, ask and answer these questions about what you do at home.

- Tu aimes quelle sorte de musique?
- Est-ce que tu lis souvent?
- Est-ce que tu regardes souvent la télé?
- Tu joues souvent aux cartes et à des jeux de société?

- Qu'est-ce que tu as fait le week-end dernier à la maison?
- Qu'est-ce que tu as fait avec tes amis?

> **Grammaire** page 167
>
> **Perfect tense with *avoir***
>
> You use the perfect tense to describe actions or events that took place in the past. To form the perfect tense, use the present tense of *avoir*, and the past participle. With -*er* verbs, the past participle ends in -*é*, with -*ir* verbs it ends in -*i*.
>
> *j'ai joué* = I played
> *tu as fini* = you finished
>
> Also learn how to form questions in French. *See page 66* ➡

> **Astuce**
>
> When you say you have done an activity in the perfect tense, always try to give your opinion about the activity using *c'était* (it was) or *je l'ai trouvé* (I found it), e.g. *J'ai regardé un film à la télé, je l'ai trouvé ennuyeux.*

> Tu aimes quelle sorte de musique?

> J'adore le rap, mais je n'aime pas tellement le hip-hop.

> Est-ce que tu joues d'un instrument de musique?

Je lis / regarde souvent / rarement	des magazines / des journaux / la télé	de temps en temps / (presque) tous les jours.
Le week-end dernier / Samedi dernier / Samedi soir / Dimanche matin	j'ai mangé / j'ai joué / j'ai préparé / j'ai nettoyé / j'ai dansé / j'ai bavardé avec …	
Je l'ai trouvé / J'ai trouvé ça C'était	ennuyeux / monotone / barbant / fatigant / amusant / marrant / intéressant / utile.	
J'ai rencontré mes amis en ville	et nous avons	joué / chanté / regardé / fini.

1 ⓥ Sort these activities into three groups – music, sport, or cinema.

J'ai vu un dessin animé.	J'ai chanté dans une chorale.
J'ai fait de la planche à voile.	J'ai joué du clavier.
J'ai mangé du popcorn.	J'ai fait du patin à roulettes.
J'ai écouté de la musique sur mon lecteur mp3.	J'ai aimé les acteurs.
J'ai acheté des billets.	J'ai écrit une chanson de rap.
J'ai fait du patinage.	Je suis allé au stade.

LES VACANCES DE FÉVRIER

Qu'est-ce que les jeunes de 16 ans ont fait pendant les vacances de février? Nous avons interviewé cinq filles et garçons, qui nous ont donné des réponses très variées.

Alexandre chante dans une chorale, et il a chanté presque tous les jours. Le soir il est rentré chez lui et il a joué du clavier.

Julie est allée six fois au centre-ville, et elle a vu deux films de guerre, un film romantique et trois films policiers pendant la semaine. Et le soir elle a regardé des films d'horreur en DVD.

Guillaume a fêté son anniversaire récemment, et il a reçu beaucoup d'argent. Il est allé au centre commercial avec ses copains et il a acheté un nouvel écran, un clavier et une souris.

Amina est allée quatre fois à la piscine olympique. À chaque fois elle a nagé pendant deux heures.

Maxime a fait du cheval en Espagne avec sa sœur. Elle avait peur parce que l'année dernière elle est tombée, mais cette fois il n'y a pas eu de problèmes.

2a 📖🎧 Write the name of the person who is interested in each of these activities.

1 le cinéma
2 l'informatique
3 l'équitation
4 la musique
5 la natation

2b 📖🎧 Note whether each of these statements is true (T), false (F) or not mentioned (?) according to the article.

1 Alexandre played the trumpet every evening.
2 Julie enjoyed the romantic film.
3 Guillaume has recently celebrated his birthday.
4 Amina spent four hours in the water.
5 Maxime went abroad.

3a 🎧 Listen to Section A and choose the correct expression to fill the gap.

1 Olivier saw a comedy film   science-fiction film   romantic film .
2 He went alone   with his friends   with his girlfriend .
3 Next week it's his birthday   brother's birthday   sister's birthday .
4 Richard's team won   lost   drew .
5 Next weekend he's going out with his friends   dad   uncle .

3b 🎧 Listen to Sections A and B and fill in the table with the activities each person did last weekend and what they are going to do next weekend.

	Last weekend	Next weekend
Olivier		
Richard		
Danielle		
Jasmine		

4a **G** Fill in the correct form of *être*.

1 Il _____ parti à la piscine sans nous.
2 Est-ce que tu _____ sortie hier soir, Anne-Marie?
3 Ils _____ restés au café pendant une heure.
4 Je m'appelle Jacqueline. Je _____ allée au centre sportif.

4b **G** Select the correct past participle.

1 Les filles sont arrivé   arrivés   arrivées au stade avant nous.
2 Elle est tombé   tombée   tombées sur la glace.
3 Vous êtes rentré   rentrées   rentrés à quelle heure, les garçons?
4 Elles sont allé   allés   allées au concert ensemble.

5 ✏ 🌐 Write an account of a busy Saturday.

- ■ Say where you went on Saturday afternoon and why.
- ■ Say who you went with.
- ■ Say what you did and what you thought of it.
- ■ Say what you did on Saturday evening and what you thought of it.
- ■ Say what you thought of the day and why.

Samedi après-midi / soir	je suis allé(e) au cinéma / au stade / à la piscine / en ville	avec mes copains / copines / ma famille / mon frère / ma sœur / tout(e) seul.
On a / Nous avons	fait du shopping / acheté des CD / vu un film qui s'appelle… / joué au … / dansé / mangé au restaurant.	
C'était (vraiment / un peu) Dans l'ensemble, c'était	marrant / fantastique / barbant / une perte de temps / amusant / relaxant / fatigant / ennuyeux	parce que …

Grammaire · *page 167*

Perfect tense with *être*

The perfect tense of some verbs is formed with the present tense of *être* instead of *avoir*. The past participle then agrees with the subject of the sentence.

Elle est arrivée.   She has arrived.

être	past participle
je suis	tombé(e)
tu es	monté(e)
il est	parti
elle est	arrivée
nous sommes	allé(e)s
vous êtes	rentré(e)s
ils / elles sont	resté(e)s

Also learn how to form negative perfect tense sentences.

See page 66 ➡

Stratégie

✏ You can use two different tenses in the same sentence. The first part of the sentence can be in the present tense to say what you normally do, and the second part in the perfect to say what you did recently.

Normalement, je sors avec ma sœur, mais hier je suis sortie avec mes copines.

Astuce

When writing French, if you are describing what you do or have done, it is useful to include time expressions such as *souvent / tous les jours / de temps en temps*, e.g. *Je vais souvent au café.*

---

kerboodle!

2.3 L'argent et le shopping

Un nouveau centre commercial

Venez au nouveau centre commercial Clair-Soleil. Il est moderne, il est pratique, le choix est énorme et les prix sont bas!

Il y a cinq restaurants, un bowling, un cinéma et environ cinquante magasins extrêmement différents: on peut y acheter des équipements de sport, des vêtements, des frigos, des télés, des machines à laver …

Il y a quelque chose pour toute la famille, il y a même des jouets pour les enfants.

Nos clients disent …

Carole Machin

Tout le monde parle du centre Claire-Soleil! Samedi je vais y aller avec mon cousin, je vais acheter un cadeau pour son anniversaire.

N'oubliez pas pour les automobilistes, le parking est gratuit!

Thomas Deniau

Samedi dernier, je suis allé au nouveau centre commercial Clair-Soleil. C'est fantastique! J'ai pris le bus pour y aller, c'est pratique.

Nadine Lescaut

Je suis allé à Clair-Soleil samedi dernier et j'ai beaucoup aimé le choix de magasins, c'est vraiment super et donc je vais y retourner le week-end prochain.

1a 📖🎧 Read the information in the top half of the poster and decide whether the statements are true (T), false (F) or not mentioned in the text (?).

1 The prices are high.
2 There is nowhere to eat in the centre.
3 There are about fifty shops.
4 You can buy electrical goods.
5 The centre is near a motorway.

1b 📖🎧 Read the customer comments in the bottom half of the poster and decide whether the statements are true (T), false (F) or not mentioned in the text (?).

1 Carol is going to buy a birthday present for her cousin.
2 Thomas has already been to the centre three times.
3 He went there by car.
4 Nadine liked the choice of restaurants.
5 She wants to go back to the centre.

2a 🎧 Listen to Section A and correct the mistakes in the following sentences.

1 Laurie receives 20 euros a week pocket money.
2 She buys clothes, make-up and socks.
3 Nathan obtains money by washing the windows.
4 He wants to buy himself a new bike.
5 Maude bought a new violin recently.

2b 🎧 Listen to Section B and choose the correct answer.

1 Simon likes buying books   DVDs   computer games .
2 Next weekend he wants to buy presents for his family   friends   girlfriend .
3 David likes big department stores   smaller shops   the market .
4 He thinks the prices in small shops are more expensive than   cheaper than   about the same as bigger shops.
5 Nicolas likes the shopping centre because there is plenty to do   he never tires of shopping   there are fewer people there .

3 Ⓖ Add the correct irregular past participle, choosing from the grammar box.

1 Il a _____ un Coca au MacDo du centre commercial.
2 Tu as _____ du shopping au centre-ville?
3 J'ai _____ un bon film au cinéma.
4 J'ai _____ une publicité pour un nouveau magasin de jouets.
5 Elles ont _____ le bus pour aller au marché.
6 J'ai _____ mes nouveaux vêtements.

4 🗨 🔊 Work with a partner. First decide whether each of the following answers are past, present or future. Next work out what the questions were. Finally adapt the answers to talk about yourself. Add some information in a different time frame.

▪ Je reçois dix livres par semaine.
▪ Je reçois de l'argent de mes parents et de mes grands-parents.
▪ Je fais des économies (quatre livres par mois).
▪ Le week-end prochain, je vais faire du jardinage pour mes parents.
▪ J'ai acheté un pantalon et une nouvelle paire de chaussures.

Tu reçois de l'argent de poche?

Je reçois dix livres par semaine.

Je reçois de l'argent	de mes parents / quand je fais du travail.	
Je fais des économies	parce que j'ai l'intention d'acheter … / parce que je veux partir en vacances.	
Pour gagner de l'argent je vais	laver la voiture / faire du baby-sitting.	
J'ai acheté	un nouveau blouson / un cadeau pour …	
J'aime mieux les petits magasins / les centre commerciaux	parce que / qu' car	il y a plus de choix / c'est moins cher / le service est bon.
Je vais acheter quelque chose	pour l'anniversaire de ma mère / mon copain.	

Ⓖ Grammaire *page 174*

Perfect tense: irregular verbs

Many verbs have irregular past participles. Copy and learn the table below, making an extra column with English translations.

avoir	past participle
j'ai	*eu (avoir)*
tu as	*lu (lire)*
il a	*vu (voir)*
elle a	*mis (mettre)*
on a	*bu (boire)*
nous avons	*pris (prendre)*
vous avez	*reçu (recevoir)*
ils / elles ont	*fait (faire)*

Also learn about *ça* and *ce*.

See page 66 ➡

🗨 Stratégie

When you are speaking, try to use all three time frames, e.g. if you are asked how much pocket money you receive, say how much you get now, what it is going up to in the near future and what you have bought recently.

Je reçois > Je vais recevoir > J'ai acheté

Astuce

Remember, to ask a question in conversation, all you need to do is make sure your voice rises towards the end of the sentence, e.g. *Tu reçois de l'argent de poche?*

kerboodle!

La mode

1 **V** Look at the sale sign. How much would you pay for the following?

jacket   socks   shoes

shirt   trousers   dress

skirt

Soldes!

Offre spécial

pantalons	25 euros
jupes	20 euros
robes en coton	30 euros
vestes	45 euros
chaussures	29 euros
chaussettes	5 euros
chemises	5 euros

La taille zéro

A Dans la presse on parle souvent de la taille zéro américaine. Dans les magazines et à la télé on voit des top models et des célébrités très, très minces.

B Selon les experts, c'est la mode qui est responsable de l'anorexie. La presse pour les adolescentes a beaucoup de photographies de top models, d'articles sur les régimes, de produits de beauté et de vêtements élégants.

C Beaucoup de jeunes filles veulent imiter ces top models et les magazines donnent l'impression qu'il faut devenir mince pour être belle. Les jeunes filles deviennent donc anorexiques ou boulimiques car elles voudraient être comme les top models.

D La réalité de l'anorexie est affreuse. Dans son livre *Ce matin, j'ai décidé d'arrêter de manger,* Justine nous dit comment, à 14 ans, elle a commencé un régime «pour être belle» et elle a fini par perdre 36 kilos.

E Certaines villes ont décidé de combattre ce problème. Les top models trop minces ou trop jeunes ne sont pas admises dans les défilés.

F Le ministre de la Santé a dit: «L'image de la femme idéale dans les magazines de mode n'existe pas. On aime toutes les filles, grosses ou minces, mais surtout naturelles!»

2 Read the article and choose a summary for each paragraph (A–F).

1 Some cities ban models who are too thin.
2 The opinion of a politician on the appearance of the ideal woman.
3 A first-hand account of what anorexia is like from a young victim of the illness.
4 Fashion can be a cause of anorexia.
5 Size zero and skinny models are often seen in the media.
6 Young girls think that they need to be thin to be beautiful.

> When you come across a word you do not recognise, you need to use the context and the surrounding words you do know to work out the meaning. For example, in the sentence *le top model porte un gilet chic,* you can assume that *gilet* is an item of clothing because a model is wearing it (*porte*) and it is described as smart (*chic*).

Stratégie

2 **G** With a partner, make these sentences comparative by choosing a word that matches your opinion – *plus*, *moins* or *aussi*. Say if you agree with your partner's opinion (*c'est vrai / je ne suis pas d'accord*).

Exemple: La radio est plus amusante que le cinéma.

1 Les ordinateurs sont _____ pratiques que les téléphones portables.

2 La lecture est _____ amusante que la musique.

3 Les textos sont _____ faciles que les e-mails.

4 Les portables sont _____ utiles que les lecteurs mp3.

5 Les films romantiques sont _____ intéressants que les films d'horreur.

6 La musique est _____ relaxante que le sport.

3 Link the statements (1–6) that you hear to the concerns expressed below. You can use the same letter more than once.

a health issues

b crime

c irritating noise

d false identity issues

e expense

> ### Grammaire | page 162
>
> **Comparative adjectives**
>
> Use the words *plus, moins* or *aussi* (as), followed by an adjective, then *que* and the thing you are comparing.
>
> *La télé est moins (plus) utile qu'Internet.* TV is less (more) useful than the internet.
>
> Exception: *meilleur* = better
>
> *Les DVD sont meilleurs que les vidéos.*
>
> DVDs are better than videos.
>
> Also learn about using the pronoun *on* with impersonal expressions, as well as using it to mean 'we'. *See page 67* ➡

4 With a partner, answer these questions about new technology. One of you plays the part of someone who loves new technology, the other dislikes it. When your partner has given their opinion, ask them why (*pourquoi?*) or why not (*pourquoi pas?*).

- Tu utilises souvent un téléphone portable?

- Quels sont les avantages ou les dangers d'Internet?

- Que penses-tu de la télé par satellite ou par câble?

- Est-ce que tu utilises un lecteur mp3?

- Est-ce que tu envoies souvent des messages électroniques?

> ### Stratégie
>
> When you have given your opinion, it is a good idea to give a reason why you hold that view. Useful phrases for adding a reason are *parce que / car / pour cette raison / à cause de cela*. So if you say something like *la télé est bête* you could add *parce qu'il y a trop de jeux*.

> Tu utilises souvent un téléphone portable?

> Oui, assez souvent.

> Pourquoi?

> J'appelle souvent mes parents et j'envoie des textos à mes amis.

> ### Astuce
>
> When you use adjectives in French, always try to add a quantifier such as *très / assez / trop*, e.g. *c'est trop cher, c'est assez amusant* etc.

	Avantage	Désavantage
(téléphone) portable	On peut contacter ses parents ou envoyer des textos.	C'est trop cher. Les sonneries m'énervent.
Internet	C'est pratique pour le shopping ou les devoirs.	On peut passer trop de temps devant l'ordinateur.
télé par satellite	Il y a plus de choix.	Il y a beaucoup de mauvaises émissions.
lecteurs mp3	La musique c'est relaxant.	Il est facile de les perdre.

kerboodle!

Free time and the media

Femme | Bébé Enfant | **Jeune 10–18** | Homme | Chaussures | Sport | Accessoires

Offres de la semaine!

De nouveaux prix pour une semaine seulement! Désirez-vous profiter de ces offres? Vous avez 7 jours!

Cliquez sur la description pour voir la photo.

1 Veste grise en laine garçon
16,44€

6 Gilet long filles, en laine, ceinture, sans manches
10,46€

2 T-shirt, coton, manches longues garçon
15,90€

7 Chemise blanche en polyester garçon, manches longues
6,96€

3 Chaussures noires en cuir filles
10,00€

8 Jean noir en coton garçon, slim
13,69€

4 Jean bleu filles, standard
15,00€

9 Parka fille, capuche
16,47€

5 T-shirt coton filles, manches longues
7,14€

10 Sweat garçon à capuche
7,96€

Christophe – un client satisfait

Je déteste aller dans les magasins! J'ai donc comparé vos prix à ceux des grands magasins en ville, et quand j'ai vu les résultats, j'ai choisi ces vêtements par Internet. Pour moi, il est important de trouver des articles de bonne qualité, mais qui ne sont pas trop chers. Et, en plus j'ai fait des économies, car je n'ai pas payé le bus pour aller faire mon shopping. J'ai fait mes achats en ligne mardi après-midi. Mon frère aussi a acheté des vêtements. Il a choisi un jean et un pull. Jeudi matin, ils sont tous arrivés à la maison. Quel service de qualité! Je vais revenir sur ce site web, avant de partir en vacances en juillet.

Merci! Christophe (étudiant, Bordeaux)

1a 📖🎧 Look at the clothes shopping website and answer the following questions in English.

1 For how long are these offers available?
2 What happens if you click on the description of an item?
3 How much would you pay for:
   a the two items with a hood?
   b the item with a belt?
   c the footwear?
   d the narrow-legged jeans?
   e the long-sleeved item for girls?
4 Robert is allergic to man-made fabrics, so has to wear clothes made of natural materials. Describe in detail, in English, the three items of clothing on the list that he can wear.

1b 📖🎧 Read the message sent in by Christophe. Complete the sentences in English.

1 Before deciding to buy from the website, Christophe _____.
2 His two main considerations when buying clothes are _____.
3 He also saved money because _____.
4 The order included clothes for _____.
5 The clothes arrived _____ after ordering.
6 He expects to use the website again before _____.
7 He probably does not have much money because _____.

2a 🎧 Listen to the whole conversation, and put the following activities in the order that Solange did them at the weekend (1–5). She mentions them in the order she did them.

1 homework
2 reading
3 shopping
4 went to a party
5 watched a film

2b 🎧 Now listen again in detail. Which three sentences are correct?

1 Delphine travelled home by coach.
2 She was met by her father.
3 Her mother thinks her shoes are too high.
4 On Saturday evening they went to a party.
5 Solange was distracted from her homework by reading magazines because she was ill.
6 Delphine has to revise for a test in geography.

Vocabulaire	
la capuche	hood
la ceinture	belt
en cuir	leather
en laine	woollen
l'étudiant (m)	university student
la manche	sleeve
revenir	to come back

Irregular past participles *Grammaire* page 167

Both the reading and listening texts contain verbs in the perfect tense, some of which use *être*, or have irregular past participles. Find the example using *être*, in Christophe's section of the reading, and three in the first part of the conversation between the two girls. How many irregular past participles can you pick out in the rest of the listening text?

AQA *Examiner's tip*

Look at the sentences in advance, and work out which part, if any, is likely to be wrong, e.g. in question 1 it is likely to be the means of transport.

G Free time and the media

Est-ce que ... ? and *Qu'est-ce que ... ?*;
Negatives with the perfect tense; *Ça* and *ce*

1a 📖 Match the French and the English.

1	Tu as pris des photos.	a	You went out to a restaurant last night.
2	Elle aime les sports d'hiver.		
3	Tu as dansé avec mon frère.	b	Nabila went windsurfing in Morocco.
4	Il a regardé un film d'horreur.	c	You danced with my brother.
5	Vous êtes allés au restaurant hier soir.	d	He watched a horror film.
6	Nabila a fait de la planche à voile au Maroc.	e	She likes winter sports.
		f	You took photographs.

1b ✏ Now change the statements into questions that have the following meanings in English, using *Est-ce que ...?*, *Est-ce qu' ...?*, *Qu'est-ce que ...?* or *Qu'est-ce qu' ...?* The first two are done for you.

1 What did you take? > *Qu'est-ce que tu as pris?*
2 Does she like winter sports? > *Est-ce qu'elle aime les sports d'hiver?*
3 Did you dance with my brother? >
4 What did he watch? >
5 Did you go to a restaurant yesterday evening? >
6 What did Nabila do? >

2 ✏ Rewrite the following questions with the words in the correct order.

1 Je / sortie /ne / pas / suis / hier soir.
2 n' / pas / a / fait / Elle / les courses.
3 n' / pas / Il / a / trouvé / ça amusant.
4 n' / Tu / es / pas / tombé / sur la glace.

3 ✏ Complete with *ça* or *ce* or *c'*, then match each one to the correct English translation.

1 ___f___ n'est pas très cher!   •a Are you OK?
2 ___d___ n'est pas assez!   b Do you like it?
3 ___c___ va?   c It's not going well!
4 ___e___ est trop cher.   d That's not enough!
5 Tu aimes ___b___?   e That's too expensive.
6 ___c___ ne va pas!   f It's not very expensive!

Est-ce que ...? and **Qu'est-ce que ...?**

Grammaire page 169

■ In French, you can change statements into questions by adding *Est-ce que* (or *qu'* before a vowel) at the beginning of the sentence and a question mark at the end.
 Statement:
 Il part aux États-Unis. He's leaving for the United States.
 Question:
 Est-ce qu'il part aux États-Unis? Is he leaving for the United States?

■ The French equivalent of 'what...' is usually *Qu'est-ce que ...?*
 Qu'est-ce que c'est? What is it?
 Qu'est-ce que tu veux? What do you want?

Negatives with the perfect tense

Grammaire page 167

To make a negative statement in the perfect tense, *ne / n'* comes before the form of *avoir / être* and *pas* comes straight after.

Il a regardé la télé.	He watched TV.
Il n'a pas regardé la télé.	He didn't watch TV.
Je suis sorti.	I went out.
Je ne suis pas sorti.	I didn't go out.

Ça and **ce**

Grammaire page 162

■ *Ce* means 'that' or 'those' or 'it', and it is usually followed by a form of *être*. It is shortened to *c'* in front of a vowel.

C'est un fruit.	That's a fruit.
Ce sont des légumes.	Those are vegetables.

■ *Ça* is used in various phrases:

Ça va?	Are you okay?
Ça ne va pas.	It's not going well.
Tu aimes ça?	Do you like it?

Aimer and *détester*; *On* meaning 'we' or 'people'

4 ✏ Complete the captions to go with each set of pictures using the list below.

Grammaire page 170

> **Aimer and détester**
>
> When *j'aime* or *je déteste* or *je préfère* is followed by a verb, that second verb is in the infinitive.
>
> *J'aime porter une robe.*
> I like wearing dresses.
>
> *Je déteste faire les magasins.*
> I hate shopping.
>
> *Je préfère aller à la patinoire.*
> I'd rather go ice skating.

1 Je déteste _____,
  je préfère _____.

2 J'aime _____,
  mais je préfère _____.

Grammaire page 164

> **On meaning 'we' or 'people'**
>
> ■ Most French people use *on* to mean 'we' in casual speech.
>   *On sort ce soir.*
>   We are going out tonight.
>
> ■ *On* can also be the equivalent of 'people' or 'they' or the impersonal 'you'.
>   *On dit que c'est bien.*
>   People say it is good.
>
>   *Comment dit-on "computer" en français?*
>   How do you say 'computer' in French?'

3 Je n'aime pas _____,
  je préfère _____.

4 Je déteste _____,
  je préfère _____.

écouter de la musique	faire les magasins	porter une robe	porter un jean
jouer au ping-pong	aller à la piscine	regarder la télé	faire du judo

5 📖 Choose the best English translation in each case.

1 On va où?
  a Where are we going?
  b Where are they going?

2 On dit que les portables sont dangereux.
  a We say that mobiles are harmful.
  b They say mobiles are harmful.

3 Est-ce qu'on peut se faire des amis sur Internet?
  a Can we become friends on the Internet?
  b Can you make friends on the Internet?

4 On ne doit pas rester trop longtemps devant son ordinateur.
  a You mustn't sit in front of your computer for too long.
  b He mustn't sit in front of his computer for too long.

5 Qu'est-ce qu'on fait ce soir?
  a What are we doing tonight?
  b What are people doing tonight?

6 On va à la piscine?
  a Shall we go swimming?
  b Are they going for a swim?

Free time and the media

Ce que j'ai fait chez moi ➡ *pages 54–55*

les	*actualités (f)*	the news
	aider	to help
la	*bande dessinée*	cartoon strip, comic book
	bavarder	to chat, talk
des	*chanteurs (m)*	singers
	chatter sur MSN	to chat on instant messenger
les	*devoirs (m)*	homework
	écouter	to listen to
une	*émission*	programme
le	*feuilleton*	series, soap opera
	gagner	to earn
le	*jardinage*	gardening
le	*jeu*	game
un	*jeu de société*	board game
le	*journal*	newspaper
un	*lecteur mp3*	mp3 player
la	*lecture*	reading
	lire	to read
les	*mauvaises nouvelles (f)*	bad news
	promener le chien	to walk the dog
	ranger ma chambre	to clean my room
	regarder	to watch
	surfer	to surf
des	*vedettes de cinéma (f)*	cinema stars

Les loisirs ➡ *pages 56–57*

	aller à la pêche	to go fishing
un	*appareil-photo*	camera
	chanter	to sing
le	*clavier*	keyboard
la	*chorale*	choir
le	*cyclisme*	cycling
	dépenser	to spend
	faire du cheval	to go horseriding
	faire du patinage sur glace	to go iceskating
	faire du ski	to go skiing

	faire une promenade	to go for a walk
les	*films de guerre (m)*	war films
les	*films d'horreur (m)*	horror films
les	*films de science-fiction (m)*	science fiction films
les	*films policiers (m)*	detective films
les	*films romantiques (m)*	romantic films
	nager	to swim
	prendre des photos	to take photos
les	*sports d'hiver (m)*	winter sports
	sortir	to go out, leave
	tomber	to fall
le	*VTT (vélo tout terrain)*	mountain bike

L'argent et le shopping ➡ *pages 58–59*

	acheter	to buy
à l'	*avenir*	in the future
l'	*argent de poche (m)*	pocket money
	bas(se)	low
la	*boucherie*	butcher's shop
la	*boulangerie*	bakery
la	*boutique*	boutique
un	*cadeau*	present
un	*centre commercial*	shopping centre
la	*charcuterie*	pork butcher's shop and delicatessen
des	*chaussures (f)*	shoes
	cher (-ère)	dear, expensive
le	*choix*	choice
le	*client*	client, customer
l'	*épicerie (f)*	green grocer's shop
	faire des économies	to save up (money)
le	*frigo*	fridge
	gratuit(e)	free
des	*jouets (m)*	toys
la	*machine à laver*	washing machine
les	*magasins (m)*	shops
le	*maquillage*	make-up
le	*marché*	market

la	pâtisserie	cake shop
la	pharmacie	pharmacy
les	prix (m)	prices
la	publicité	publicity
	recevoir	to receive, get
	varié(e)	varied
les	vêtements (m)	clothes

1 Ⓥ Here is a shopping list. Where would you go for these items?

> de l'aspirine
> du jambon
> du bifteck
> une tarte aux cerises
> un kilo de pommes de terre
> un paquet de sucre
> une baguette et quatre croissants

la boucherie l'épicerie la boulangerie

la pâtisserie la pharmacie le marché

la charcuterie

La mode ➡ pages 60–61

	affreux (-euse)	hideous, horrible
	chic	stylish
un	collant	tights
en	coton	(made) of cotton
la	cravate	tie
des	défilés de mode	fashion show
	gros(se)	fat
un	manteau	coat
	mince	thin
	large	wide, broad
la	mode	fashion
	perdre	to lose
	porter	to wear / carry
les	produits de beauté (m)	beauty products
un	pull	jumper

le	pyjama	pyjamas
un	sac à main	handbag
les	soldes (m)	the sales
la	taille	size
une	veste	jacket

Les nouvelles technologies ➡ pages 62–63

	aller sur un site	to go to a website
l'	avantage (m)	advantage
le	désavantage	disadvantage
	en ligne	online
	envoyer	to send
des	étrangers (m)	strangers
les	inconvenients (m)	disadvantages
le	jeu	game
un	jeu vidéo	video game
le	lecteur DVD	DVD player
les	messages électroniques (m)	electronic messages
l'	ordinateur (m)	computer
la	presse écrite	the press
des	renseignements (m)	information
la	sonnerie	ringing
le	(téléphone) portable	mobile phone
des	textos (m)	texts
	utiliser	to use

2 Ⓥ What is your opinion of the following?

la télé par satellite   les forums sur Internet

les ordinateurs portables   les lecteurs mp3

la radio   la presse écrite

les messages électroniques

la sonnerie des téléphones portables

Ça m'énerve!

Ça ne me'intéresse pas spécialement.

J'aime ça.

2.6 Vive les vacances!

Objectifs

Talking about holiday preferences

How to say 'to' or 'in' a country

Using what you know

1 **V** Choose the odd one out.

1	ski nautique	voile	natation	promenade en bateau	cyclisme
2	la Chine	la France	le Portugal	la Russie	la Belgique
3	la montagne	la plage	le ski	les sports d'hiver	la neige
4	le pique-nique	le camping	l'hôtel	le logement	la villa
5	la cuisine	les glaces	le pique-nique	le restaurant	le bord de la mer

Sondage: les vacances que je préfère ...

77% des Français aiment passer leurs vacances au bord de la mer, comme Valérie ...

«Je pars en vacances avec ma famille. Tous les ans on va au bord de la mer, pas loin de Bordeaux. J'adore bronzer sur la plage et nager dans la mer. L'année dernière, il faisait trop chaud.»

35% aiment passer des vacances à la campagne, comme Églantine ...

«Moi, j'aime les vacances à la campagne parce que j'adore le calme et l'air est pur. Ma famille a passé des vacances en France. Mon père veut aller au Portugal mais il fait trop chaud, je crois. J'aime faire des promenades en forêt avec mes parents; j'aime aussi faire des pique-niques dans la nature. Je n'aime pas aller au bord de la mer en été car je trouve qu'il y a trop de monde sur les plages et on dit que bronzer est mauvais pour la santé.»

23% aiment partir à l'étranger, comme Guillaume ...

«J'aime partir à l'étranger parce que je veux connaître des cultures différentes. La plage, ça va mais j'aime surtout rester dans une grande ville parce que j'adore visiter les musées et les monuments historiques. L'année dernière, je suis allé en Angleterre et j'ai visité Londres. Il y avait beaucoup de choses à faire et c'était vraiment intéressant mais malheureusement il fait mauvais presque tous les jours.»

57% aiment les sports d'hiver, comme Safina ...

«Je n'aime pas partir au mois d'août, pendant les grandes vacances parce qu'il fait souvent trop chaud. Je préfère partir à la montagne pour faire du ski. Quand je suis en vacances, j'aime me relaxer. J'aime partir avec mes amies parce que j'ai plus de liberté. Je ne m'entends pas bien avec mes parents. L'année prochaine je voudrais aller aux États-Unis, à New York.»

2a 📖 🎧 Read the report. Choose the correct photo.

1 Je vais à la montagne dans les Alpes.
2 J'aime passer mes vacances à la campagne.
3 Cette année, je reste chez moi.
4 J'aime passer le week-end dans une grande ville.
5 Je vais toujours au bord de la mer.

2b 📖 🎧 Read the report again. Who says the following?

1 I love peace and quiet.
2 I like sunbathing.
3 I'm interested in foreign culture.
4 Sunbathing is bad for you.
5 I think it is important to relax on holiday.

3 🎬 🎧 Watch the video or listen to the audio track for Sections A and B and decide which statements are true (a, b or c).

1 a Océane likes holidays in the country.
   b She likes city breaks.
   c She likes going to the seaside.

2 a She likes sunbathing.
   b She likes water sports.
   c She likes shopping.

3 a Nicolas doesn't like Spanish food.
   b He likes going to Spain.
   c He doesn't like cooking.

4 a Nicolas prefers to stay in a holiday apartment.
   b He likes camping.
   c He prefers to stay in a hotel.

5 a Nicolas prefers going on holiday with his family.
   b His parents are not very nice to him.
   c Last year he stayed at home.

6 a The weather was awful.
   b He visited a farm.
   c He did not enjoy visiting the farm.

7 a He would like to stay in a luxury apartment.
   b He would like a sea view.
   c He wants to stay there for a week.

4 🄶 Fill in the correct preposition *en*, *au*, *aux* or *à*.

1 Je veux aller _____ États-Unis.
2 Mes grands-parents habitent _____ Canada.
3 Je vais faire du shopping _____ New York.
4 Cette année je vais à Rome _____ Italie.
5 En juillet, je suis allé _____ pays de Galles.
6 Je voudrais aller _____ Caraïbes.

5 🗨 🌐 Ask as many people as possible in the class these questions about their holiday preferences. Report back your findings to your partner. Use the box below to help.

- Où est-ce que tu aimes partir en vacances et pourquoi?
- Quelle sorte de logement préfères-tu?
- Comment est-ce que tu aimes voyager? Pourquoi?
- Qu'est-ce que tu aimes faire en vacances?
- Tu aimes mieux partir en vacances en famille ou avec des amis? Pourquoi?
- Où es-tu parti(e) l'année dernière? C'était comment?
- Comment sont tes vacances idéales? Pourquoi?

Grammaire *page 170*

How to say 'to' or 'in' a country

If you want to say 'to' or 'in' a country in French, you need to know the gender of the country. Feminine countries (*la France, l'Angleterre, l'Espagne*) take *en*.

Masculine countries (*le Portugal, le Canada*) take *au*. If the country is plural (*les États-Unis*) use *aux*. Cities take *à*.

Je vais à Londres. I am going to London.

Also learn how to recognise some useful verbs in the imperfect tense.   *See page 80* ➡

Stratégie

🗨 When speaking French, avoid guessing at words you do not know. Use what you are sure is correct. If you are talking about holidays, for example, and you stayed in a campsite but you forget the French for campsite, it is better to say *je suis resté(e) dans un hôtel* rather than making up a word that may be incorrect.

Astuce

Don't forget: if someone says *je suis allé en France avec mes parents*, when reporting back you need to say *Il est allé en France avec ses parents*.

Alison aime partir en Espagne, parce qu'il y fait chaud.

Elle préfère loger dans un hôtel.

Elle préfère voyager en avion, parce que c'est rapide et pratique.

En vacances, elle aime aller à la plage pour bronzer et nager.

Elle aime aller en vacances avec sa famille, parce qu'elle s'entend bien avec ses frères.

L'année dernière, ils sont allés dans le nord de l'Espagne. C'était vraiment intéressant.

Pour ses vacances idéales Alison voudrait partir en Chine.

Les vacances des Français

Les Français aiment les vacances et détestent le travail. C'est vrai? C'est un peu inexact mais les Français adorent leurs vacances.

La destination la plus visitée en hiver est la montagne parce que le ski redevient de plus en plus populaire.

Mais en été, plus de 35 millions de Français partent en vacances sur les plages de la Méditerranée ou de l'Atlantique.

Pour les gens qui aiment le calme, il y a la campagne. Au printemps et en automne, on peut y faire des promenades, aller à la pêche dans les rivières, ou nager dans les lacs. Les gens qui vont à la campagne y reviennent souvent.

En général les Français préfèrent rester en France. Seulement 15% des Français ont visité un pays étranger pendant leurs vacances. Beaucoup de personnes pensent que les voyages en avion sont mauvais pour l'environnement.

A

B

C

1a 📖 🎧 🌐 Place the letters of the three photos in the order in which they are mentioned in the article.

1b 📖 🎧 🌐 According to the article, decide whether the following statements are true (T), false (F) or not mentioned (?).

1 The French don't like going on holiday.
2 Skiing is becoming more popular.
3 More people go to the Atlantic coast than the Mediterranean.
4 According to the article, there is nothing to do in the countryside.
5 Spain is the most popular foreign destination.
6 Many people are worried about the effects of flying on the environment.

📖 **Stratégie**

Verbs beginning with *re-* (such as *revisiter*) often mean to do something again: *revenir* (to come back), *revoir* (to see again). Many adjectives beginning with *in-* (such as *inexact*) are the equivalent of the English *un-*, e.g. *inconfortable* (uncomfortable), *inutile* (useless). Look out for these when reading or listening to French. Look for examples in the reading passage above.

2a 🎧 Listen to the holiday plans and match the numbers (1–4) with the locations.

    a seaside   **b** mountains   **c** city break   **d** countryside

2b 🎧 Listen again and write down what activities the speakers (1–4) did last year and what they want to do next time. If two activities are suggested, write them both down.

3a **G** Fill in the gaps in the table below. Use the verb tables on page 176 to help you if you need to. Remember that *réserver* takes *avoir* in the perfect tense, and *rester* takes *être*.

infinitive	translation	past	present	future
réserver	to reserve, book	j'	je réserve	je
rester	to stay	je	je reste	je

3b **G** Choose the correct tense to complete the sentence. Look carefully at the clues at the beginning which will help you to decide.

  1 Tous les ans, je _____ en vacances en Normandie. (aller)

  2 Il y a deux ans, nous _____ la Bretagne. (visiter)

  3 L'année prochaine, je _____ une chambre familiale avec demi-pension. (réserver)

  4 Hier, les enfants _____ une promenade à vélo. (faire)

  5 La semaine dernière, nous _____ dans une grande villa. (rester)

  6 Dans deux ans, je _____ aux États-Unis. (voyager)

4 ✏ Compare the holiday you took last year with your plans for this year.

    ▪ Say where you stayed last year and what you intend to do this year.

    ▪ Describe what you did and what you intend to do.

    ▪ Say who you went with and who you are going with this time.

    ▪ Say where you stayed and where you would like to stay this year.

    ▪ Include your opinion about last year's activities, and what your hopes for this year are.

Grammaire *page 166*

Using past and future tenses

Learn how to use verbs in the perfect, present and future tenses.

J'ai visité l'Italie.	I visited Italy.
Je visite l'Italie.	I am visiting Italy.
Je vais visiter l'Italie.	I am going to visit Italy.

Faire and *aller*

j'ai fait > je fais > je vais faire

je suis allé > je vais > je vais aller

Also learn about using the superlative. *See page 80* ➡

Astuce

When speaking or writing about the past or the future in French, be careful not to get confused between *dernier* (last) and *prochain* (next). *L'année dernière je suis allé en Italie* but *L'année prochaine je vais aller en Espagne*.

Last holiday	Next holiday
L'année dernière, je suis allé(e) …	Cette année, je vais aller …
L'été dernier j'ai fait / joué / visité …	Cette année, je vais faire / jouer / visiter …
La dernière fois que je suis parti(e) en vacances j'y suis allé(e) avec …	La prochaine fois je vais partir avec …
Je suis resté(e) / j'ai logé dans une villa …	La prochaine fois je voudrais loger dans …
Je suis resté(e) à la maison, et j'ai fait des activités dans ma région.	Je ne sais pas encore ce que je voudrais faire cette année, mais je rêve de …
C'étaient les vacances les plus amusantes / relaxantes / ennuyeuses de ma vie.	Cette année j'espère passer des vacances sportives / intéressantes / relaxantes.

Que faire en vacances?

1 **V** Match the following words to their English equivalent.

1	l'alpinisme	a	guided visit
2	l'escalade	b	tourist information office
3	une station thermale	c	a dish
4	une visite guidée	d	mountaineering
5	le syndicat d'initiative	e	a craftsman
6	un artisan	f	a spa resort
7	un plat	g	rock climbing

En vacances, qu'est-ce que tu voudrais faire?

A Alpinisme, escalade, moto-neige. Essayez une nouvelle activité tous les jours dans notre centre de vacances, qui se trouve à dix kilomètres du mont Blanc dans les Alpes.

B Vous voulez vous sentir en bonne forme? Faites un séjour dans notre station thermale. On offre des massages à prix réduits. Pourquoi pas ne profiter de cette offre spéciale? C'est bon pour la santé.

C Fatigué de la ville? Louez un de nos gîtes et faites des promenades pour profiter d'agréables moments dans le calme et la tranquillité. Ou bien essayez la pêche.

D Naviguez doucement sur le canal dans un de nos bateaux. Vous avez la possibilité de vous relaxer en regardant de beaux paysages ou vous pouvez faire des arrêts pour faire du shopping dans les grandes villes qui se trouvent au bord du canal.

E Vous avez toujours un guide à la main, vous recherchez donc les sites et les curiosités, les musées et les monuments historiques. Visites guidées possibles en plusieurs langues – consultez le syndicat d'initiative ou l'office de tourisme de la ville la plus proche.

F Allez voir les grands artisans de la région qui font le même travail de père en fils. Si vous préférez, essayez les plats traditionnels de la région.

2a 📖📖🎧 Choose a title for each section of the text (A–F).

1 Holidays on water
2 Rural holidays in the middle of nature
3 Holidays based on traditions and crafts
4 Cultural holidays
5 Active holidays
6 Holidays to make you feel good

2b 📖🎧 Decide whether each of the statements below is true (T), false (F) or not mentioned (?) according to the holiday brochure.

1 Le centre de vacances se trouve au bord de la mer.
2 Les massages dans la station thermale sont moins chers que d'habitude.
3 Les gîtes se trouvent dans le centre de la France.
4 On ne peut pas quitter le bateau pendant son séjour sur le canal.
5 Les visites guidées sont seulement en français.
6 Les artisans du présent font le même travail que les artisans du passé.

3a 🎧 Link each speaker (1–5) to the corresponding picture (A–E).

3b 🎧 Listen again and choose the correct sentence ending for each speaker.

1 This girl likes swimming   sunbathing   winter sports .
2 At the end of the day, this boy prefers to go for a walk   stay at home   eat out .
3 This boy wants to visit a city   go fishing   do his schoolwork .
4 This girl likes theme parks   staying in France   staying in a hotel .
5 This boy likes canal holidays   is going away for a week   is not looking forward to going away .

4 Ⓖ Work with a partner, and decide which order these sentences should go in to make sense (1–6).

a Enfin, j'ai bu une tasse de café et j'ai demandé l'addition.
b Une heure plus tard, j'ai décidé de prendre un dessert.
c D'abord, je suis allé à un restaurant marocain.
d Ensuite, je suis rentré à l'hôtel après ce délicieux repas.
e Puis, après avoir lu la carte, j'ai choisi une entrée, un plat principal et une boisson.
f Le lendemain, on est allé à un restaurant chinois.

5 ✏️🌐 Write about one day of your holiday (real or imaginary).

▪ Say what you did first and give your opinion of the activity.
▪ Say what you did later in the day and why.
▪ Say what you did after that and give your opinion.
▪ Say what you did in the evening and why.

D'abord / Au début j'ai	fait de la voile / visité la ville / visité un monument / mangé au restaurant / fait les magasins / rencontré mes amis / bronzé sur la plage	c'était / je l'ai trouvé intéressant / j'ai trouvé ça ennuyeux / fatigant.
Ensuite / Puis / Après j'ai		parce que j'aime faire des activités sportives / la cuisine italienne.

Time expressions in the past Ⓖⓡⓐⓜⓜⓐⓘⓡⓔ *page 163*

When you are writing in the past tense, use adverbs to structure what you want to say. *D'abord* and *au début* both mean 'first' or 'at the beginning'; *ensuite*, *après* and *puis* mean 'next' or 'afterwards'; *enfin* and *à la fin* both mean 'finally'. You can also use time expressions such as *une heure plus tard* (an hour later).

✏️ When writing about holiday activities try to sequence your answer. Use the days of the week (*lundi j'ai nagé*), words like *le lendemain* (the next day) or expressions like *deux jours plus tard* (two days later), *au début* / à la fin de la semaine (at the start / end of the week) and *le matin* / *l'après-midi* / *le soir*. **Stratégie**

Remember you use the perfect tense for saying what you did and the imperfect for descriptions in the past. *J'ai bu un coca dans un café. Le café était petit et joli. Il y avait des tables devant.* **Astuce**

2.9 Les excursions

Objectifs

Getting around

Telling people what to do

Listening for gist

On vous propose ...

1 **Appréciez Paris à bord d'un bateau au design moderne pour une promenade d'une heure quarante-cinq minutes.** Écoutez notre nouvelle animation musicale! Déjeuner servi entre 13h et 14h30 (cinquante euros en plus). Départ du Pont de l'Alma. Vous y allez en métro ou en RER (station à cinq minutes). Arrivée Bercy. Achetez des billets simples ou aller et retour.

2 **Une visite de la maison et du jardin de Claude Monet, l'artiste impressionniste.** Départ de l'office de tourisme en car grand tourisme. Déjeuner au restaurant à Giverny. Continuation vers Rouen et visite guidée de la ville. Dîner et hôtel compris.

3 **Un vol à bord d'un hélicoptère d'une durée de 15 min, 30 min ou 45 min, selon votre choix ...** Ce voyage en hélicoptère est garanti inoubliable. Vous pouvez voler au-dessus de tous les monuments de Paris – la Tour Eiffel, La Défense etc! Pour 2 personnes (les enfants ne sont pas admis). Départ de l'aéroport d'Orly.

A

B

C

1a 📖🎧 Match each activity (1–3) to the correct photo (A–C).

1b 📖🎧 Read the sentences and decide if the information is true (T), false (F) or not mentioned (?).

1 La promenade sur la Seine est dans un vieux bateau.
2 Le déjeuner en bateau n'est pas compris.
3 La visite de la maison de Monet dure une heure.
4 On mange à Rouen et on y passe aussi la nuit.
5 Le vol en hélicoptère est cher.
6 Les enfants ne peuvent pas faire la promenade en hélicoptère.

2 **Ⓥ** Sort the following words into four groups – air travel, road travel, train travel or travel by sea. (Some words fit in more than one category).

| le vol | la salle d'attente | les feux rouges | un horaire |

| un sens interdit | l'autoroute | stationner | la voie |

| composter | le bateau | le port | la gare routière |

| la gare SNCF | l'aéroport | l'hôtesse de l'air | le trottoir |

3a 🎧 🔊 Listen to the speakers (1–6) and choose the correct word to explain how each one is travelling.

> en voiture   en train   en bateau
> en avion   à pied   en bus

🎧 Don't be put off if you do not understand everything you hear. Picking out the gist of what you've heard can gain you marks. In the listening task, there are several key words in each question to give you an idea of what means of transport is being used, e.g. *autoroute*, *station-service* and *parking* indicate road transport as the subject.

Stratégie

3b 🎧 🔊 Listen again and answer the questions in English.

1 What was the problem on this journey?
2 What caused the delay?
3 Where exactly was the friend?
4 What went wrong here?
5 What two problems are mentioned?
6 Why did they end up in the village?

4 Ⓖ With your partner, choose the correct verb from the list below (right) to go in the gap. Then convert it to the imperative and instruct your partner to carry out the action.

1 _____ le musée de la pêche!
2 _____ à l'arrêt du car devant la gare.
3 _____ du shopping dans notre magasin de souvenirs.
4 Taxi ou bus? _____ le moyen de transport le plus pratique.
5 _____ aux feux et _____ à gauche au rond-point.
6 Pour aller au centre-ville, _____ un taxi.

> arrêter   tourner   aller
> visiter   prendre
> choisir   faire

Telling people what to do

To tell someone what to do (politely), use the *vous* form of the present tense without the *vous*. This form of the verb is always used for telling more than one person what to do.

Choisir >

Choisissez notre ville. Choose our town.

Faire >

Faites une promenade en bateau. Go on a boat trip.

Also learn about the correct words after *à* and *de*.

See page 81 ➡

Grammaire *page 168*

5 💬 With a partner, ask and answer these questions about travelling to and getting around on holiday.

- Comment as-tu voyagé pour aller en vacances et pourquoi?
- Le voyage a duré combien de temps?
- Qu'est-ce que tu as fait pendant le voyage?
- Tu as fait des excursions en vacances? Qu'est-ce que tu as visité?
- Tu as loué un vélo / fait des randonnées?
- Quel est ton moyen de transport préféré et pourquoi?

Comment as-tu voyagé pour aller en vacances et pourquoi?

J'ai voyagé en avion parce que c'est plus rapide, mais c'est mauvais pour l'environnement.

J'ai voyagé	en voiture / en avion	parce que c'est pratique / rapide / pas trop cher / plus confortable que …
Le voyage a duré / On est parti à / arrivé à	(environ) … heures.	
Pendant le voyage, j'ai lu un livre / joué aux cartes avec … / mangé … et	je l'ai trouvé / je trouvé ça ennuyeux / fatigant / (trop) long / (assez) agréable.	
On a fait une excursion en car / loué des vélos / fait des randonnées à pied / en voiture / en avion et	c'était (vraiment) amusant / intéressant / fatigant / ennuyeux.	
Je préfère voyager en …	parce que c'est confortable / pratique.	

When speaking French you can use exclamations to make what you say more interesting. *Quel dommage!* (What a shame!), *Quelle surprise!* (What a surprise!), *Quelle horreur!* (How awful!), *Quelles vacances!* (What a holiday!).

Astuce

Holidays

Vannes, le 9 mars

Monsieur,

Hier, je suis rentré de mon séjour de deux semaines à la Martinique. Je ne suis pas très content. Voilà pourquoi:

Nous avons attendu deux heures dans le car avant notre départ pour l'hôtel. Le chauffeur n'est pas arrivé.

Nous avons réservé une chambre à deux lits avec salle de bains pour nos enfants. Nous avons trouvé une chambre avec un grand lit sans salle de bains.

La plage n'était pas à côté de l'hôtel, contrairement à ce qui est mentionné dans la brochure. Elle est à vingt minutes à pied.

Les excursions n'étaient pas bien organisées et souvent elles ont été annulées sans excuses.

Après tous ces problèmes, je vous demande de me rembourser une partie de la somme que nous avons payée avant nos vacances.

Je vous prie de recevoir, Monsieur, l'expression de mes salutations distinguées,

J. Crougneau

1a 📖🎧 Read the letter from Mr Crougneau and note the missing word in the following sentences in English.

1 Jean Crougneau wrote the letter on _____.

2 He has just returned from _____ weeks' holiday.

3 He went to _____.

4 He travelled from the airport by _____.

5 He stayed in a _____.

1b 📖🎧 Decide whether the following statements are true (T), false (F) or not mentioned (?).

1 The journey from the airport to the hotel took two hours.

2 They were expecting *en suite* facilities with a bath.

3 The beach was a long way from the hotel.

4 The hotel had an indoor swimming pool.

5 They went on excursions every day.

6 They expect a complete refund of the price of their holiday.

2a 🎧 Mr Crougneau's daughter, Éloïse, is talking to her friend, Nadine, about her holiday. Listen to the beginning of the conversation. Which three of the following items are mentioned?

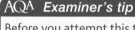

a **27** Tuesday

b **29** Thursday

c

d

e

f

AQA *Examiner's tip*

Before you attempt this type of listening task, look at the pictures, and try to anticipate the key words that you might hear linked to the pictures. Think about the differences between the ones that are similar. The first two, for example, focus on the date.

Perfect tense

Both comprehension tasks use the perfect tense. Can you identify six examples in the reading task, including two that use *être*?

Grammaire page 167

2b 🎧 Éloïse goes on to describe how she spent her birthday this year, while in Martinique. Listen to each part of the conversation, and choose the correct word to complete the sentence.

1 She went diving in the morning afternoon evening .

2 She saw fish that were large colourful dangerous .

3 At the restaurant, she chose a main course of chicken fish pork .

4 For dessert, she had a banana ice cream cake .

5 She drank beer lemonade fruit juice .

Vocabulaire

annuler	to cancel
essayer	to try
joli(e)	pretty
parfumé(e)	flavoured
la plongée	diving
le séjour	stay

(G) Holidays

Imperfect tense; Superlatives; Commands (*tu* form)

1 ✎ Complete the following sentences with verbs in the imperfect chosen from the list below.

1 Il y _____ du soleil à Marseille.

2 J'ai dormi sous la tente. C'_____ amusant!

3 Hier, il _____ , alors je suis allée au musée d'art moderne.

4 Je ne suis pas sortie parce qu'il _____ trop froid.

5 Je ne suis pas allé à la plage, car il _____ mauvais temps.

6 Il _____ quand je suis arrivée dans les Alpes. C'_____ beau!

| avait | était | était | faisait | neigeait | pleuvait | faisait |

> **Imperfect tense**
>
> Use the imperfect tense to describe what something was like in the past.
>
> *C'était super!* It was great!
>
> *Il faisait froid.* It was cold.
>
> *Il y avait du soleil.* It was sunny.
>
> *Il pleuvait.* It was raining.
>
> *Il neigeait.* It was snowing.
>
> *Grammaire* page 167

2 📖 Match the French and the English.

1 Les TGV sont les trains les plus rapides.

2 La plage de La Baule est la plus longue d'Europe.

3 Le Concorde était l'avion le plus rapide du monde.

4 Nous avons mangé dans le meilleur restaurant de la ville.

5 Je passe mes vacances dans la plus jolie maison de la région.

6 Est-ce que la tour Eiffel est le monument le plus visité de Paris?

a the most popular monument

b the fastest aeroplane

c the best restaurant

d the prettiest house

e the longest beach

f the fastest trains

3 ✎ Underline the imperative (command) in the following sentences, then translate each one into English.

Exemple: <u>Achète</u> *des bananes!* Buy bananas!

1 Visite le port!

2 Loue un vélo!

3 Va à la pêche!

4 Prends un bus!

5 Ne rentre pas trop tard!

6 N'oublie pas le billet!

> **Superlatives**
>
> ■ To say 'the most', use *le / la / les plus* + adjective.
> *C'est la plus belle chambre.* It is the most beautiful room.
>
> ■ To say 'the best', use *meilleur / meilleure / meilleurs / meilleures*.
> *C'est le meilleur camping.* It is the best campsite.
>
> *Grammaire* page 162

> **Commands (*tu* form)**
>
> ■ Use an imperative (command) when giving orders or instructions.
>
> ■ Use the *tu* form when speaking to someone your own age or someone you know very well. This is usually the *tu* form of the present tense. However, with -*er* verbs, remove the 's' at the end.
> *Tu vas à la piscine.* You go to the swimming pool.
> > *Va à la piscine!* Go to the swimming pool!
>
> *Grammaire* page 168

Commands (*vous* form); Prepositions with *à* and *de*

4 ✏ Write a command to go with these pictures, making sure you are using the *vous* form. The imperatives you need are in the word snake at the bottom.

1 _____ un bus!

2 _____ un vélo!

3 _____ à l'heure!

4 _____ à la pêche!

> ### Commands (*vous* form)
> Use the *vous* form of the imperative (normally ending in -ez) when speaking to someone you don't know very well or to more than one person.
>
> *Allez au camping!* — Go to the campsite!
> *Achetez des cartes postales!* — Buy some postcards!
> *Prenez l'ascenseur!* — Take the lift!
>
> *Grammaire page 168*

5 _____ la tour Eiffel!

6 _____ au restaurant!

allezrentrezprenezlouezmangezvisitez

5 📖 Choose the correct preposition.

1 Il a dormi **à l'** **au** château.
2 Il se baigne **au** **à la** plage.
3 Je vais à pied **au** **à l'** hôtel.
4 Elle traverse toujours **aux** **des** feux.
5 Je vais t'appeler **du** **des** dortoir.
6 Il part **des** **du** guichets là-bas.
7 Le bus va **de la** **à la** plage.
8 Je reviens **du** **de l'** étranger.

> ### Prepositions with *à* and *de*
> *À* can mean either 'at' or 'to'. Remember also that:
> - *à + le* changes to *au*
> - *à + l'* remains *à l'*
> - *à + la* remains *à la*
> - *à + les* changes to *aux*
>
> *J'arrive au restaurant.* — I arrive at the restaurant.
> *Je traverse aux feux.* — I cross at the traffic lights.
>
> The French for 'from' is *de*. Also remember that:
> - *de + le* changes to *du*
> - *de + l'* remains *de l'*
> - *de + la* remains *de la*
> - *de + les* changes to *des*
>
> *J'appelle du bureau.* — I am calling from the office.
> *J'arrive de l'aéroport.* — I come from the airport.
>
> *Grammaire page 167*

Holidays

Vive les vacances! ➡ *pages 70–71*

une	belle vue	fine view
le	bord de la mer	seaside
	bronzer	to sunbathe
la	campagne	countryside
le	Canada	Canada
les	Caraïbes (f)	the Carribbean
la	Chine	China
l'	Espagne (f)	Spain
les	États-Unis (m)	United States
l'	étranger (m)	foreigner
à l'	étranger	abroad
	faire du camping	to go camping
	faire du ski	to go skiing
l'	Italie (f)	Italy
le	logement	housing
la	montagne	mountain
des	monuments historiques (m)	historic monuments
le	pays de Galles	Wales
le	pique-nique	picnic
la	plage	beach
la	planche à voile	windsurfing
se	relaxer	to relax
le	ski nautique	water skiing
	trop de monde	too many people
les	vacances (f)	holidays

Des projets de vacances ➡ *pages 72–73*

en	automne	in autumn
le	balcon	balcony
le	camping	camping
la	caravane	caravan
la	chambre familiale	family room
la	colonie de vacances	holiday camp
la	demi-pension	half board
le	dortoir	dormitory
en	été	in summer

	étranger(-ère)	foreign
	faire de la planche à voile	to go windsurfing
	faire de la voile	to go sailing
le	gîte	gite
en	hiver	in winter
la	location	hiring
	louer	to hire
le	pays	country
la	pension complète	full board
au	printemps	in spring
	redevenir	to become again
	réserver	to reserve
	revisiter	to revisit
le	séjour	stay
le	terrain de camping	campsite

1 **V** Choose accommodation for the following from the list below.

1 Une famille avec quatre enfants pleins de vitalité. Le père a acheté une nouvelle tente.

2 Une célébrité en visite à Paris.

3 Deux étudiants qui n'aiment pas faire du camping mais qui n'ont pas beaucoup d'argent. Ils aiment dormir dans des dortoirs.

4 Un monsieur qui a gagné à la loterie et qui veut passer des vacances au bord de la mer.

5 Un groupe de jeunes qui veulent faire des activités sportives et veulent un logement avec pension complète.

6 Une famille qui n'aime pas les tentes mais qui trouve les hôtels trop chers.

une auberge de jeunesse

un appartement avec un balcon et une vue sur la mer

un terrain de camping   une caravane

un grand hôtel de luxe   une colonie de vacances

Que faire en vacances? ➡ *pages 74–75*

l'	alpinisme (m)	mountaineering
l'	artisan (m)	craftsman
le	bateau	boat
	bienvenue	welcome
une	boisson	drink
en	bonne forme	in good shape
l'	entrée (f)	starter
l'	escalade (f)	rock climbing
	louer un gîte	to hire a gite
l'	office de tourisme (m)	tourist information office
la	pêche	fishing
le	plat du jour	dish of the day
le	plat principal	main course
les	plats traditionnels (m)	traditional food
des	randonnées (f)	walks, hikes
se	sentir	to feel
des	sports nautiques (m)	water sports
une	station thermale	thermal spa
les	spécialités de la région (f)	the specialities of the region
le	syndicat d'initiative	tourist information office
la	tasse	cup
une	visite guidée	guided tour

Les excursions ➡ *pages 76–77*

l'	aéroport (m)	airport
l'	arrêt (m)	stop
l'	arrivée (f)	arrival
l'	autoroute (f)	motorway
les	bagages (m)	baggage
	bienvenue	welcome
un	car	coach
	composter	to stamp
	compris(e)	inclusive
	durer	to last
l'	essence (f)	petrol
la	gare routière	coach station

l'	horaire (m)	timetable
l'	hôtesse de l'air (f)	air stewardess, flight attendant
la	location de voitures	car hire
	manquer	to miss
	pénible	hard, tiresome
le	permis	permit, licence
un	pique-nique	picnic
un	terrain de jeux	playground
	tous les jours	every day
un	retard	delay
	sain et sauf	safe and sound
la	salle d'attente	waiting room
	sauf	except
un	sens interdit	one-way street
	stationner	to park
la	station-service	service station
le	tarif réduit	reduced price
	traverser	to cross
le	trottoir	pavement
un	vol	flight
	voler	to fly

Extra holiday vocabulary

l'	addition (f)	bill
l'	agence de voyages (f)	travel agent, agency
l'	aller retour (m)	return ticket
l'	aller simple (m)	single, one-way ticket
l'	avion (m)	aeroplane
le	bureau de renseignements	information office, desk
le	carnet	ticket
la	carte postale	postcard
le	départ	departure
le	menu	menu
la	mer	sea
le	passager	passenger
le	service (compris)	service charge (included)
le	tourisme	tourism
la	valise	suitcase

2 En vacances

You are on holiday in France. You have agreed to take part in a survey about holidays. Your teacher will play the part of the person carrying out the survey and will ask you the following:

1 personal details
2 details about your accommodation
3 why you chose the area
4 what you did yesterday
5 what you have planned for today
6 where you intend to holiday next
7 !

! Remember you will have to respond to something that you have not yet prepared.

> **AQA Examiner's tips**
>
> Start off with *Je m'appelle* ...
> Remember that *j'ai* = 'I have' and *je suis* = 'I am'. However, you should use *j'ai* when saying your age. For saying how you travelled and how you arrived, use the perfect tense, e.g. *j'ai voyagé, je suis arrivé.*

1 Personal details
- say your name, age and nationality
- say how you travelled and when you arrived
- say how long you are staying for
- give details about your family

> **AQA Examiner's tips**
>
> Now, start your plan. Write a maximum of six words. Here are some suggested words for the first section.
> *nom, âge, nationalité, voyager, rester, famille*
> Remember that the maximum number of words allowed in your plan is 40, so two of your sections will need to be limited to five words. You can use *voyagé* (travelled) and *resté* (stayed) if you prefer – infinitives or past participles are allowed.

2 Details about your accommodation
- say where your hotel is situated
- describe the hotel facilities
- describe your room
- say what you think of the standard of accommodation

> **AQA Examiner's tips**
>
> Use *se trouve* for the location of the hotel. Say where it is in relation to other places, e.g. *L'hôtel se trouve près de la plage.*
> Show initiative when you describe the hotel facilities, e.g. mention a swimming pool, say that you like swimming, say that you go swimming at home every week, say you are generally quite sporty, you also like playing tennis etc.

3 Why you chose the area
- say why you chose the area
- say what you enjoyed visiting last time you came
- compare it to your own area at home
- say which area you prefer

> **AQA Examiner's tips**
>
> You can use the present tense to say why you chose the area, e.g. *d'habitude, il fait beau.*
> In order to say what you enjoyed visiting, you will need to use two verbs, the first one in the past, the second one in the infinitive, e.g. *j'ai aimé aller.*
> Keep the comparison simple, e.g. *dans ma ville, il n'y a pas de* ...
> Use French words only on your plan. Not only will they provide you with a reminder of what to say next, they will also help you with what you want to say.

4 What you did yesterday
- say where you went yesterday morning
- say what you thought of it
- say what you did for the rest of the day
- say what others in your family did

When giving your opinion, use *j'ai aimé ...* and *je n'ai pas aimé ...*

Vary your vocabulary. Use different verbs for different people, e.g. *aller, rester, visiter, faire* in the perfect tense.

Hyphenated words, e.g. *après-midi*, count only for one word in your plan.

5 What you have planned for today
- say what your own plans for today are
- say why you chose those activities
- say what you will do if it rains
- say what others in your family want to do today

Use *je voudrais / j'aimerais* + verb in the infinitive to explain your own plans.

Use *s'il pleut* to introduce what you will do if it rains.

Use *il / elle voudrait / aimerait* + infinitive to introduce what others would like to do. Although the spelling is different from *aimerais / voudrais*, the sound is the same.

Remember there is no limit to the number of visuals you can have on your plan.

6 Where you intend to holiday next
- say where you intend to holiday next
- say why you have chosen that particular destination
- say how long you would like to go for
- say what you would like to do / visit there

Use a variety of ways to introduce a future event, e.g. *j'ai l'intention de / j'espère / je voudrais / je vais / j'aimerais*.

All of these phrases are followed by a verb in the infinitive, e.g. *j'ai l'intention d'aller ...*

If you need to use more than six words in your plan, do so, but remember that you will have to use fewer than six words elsewhere to compensate.

7 **!** A conclusion to the survey might be about:
- what you think of the facilities on offer
- how the resort could be made more appealing to various groups of people: adults, teenagers, families with young children etc.
- whether what is on offer is good value for money
- what your ideal holiday would be like

Choose which **two** options you think are the most likely, and for each of these, note down **three** different ideas. In your plan, write three words that illustrate each of the two most likely options. For the second option you might choose: *adultes, jeunes, familles*. Learn these two options using your reminder words. Remember to check the total number of words you have used. It should be 40 or fewer.

You should now have completed your plan and prepared your answers. Give your plan to your teacher for feedback. Compare your answers to the online sample version – you might find some useful hints to make yours even better.

2 ✏ Mes loisirs

You are writing an e-mail to your French friend Sabine who has asked you:

1 what you do with your free time when you stay in
2 what you do when you go out
3 how much money you receive and from whom
4 how you like spending your money
5 if you have a mobile phone
6 if you are interested in fashion
7 if you are sporty

AQA Examiner's tips

Start off with *j'aime écouter* …
Check which verbs take *être* in the perfect tense, e.g. to say 'I went up to my room and I watched TV' you need to use an *être* verb (*je suis monté*) and an *avoir* verb (*j'ai regardé*). See grammar section page 167.
Use *j'ai invité … chez moi* to say you had a friend to visit.

1 **What you do with your free time when you stay in**
   - talk about music you listen to and / or play
   - mention TV and what you watched last night
   - say what you like doing on the computer
   - mention last time you had a friend to visit

AQA Examiner's tips

Now, start your plan. Write a maximum of six words. *musique, télé (hier), ordinateur (activités), copains* Although you are using six words, you don't necessarily need to illustrate six ideas. In this case, two words illustrate one idea, i.e. *télé (hier)*. That allows you to define more precisely what you will be saying, i.e. what you watched yesterday.

2 **What you do when you go out**
   - say where you go and when
   - say who you go with
   - say what you did last time you went out
   - say what time you had to be back in and what you thought of that

AQA Examiner's tips

Use *j'ai dû rentrer à* to say when you had to be back.
Use *c'était* to say what you thought of having to be back in at that time.
Sometimes, proper nouns are the best way of summarising what you want to say. Don't be afraid of using them in your plan.

3 **How much money you receive and from whom**
   - say how much money you receive each week
   - say whether it is pocket money or whether you earn it
   - say whether you think it is enough
   - compare how much pocket money you get with what your brothers / sisters / friends get

AQA Examiner's tips

Use *me donne* to say 'gives me' and *gagne* for 'earn'.
Use *reçoit / reçoivent* when writing about what others get (but *je reçois*).
Your plan is there to act as a reminder of what you wrote for the bullet points in your preparation for the task. Try to memorise the connections between your list of words and what they represent.

4 How you like spending your money
- say how much you regularly save and what for
- say what you usually buy with your money
- say how you spent your money last month
- say what you would do if you won the lottery

AQA Examiner's tips

Use *économiser* for 'save'.
Start the last bullet point with *si je gagnais à la loterie, je voudrais …* You can also use *j'aimerais*.
If you want to use numbers in your plan, write them in words.

5 If you have a mobile phone
- say whether you have a mobile phone and when you got it
- say what you do with it
- say how much you spend monthly on using your mobile
- say what you think of your mobile

AQA Examiner's tips

Use *un portable* for 'a mobile phone'.
Use *je paie / ça coûte / je dépense* to say how much you spend. The word for pounds is *livres*.
Remember to include verbs in your plan. In this way you won't be tempted to use words like *c'est* too often.

6 If you are interested in fashion
- say what clothes you like wearing
- say whether fashion is important to you
- mention a fashionable item you bought recently
- say why it is difficult to keep up with fashion

AQA Examiner's tips

Use *à la mode* for 'in fashion'.
Remember that fashion can be about things other than clothes, e.g. jewellery, bags etc.
Remember that the seven headings in the task itself also act as a reminder of what you have to say. Make a link between those headings and your own six words by having the task and your plan next to each other on the day when you have to write the task.

7 If you are sporty
- say which sports you like and dislike
- say whether you walk and / or cycle in order to keep fit
- say whether your diet helps your fitness
- say whether it is important to play sport and be fit

AQA Examiner's tips

Use *jouer au* + sports to say which sports you play.
If you want to say 'it is important to play + sport' use *il est important de jouer* + sport. Note that the second verb is in the infinitive, e.g. *jouer, faire*.
Remember to check the total number of words you have used in your plan. It must be 40 or fewer.

You should now have completed your plan and prepared your answers. Compare your work with the online response to the task – you might find some useful hints to make yours even better.

1 Choose the correct sentence ending.

Quand je reste à la maison, j'aime …

a sortir   b regarder la télé

c manger au restaurant   d jouer au foot au parc

2 Choose the correct sentence ending.

Avec un téléphone portable il est impossible …

a de parler à ses amis   b de prendre des photos

c de faire de la natation   d d'envoyer des textos

3 Choose the correct form of the verb to complete this sentence.

Je ne _____ pas allé au concert.

a ai   b a   c suis   d est

4 In which of the following sentences is someone talking about what they are going to do in the future?

a Je suis rentrée hier.

b Je suis allé en France l'année dernière.

c Je vais aller à Paris en juillet.

d Je n'ai jamais vu les pyramides.

5 Which of the following contains a past tense?

a Je vais passer mes vacances en Italie.

b Je vais bronzer au bord de la piscine.

c J'ai mangé un gros gâteau au chocolat.

d Je vais acheter des souvenirs.

6 Find the correct French translation for the following sentence.

I'm going to go to the United States.

a Je vais partir au pays de Galles.

b Il va visiter les États-Unis.

c Elle va passer huit jours en Amérique.

d Je vais aller aux États-Unis.

Le sais-tu?

Le vélo est le sport le plus populaire en France. Connais-tu le nom de la grande course cycliste qui se passe chaque été en France? Les Français ont un surnom pour le vélo, ils l'appellent *la petite reine* (the little queen).

Le sais-tu?

Paris est la première destination touristique du monde.

90% des Français restent en France pour leurs vacances. Au mois d'août, presque tout le monde part en vacances. Il y a donc beaucoup de voitures sur les autoroutes françaises. Connais-tu des villes touristiques françaises?

3 Home and environment

Compass points; house types and locations

1 📖🎧✏️ Look at the map to check which three of the statements are true. Correct the statements that are false.

1 Calais est dans le sud de la France.
2 Bruxelles est dans le centre de la Belgique.
3 Marseille est dans le sud de la France.
4 Genève est dans l'est de la Suisse.
5 Bordeaux est dans le sud-est de la France.
6 Rouen est dans le nord-ouest de la France.

2a 📖🎧 Match each person with the correct pictures (two need two pictures each, and two need one picture each).

J'habite un vieil appartement en centre-ville. C'est nul! Je rêve d'un chalet à la montagne …

Nadia

J'habite à la campagne. On a une vieille maison dans un village sympa.

Mehdi

Quand je suis chez mon père, j'habite un appartement moderne en centre-ville. Chez ma mère, c'est une petite maison individuelle dans la banlieue de Nantes.

Théo

Rose

J'habite une grande maison au bord de la mer. C'est dans une petite ville touristique.

2b 💬 Work in pairs. Partner A chooses to be one of the four people above. Partner B asks yes/no questions to guess who it is.

Exemple:

Tu habites un appartement?

Non.

Tu es Mehdi?

Tu habites à la campagne?

Oui.

Rooms in house; furniture and prepositions

1a 📖 🎧 Read Rose's email about her new house, then match each question (1–5) with the correct answer (a–e).

De:	Rose
À:	Théo
Sujet:	Ma nouvelle maison

Au rez-de-chaussée, il y a l'entrée, un petit salon et une super grande cuisine! Il y a aussi des toilettes et puis l'escalier pour monter au premier étage où il y a un grand salon et la chambre de mes parents. Au deuxième étage, il y a ma chambre, la chambre d'Émilie et puis la salle de bains.

1 Où est la chambre des parents?
2 Il y a combien de chambres?
3 Il y a combien de salons?
4 Où est la salle de bains?
5 Où sont les toilettes?

a Il y en a trois.
b Il y en a deux.
c Au rez-de-chaussée.
d Elle est au premier étage.
e Elle est au deuxième étage.

1b ✏ Adapt Rose's email to describe your own house, or an imaginary house of your dreams.

2a 📖 🎧 Look at the picture and choose the correct ending for each of the following sentences.

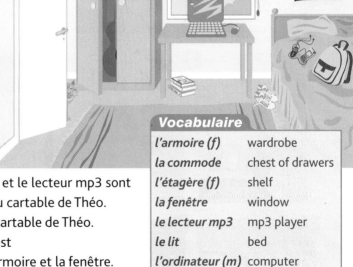

1 La table est
   a devant la fenêtre.
   b sur la fenêtre.

2 Les livres sont
   a sur les étagères.
   b sous la table.

3 Le cartable est
   a derrière le lit.
   b sur le lit.

4 Les baskets sont
   a à côté du lit.
   b sous le lit.

5 Le portable et le lecteur mp3 sont
   a à côté du cartable de Théo.
   b dans le cartable de Théo.

6 La guitare est
   a entre l'armoire et la fenêtre.
   b dans l'armoire.

7 Le chat est
   a derrière la porte
   b derrière le lit.

2b 🗨 Work in pairs. Partner A makes one statement about Théo's bedroom. Partner B says whether it is true or false. Then swap parts.

Exemple: **A** La guitare est dans l'armoire.
B C'est vrai!

Helping at home; daily routine

1 📖🎧 Find the correct picture for each line of text.

1 Quelquefois, je mets la table.
2 C'est mon père qui fait la cuisine.
3 Je ne fais jamais la vaisselle chez ma mère.
4 Mon beau-père fait les courses deux fois par semaine.
5 Mes petits frères rangent leur chambre de temps en temps.
6 Chez mon père, je fais souvent le ménage et je nettoie les toilettes.

a

b

c

d

f

e

2a 📖🎧 Read what Alice says about her twin sister, then decide whether the following pictures show Alice or Manon.

Je partage ma chambre avec Manon, ma sœur jumelle, et c'est l'horreur! Manon se lève à six heures et demie. Moi, je me lève à sept heures et quart.

Manon prend une douche, puis elle s'habille très lentement. Moi, je me lave, puis je m'habille et hop! je pars au collège.

Le soir, je fais mes devoirs avant le dîner. Manon fait ses devoirs après le dîner, puis elle se couche à dix heures. Moi, je regarde la télé et puis je lis ou j'écoute de la musique dans ma chambre. Mais Manon n'est pas contente: elle veut dormir. Ça m'énerve!

1 — 6:45

2 — 7:05

3 — 7:15

4 — 22:05

5 — 22:15

6 — 22:30

Vocabulaire

les courses (f)	shopping
la cuisine	cooking
de temps en temps	from time to time
jamais	never
le ménage	housework
mettre la table	to lay the table
nettoyer	to clean
quelquefois	sometimes
ranger sa chambre	to tidy one's bedroom
rarement	rarely
souvent	often
tous les jours	every day
une fois par semaine / mois	once a week / month
la vaisselle	washing-up

Faire

Faire is irregular.

faire = to make or do

singular	plural
je fais	*nous faisons*
tu fais	*vous faites*
il / elle / on fait	*ils / elles font*

Grammaire page 176

2b 💬 Compare your daily routine with your partner.

Exemple: A Je me lève à sept heures et quart. Et toi?
B Moi, je me lève à

Home activities; perfect tense

1 📖🎧 Read about Mimi's typical day and put the following pictures in the correct order.

> «D'habitude, je me lève à six heures et demie et je vais à la piscine où je nage pendant une heure. Après, je prends une douche. Ensuite, je rentre à la maison et je prends mon petit déjeuner.»

> «Normalement, le matin je suis dans mon studio. Je joue de la guitare, je chante et j'écris des chansons. À treize heures, je mange une salade et je bois un café.»

> «Je vais chez ma grand-mère tous les jours. En général, je suis chez elle entre trois heures et cinq heures ... Le soir, je sors avec mes copains. On écoute de la musique et on s'amuse bien.»

Vocabulaire

après	after that
bien s'amuser	to have a good time
ensuite	then
entre ... et ...	between ... and ...
d'habitude	usually
en général	generally
normalement	normally
pendant	during

Perfect tense

Remember, to talk about what happened in the past in the perfect tense, use:

- *avoir* + past participle (in most cases)

j'ai nagé	I swam
on a nagé	we swam

- *être* + past participle with verbs such as *aller, venir, sortir, rester* and reflexive verbs such as *se réveiller* or *s'amuser*.

je suis sorti(e)	I went out
on est sorti(s)	we went out
je me suis réveillé(e)	I woke up

Grammaire page 167

A

B

C

D

E

2 📖🎧 Read Mimi's blog about last Friday. Then copy the phrase that describes what was different from her regular routine.

Vocabulaire

une émission de télévision	a television programme

Vendredi dernier, je me suis réveillée à six heures et demie. J'ai écouté la radio pendant une demi-heure. Puis je suis allée à la piscine. Ensuite, j'ai pris une douche, mais je n'ai pas pris de petit déjeuner. Je suis sortie. Je suis allée à Paris pour une émission de télévision. Le soir j'étais très fatiguée. Je ne suis pas allée chez ma grand-mère. Je suis rentrée à la maison.

Noël et le jour de l'An

Tu aimes Noël, Marc?

Bien sûr. C'est génial. Chaque année, le vingt-quatre décembre, ma mère et mon père préparent le repas traditionnel de Noël. J'aide un peu dans la cuisine parce qu'il y a beaucoup à faire. En général, mes deux petits cousins arrivent à quinze heures avec mon oncle et ma tante. Après le repas on passe le soir à faire la fête et tout le monde dort chez nous. Mes deux cousins, mon petit frère de cinq ans et ma petite sœur de sept ans pensent que le Père Noël existe. Le matin du vingt-cinq, ils réveillent tout le monde à cinq heures! On descend tous et les petits commencent à ouvrir leurs cadeaux tout de suite. Moi, maintenant, je fais partie des adultes mais je reçois pas mal de cadeaux quand même!

Tu réveillonnes?

Le trente et un décembre, oui. L'année dernière, j'ai réveillonné chez un de mes copains. C'était génial! On s'est retrouvé en début de soirée chez Luc. Il y avait une vingtaine de personnes et on a dansé jusqu'à six heures du matin. Au moment où on se disait «bonne année» à minuit, les parents du Luc sont venus voir si tout se passait bien. C'est là que j'ai rencontré Marine qui est toujours ma petite amie maintenant. Les réveillons, à mon avis, c'est extra.

1a 📖🎧 Read the first paragraph and answer the questions in English.

1 Who contributes to the preparation of Christmas dinner?
2 How many people there for dinner?
3 In what way do Marc's younger brother and sister make Christmas special?
4 What happens early morning on Christmas day in Marc's house?

1b 📖🎧 Read the second paragraph and decide whether these statements are true (T), false (F) or not mentioned in the text (?).

1 On réveillonne le dernier soir de l'année.
2 Trente personnes ont réveillonné chez Luc l'année dernière.
3 La fête a fini à minuit.
4 Les parents de Luc ont fait la fête avec leurs amis.

2a 🎧 Listen to Section A and correct the sentences that are wrong.

1 Suliman is 50 years old.
2 Usually, he celebrates his birthday at a restaurant.
3 This time he went to a restaurant.
4 Afterwards, he was disgusted.

2b 🎧 Listen to Section B and correct the sentences that are wrong.

1 Suliman is a Christian.
2 Eid is celebrated at the end of Ramadan.
3 During Ramadan, Suliman only eats during the day.
4 The celebrations last for three weeks.
5 This year, Suliman's family invited his uncle and aunt to their house.

3 Ⓖ Change the sentences so that they refer to what things were like last year. Use the imperfect tense.

Exemple: Il fait beau pour mon anniversaire. >
L'année dernière, il faisait beau pour mon anniversaire.

1 J'ai quatorze ans.
2 La cuisine de ma tante, c'est délicieux!
3 Je suis à la maison à Noël.
4 Il y a du monde au réveillon.
5 C'est dommage. Il est malade le jour de son anniversaire.

Common imperfect expressions

You will sometimes need to use the imperfect tense to describe what something was like, how someone was feeling or where something / somebody was. These five need learning by heart: *j'avais* (I had), *j'étais* (I was), *il y avait* (there was / there were), *c'était* (it was) and *il faisait chaud / froid* (it was hot / cold).

Also learn to recognise other imperfect verb forms.
See page 102 ➡️

Grammaire page 167

4 ✏️ 🗨️ Write a social networking site message to your friends, telling them about your birthday. Mention:

▪ When your birthday is and how old you are.
▪ How you normally spend your birthday (where, what you do).
▪ What you did for your last birthday (using the perfect tense).
▪ What you thought of it (using *faire*, *avoir* and *être* in the imperfect).
▪ What your favourite festival is (and why).
▪ What you do / did for that festival.

✏️ When writing, include what you **don't** do as well as what you do. As well as *ne … pas*, include expressions such as *ne … jamais* (never) and *ne … plus* (no more, no longer). Write three things you don't do, never do or no longer do on your birthday.

Stratégie

Mon anniversaire, c'est le …	
Normalement, pour mon anniversaire, je …	
À mon dernier anniversaire,	j'ai reçu … / mangé … je suis allé(e) …
C'était	génial / barbant etc.
Il faisait	froid / beau etc.
Ma fête préférée, c'est	Noël / Pâques / l'Aïd / la Saint-Valentin.
Je préfère … parce que …	je reçois … / on mange … / on va ….

Add more information than asked for if you can. It makes your work more interesting and will help you to gain extra marks in your exam.

Astuce

LOCATIONS VACANCES

A   Le Barroux: Maison récente avec vue sur la campagne – pour six personnes – chambres (il y en a trois) – piscine privée – à huit cents mètres du village. Grand jardin, cuisine, séjour, salle de bains, WC. Confort, machine à laver, lave-vaisselle, four à micro-ondes, frigo, congélateur, télévision, lecteur DVD. 750 euros par semaine.

B   Nice: Appartement au rez-de-chaussée – trois pièces pour quatre personnes. Deux chambres, une salle de bains, WC, salon, cuisine. Les habitants actuels y habitent depuis six ans. Commerces 4 km. Plage 500 m. 600 euros par semaine.

C   Chamonix. Chalet de montagne. Vue extraordinaire du Mont Blanc. Cinq pièces pour six personnes. Trois étages, quatre chambres, deux salles de bains. Très récent. Assez grande terrasse, balcon, sous-sol.

Équipement: frigo, four, cuisinière, lave-vaisselle, micro-ondes, aspirateur, télévision. 800 euros la semaine.

D   Immeuble de luxe. Interphone, ascenseur. Cinquième étage. Tout confort. Petite cuisine, séjour, chambre. En plein centre, à cinq minutes de l'Arc de Triomphe et à dix minutes de la Tour Eiffel. 1100 euros par semaine.

1a 📖🎧 Read the adverts and decide which would be most suitable for each of the situations below.

1. Your father would like a sea view.
2. Your brother would like a swimming pool.
3. Your mother wants to be in the countryside.
4. Your sister wants to see Paris.
5. You would prefer a holiday in the mountains.

1b 📖🎧 Read the adverts again and note which places satisfy the following situations. In some cases there are two possibilities, so write them both down.

1. There are five people in your family.
2. You want a garden.
3. There has to be a lift.
4. You want to be on the ground floor.
5. You want a dishwasher and a microwave oven.

2a 🎧 Listen to Section A. Which four of these statements are true?

1 Mani lived in Paris before moving to Marseilles.
2 He has lived in Marseilles for three months.
3 He likes living by the sea.
4 His house is close to the beach.
5 He does not have a swimming pool.
6 He really likes his house.

2b 🎧 Listen to Section B and answer in English.

1 Where do Mani's parents live?
2 How many rooms are there in their house?
3 Where are the toilets?
4 How do we know that Mani is now a rich man?

3 🄖 Complete these sentences using the information in brackets.

1 J'habite ici _____ (for three years).
2 Grég habite dans cette maison _____ (for six months).
3 J'habite dans mon appartement _____ (for a year).
4 Nous sommes dans la salle à manger _____ (for an hour).
5 Elle regarde la télé dans la salle de séjour _____ (for two hours).
6 J'habite en France _____ (since I was born).

4 🗨 🄝 Work with a partner. One partner asks the questions and the other answers. Then swap roles.

▨ Où habites-tu?
▨ Tu y habites depuis quand?
▨ Il y a combien de chambres?
▨ Quelles autres pièces y a-t-il dans la maison?
▨ Qu'est-ce qu'il y a dans les pièces?
▨ Tu habitais où avant?
▨ Tu aimes ta maison?

Habiter and **depuis** · Grammaire page 17

> **Habiter** and **depuis**
>
> Sometimes *depuis* is translated by 'for' and sometimes by 'since'. In English we use the past tense before both these words, but in French you use the present tense before *depuis*.
>
> *J'habite ici depuis ma naissance.* — I have been living here since I was born.
>
> *J'habite ici depuis six ans.* — I have been living here for six years.
>
> Also learn about how to use *en* as an object pronoun. *See page 103* ➡

> **Stratégie**
>
> 🗨 When using adjectives in your conversation, remember to add qualifiers and intensifiers such as *très* (very), *un peu* (a bit), *assez* (quite), *trop* (too) and *vraiment* (really). Example: *J'habite dans une assez grande maison.*

Où habites-tu?

J'habite dans une assez grande maison au centre-ville, avec ma famille.

J'habite dans Nous habitons dans	une (assez) grande maison (au centre-ville). un (très) petit appartement (dans un village).	
J'y habite	depuis (trois) ans / depuis ma naissance.	
Avant, j'habitais	dans le centre-ville / dans un appartement.	
Au rez-de-chaussée Dans la salle de séjour	nous avons / il y a	une cuisine / une salle de bains / une table / des chaises etc.
La maison / l'appartement	se trouve / est situé(e)	près de … / dans le centre de …
J'aime bien / Je n'aime pas	ma maison	parce qu'elle est …

> **Astuce**
>
> When giving personal information, try not just to say *je* all the time. Also use *nous* (we) and *il y a* (there is).

3.3 Là où j'habite

Les régions de France

A Valérie habite dans une maisonnette à St-Tropez, une ville très touristique à environ 50 kilomètres de Cannes, dans le sud de la France. Elle aime bien habiter ici parce qu'il fait chaud la plupart de l'année. C'est une ville qui est très animée en été, mais plus calme en hiver. Au port il y a une centaine de bateaux de luxe. Les gens qui habitent sur ces bateaux sont très riches – des vedettes de cinéma ou des chanteurs célèbres par exemple.

Qu'est-ce qu'on peut faire à St-Tropez? Eh bien, on peut aller au casino, manger dans un des restaurants chics, ou bien faire de la voile. Comme Valérie n'est pas très riche, elle n'a pas choisi ces activités hier: elle est allée à la plage avec ses copines, et le soir elle est allée au cinéma. Elle attend le mois de mai avec impatience parce qu'elle va visiter la ville de Cannes pour le festival du cinéma.

B André habite à Genève, une grande ville suisse. Cette ville est tout près de la frontière française, et on y parle français. C'est une ville très historique qui a été fondée pendant l'époque romaine, mais qui est maintenant un des plus grands centres financiers du monde. C'est une ville verte, située au bord d'un très grand lac, avec beaucoup de jardins publics. André habite dans un grand appartement au centre ville, pas loin du lac.

Qu'est-ce qu'on peut faire à Genève? Les montagnes ne sont pas loin, donc en hiver on peut faire du ski. André est content d'habiter ici parce qu'il adore skier, mais ce week-end il n'y a pas assez de neige. Ce qu'il va faire, c'est du VTT à la campagne. Quand il ne fait pas de sport, André aime jouer du saxophone. Au mois de juillet il y aura un festival de jazz à Montreux, près de Genève, et André va y participer avec d'autres jeunes musiciens.

1a 📖🎧 Read Section A and choose the expression to complete each of these statements.

1 Valérie habite dans le sud le nord l'est de la France.
2 St-Tropez est assez près de très loin de Cannes.
3 Ici on peut aller à la plage dans les montagnes à la tour Eiffel .
4 Hier soir Valérie est allée à un restaurant chic
   au cinéma à Cannes au cinéma à St-Tropez .

1b 📖🎧 Read Section B and choose the expression to complete each of these statements.

1 Genève est une petite vieille nouvelle ville.
2 À Genève on parle français anglais espagnol .
3 Genève a beaucoup de parcs de montagnes d'usines .
4 André va jouer dans un festival de cinéma musique danse .

📖 Watch out for clues about size and quantity. Examples of this are *une centaine* (**about** a hundred) and *une maisonnette* (a **small** house).

You don't need to be exact with figures. Recognise vague expressions like *environ* and *à peu près* (both meaning 'about').

Stratégie

2a 🎥🎧 Watch the video and/or listen to the audio track. Which towns do these adjectives refer to, Avignon (A) or Vitrolles (V)?

polluée   sale   animée   touristique

industrielle   grande

2b 🎥🎧 Watch / listen again. According to the conversation, which four statements refer to Avignon and which refer to Vitrolles?

1 It is quite a big town.
2 There are a lot of shops there.
3 There is a lot for tourists to see.
4 There is too much traffic in town

5 There is a lot of pollution.
6 You can watch a film there.
7 There are a lot of cafés there.
8 You can go ice skating there

3 🅖 Work in pairs. Partner A asks the questions and partner B answers.

Exemple: A Est-ce qu'on peut aller au cinéma?
              B Non, on ne peut pas aller au cinéma.

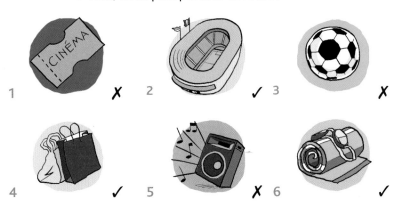

1 ✗   2 ✓   3 ✗

4 ✓   5 ✗   6 ✓

> **Ⓖrammaire** *page 169*
>
> **Saying what you can and can't do**
>
> In English, we use 'you can' or 'you can't' to mean 'people can / can't'. In the same way, the French use *on peut* and *on ne peut pas* followed by the infinitive.
>
> *On peut aller   You can go to
> au cinéma.   the cinema.*
>
> *On ne peut pas   You can't eat
> manger ici.   here.*
>
> Also learn more about adjectives that go before nouns.
>
> *See page 103* ➡

4 ✏ Write a website in French, giving information about your home town or village (or a fictional home town). Use the language box to help you with ideas.

> **Astuce**
>
> If you want to talk about a future event, instead of saying *il y a* (there is), use *il y aura* (there will be), e.g. *En juillet il y aura un festival de jazz à Montreux.*

[Name of place] est	un village / une (grande) ville / à la campagne.
	dans un vieux quartier / un quartier moderne.
Il / elle se trouve dans le /l'	nord / sud / est / ouest de …
C'est près de / pas loin de …	
[Name of place] est une ville / un village	touristique / industriel(le) etc.
Il fait	beau en été / froid en hiver etc.
Il y a	une cathédrale / une bibliothèque / une église etc.
On peut … / on ne peut pas …	visiter le parc etc.
En septembre / l'année prochaine,	il y aura un festival de …

Home and local area

• Bastia

La Corse

Salut, tout le monde!

Un petit bonjour d'Erbalunga, près de Bastia, en Corse. Je suis bien arrivé, mais le voyage en bateau était long. Il y a beaucoup de travail à faire dans la maison, mais le plus important, c'est qu'après quelques problèmes, l'ordinateur marche bien! Demain, c'est mon premier jour au nouveau collège – au secours – et c'est aussi ma fête!! J'espère que mes parents n'ont pas oublié, et qu'ils m'ont acheté un cadeau!

Je voudrais avoir des nouvelles de mes copains de Lyon!

Répondez-moi!

Guillaume

Salut Guillaume!

J'espère que ton premier jour au collège est bien passé. Ici rien n'a changé! Le prof de maths est toujours sévère. J'ai beaucoup de devoirs, alors je n'ai pas le temps de t'écrire un long message maintenant, mais parle-moi de ta nouvelle maison. Et ton village, il est comment?

Joël

1a Read Guillaume's first message since moving to Corsica and Joël's reply. Choose the correct word(s) to complete the sentences.

1 His new home is in Bastia Erbalunga Lyon .

2 He travelled to Corsica by boat plane helicopter .

3 It was important for him to get his computer music system mobile phone working.

4 He will start at his new school in two weeks next week tomorrow .

5 His first day at school is also important because it is his birthday nameday brother's birthday .

6 He wants Joël to tell him about his pets friends grandparents in Lyon.

7 Joël complains about a teacher a friend his parents .

8 He has only written a short message because he has to help at home do his homework go out .

Salut à tous mes amis!

Comment ça va à Lyon? Ici en Corse, après trois semaines, c'est le bazar!

Mon père a commencé son nouveau travail dans un lycée de Bastia et moi, je vais au collège depuis deux semaines. Il est très moderne, et les profs sont assez sympas. Je me suis déjà fait quelques amis en classe, alors ça va.

Le village où nous habitons est très petit. Ma mère l'aime bien, c'est si tranquille, mais le problème, c'est notre maison. C'est une jolie maison traditionnelle. Il y a trois chambres, et un grand jardin, mais il y a beaucoup de travail à faire dans la cuisine et la salle de bains. Depuis notre arrivée la douche ne marche pas (mais on peut prendre un bain!) et nous n'avons qu'un four à micro-ondes pour préparer les repas. Alors on mange beaucoup de salade!

Le maçon va commencer le travail lundi prochain. J'espère qu'on va finir avant l'arrivée de Joël en juillet.

À bientôt,
Guillaume

1b 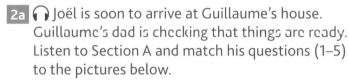 Read Guillaume's reply and find the correct ending for each sentence.

1 Guillaume arrived in Corsica …
2 He started at his new school …
3 Guillaume says the village is …
4 His mother thinks the village is …
5 The shower …
6 The microwave …
7 The builder will start work …
8 Joël will arrive …

a … works properly.
b … small.
c … two weeks ago.
d … in July.
e … peaceful.
f … three weeks ago.
g … does not work.
h … next Monday.

AQA *Examiner's tip*

When you do this sort of task, you can often see two possible endings to a sentence that are similar, e.g. c and f. Check the detail of the text carefully, before you make your choice.

2a Joël is soon to arrive at Guillaume's house. Guillaume's dad is checking that things are ready. Listen to Section A and match his questions (1–5) to the pictures below.

A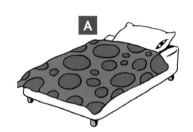

B

C 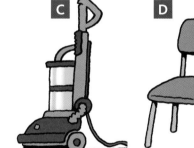 D 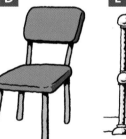 E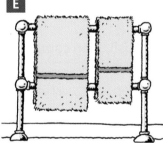

Vocabulaire

c'est le bazar	it's chaos
la fête	nameday
les fruits de mer (m)	seafood
l'horaire (m)	a timetable
le maçon	a builder
le travail	job
oublier	to forget

2b Listen to Section B. Which of the following has Guillaume done?

1 reserved seats on the 10 o'clock boat
2 been to the tourist office for information on windsurfing lessons
3 found out about trips to the mountains
4 organised a fishing trip
5 found out about buses into town
6 booked a flying lesson

Grammaire *page 168*

Depuis* and *ne … que

In the reading passage you will find an example each of *depuis*, and *ne … que*. See if you can find and understand them. Can you see a phrase which means the same as: *depuis trois semaines, c'est le bazar* or *nous avons seulement un four à micro-ondes*?

For more practice using *depuis* see page 102, and for *ne … que* see page 168. ➡

(G) Home and local area

The imperfect tense; *Depuis* + present tense

1 📖 Choose the correct translation for each sentence.

1 Je dormais quand tu as appelé.
   a I was asleep when you called.
   b I will be asleep when you call.
2 Avant, je ne regardais jamais la télévision.
   a I have never watched television.
   b I never used to watch television.
3 Elle visitait le musée quand je suis arrivée.
   a She wanted to visit the museum when I arrived.
   b She was visiting the museum when I arrived.
4 Il lavait la voiture tous les dimanches.
   a He used to wash the car every Sunday.
   b He washes the car every Sunday.
5 Quand il travaillait à Calais, il téléphonait tous les soirs.
   a When he used to work in Calais, he called every night.
   b When he worked in Calais, he called one night.
6 Quand j'habitais à la campagne, je me levais à six heures.
   a When I live in the country, I'll get up at six.
   b When I lived in the country, I used to get up at six.

2 🖊 Match the French and the English, then complete the French using words from the boxes below.

1 He has been asleep in the garden for ten minutes.
2 I have been in Paris for five years.
3 You have been working in the library for a week.
4 She has been watching the door for an hour.
5 There has been a cathedral here for 600 years.
6 We have been living in the house for six months.

a Je _____ à Paris depuis cinq ans.
b Il _____ dans le jardin depuis dix minutes.
c Tu _____ à la bibliothèque depuis une semaine.
d On _____ dans la maison depuis six mois.
e Elle _____ la porte depuis une heure.
f Il y _____ une cathédrale ici depuis 600 ans.

a	dort	habite	regarde	suis	travailles

Grammaire — page 167

The imperfect tense

The imperfect tense is used to describe what something was like in the past, or what someone used to do regularly in the past. In the singular, it usually ends in *-ais* or *-ait*. You don't pronounce the final *-s* or *-t*.

habiter	to live
j'habitais	I used to live; I lived
tu habitais	you used to live; you lived
il / elle habitait	he / she used to live; he / she lived

Grammaire — page 171

***Depuis* + present tense**

Remember to use the present tense (not the past tense) before *depuis*.

Je travaille ici depuis cinq ans.
I have worked here for five years.

Using *pouvoir*; Three irregular adjectives; *En* as an object pronoun

3 📖 Match the questions and the answers using the English in brackets to help you.

1 Il y a combien de pièces dans ta maison? (There are eight of them.)

2 Vous avez combien de chambres? (We have three of them.)

3 Il y a combien de salles de bains? (There are two of them.)

4 Comment est le garage? (There is none.)

5 Vous avez un jardin? (Yes, we have one.)

6 Vous mettez des fleurs aux fenêtres. (Yes, we do.)

a Oui, on en met!

b Il y en a huit.

c Il y en a deux.

d Oui, on en a un.

e Il n'y en a pas.

f On en a trois.

4 ✏️ Match the French and the English. Complete the French so that it matches the English, choosing between *on peut* and *on ne peut pas*.

1 _____ entrer dans l'église.

2 _____ visiter la bibliothèque.

3 _____ s'asseoir sur les pelouses.

4 _____ dormir sur le trottoir.

5 _____ descendre au sous-sol.

6 _____ monter sur le toit.

a You can visit the library.

b You cannot sit on the lawns.

c You can go down to the basement.

d You cannot sleep on the pavement.

e You can go into the church.

f You cannot go up the roof.

5 ✏️ Complete the captions with the correct adjective taken from the word snake below.

1 un _____ jardin

2 une _____ rivière

3 une _____ église

4 un _____ château

5 un _____ hôtel

6 un _____ escalier

vieillevieuxbelnouvelbellebeau

En as an object pronoun

En is used to avoid repeating a noun introduced with a number or *du / de la /de l' / des*. It goes before the verb.

Vous avez deux salles de bains? Do you have two bathrooms?

Non, on en a trois! No, we have three of them!

Grammaire page 165

Using *pouvoir*

The French for 'you can' and 'you can't' (when you mean 'people in general') is *on peut* and *on ne peut pas*. It is followed by the infinitive.

On peut jouer au foot au stade, mais on ne peut pas aller à la piscine. You can play football at the stadium, but you can't go to the swimming pool.

Grammaire page 169

Three irregular adjectives

■ These three common adjectives come before the noun: *vieux, nouveau, beau*:

un vieux musée an old museum

un nouveau centre commercial a new shopping centre

un beau tableau a beautiful painting

■ Their feminine forms are *vieille, nouvelle* and *belle*:

une nouvelle piscine a new swimming pool

■ They also have a special form which is used before a vowel or a silent h:

un vieil homme an old man

un nouvel aéroport a new airport

un bel endroit a beautiful place

Grammaire page 162

Home and local area

On fait la fête ➡ pages 94–95

l'	Aïd (m)	Eid
l'	anniversaire (m)	birthday
	ensemble	together
	faire la fête	to have a party, celebration
la	fête	party, festival
	Noël	Christmas
	Pâques	Easter
le	repas	meal
se	retrouver	to meet (up)
	réveillonner	to celebrate Christmas or New Year's Eve
	tout de suite	immediately

1 **V** Solve the anagrams and match the French words with the English ones.

1	a block of flats	a	leave isle-slav
2	the basement	b	nurse case
3	the terrace	c	gatéu ne
4	a floor	d	rasers tale
5	dishwasher	e	immune blue
6	lift	f	louse-loss

Ma maison ➡ pages 96–97

l'	ascenseur (m)	lift
le	balcon	balcony
la	cave	cellar
la	cuisinière	cooker
un	étage	floor, level
le	four à micro-ondes	microwave oven
un	immeuble	block of flats
le	lave-vaisselle	dishwasher
la	machine à laver	washing machine
une	maison individuelle	detached house
une	maison jumelée	semi-detached house
la	pièce	room

la	salle de séjour	living room
le	sous-sol	basement
la	terrasse	terrace

2 **V** With a partner, work out which sentence goes with which festival.

1	Noël	a	On offre une carte à la personne qu'on aime.
2	L'Aïd	b	La fête dure trois jours.
3	Pâques	c	On fait un réveillon.
4	Le Nouvel An	d	On se dit «bonne année».
5	La Saint-Valentin	e	On donne des cadeaux et on en reçoit.
6	La Saint Sylvestre	f	Il y a des œufs en chocolat.

Là où j'habite ➡ pages 98–99

	animé(e)	busy, lively
la	bibliothèque	library
la	boîte de nuit	nightclub
le	champ	field
le	club des jeunes	youth club
l'	époque (f)	era, period of time
	fonder	to set up, to found
l'	habitant (m)	occupant, inhabitant
	historique	historical
le	jardin public	park
le	métro	underground (train)
le	musée	museum
	propre	tidy, clean / own
le	quartier	area
la	rivière	river
le	terrain de sport	sports field
l'	usine (f)	factory
	touristique	tourist

3 **V** Work in a group. Imagine you are moving house to a different town. Which of these adjectives would make you feel as if it was the right town for you? Choose your top five and put them in order.

pittoresque	touristique animée fleurie
industrielle	calme historique moderne

Prepositions

	à	in, at, to
	au-dessous de	above
	au-dessus de	below
	autour de	around
	avec	with
au	bord de	by, at
au	bout de	at the end of
	contre	against
à	côté de	by the side of
	dans	in
	de	of, from
en	dehors de	outside of
	depuis	since, for
	derrière	behind
	devant	in front of
	en	in, to
	entre	between
en	face de	opposite
au	fond de	at the bottom of
au	lieu de	instead of
	jusqu'à	as far as
	malgré	despite
au	milieu de	in the middle of
	parmi	among
	pour	for
	près de	near to
	sans	without
	selon	according to
	sous	under
	sur	on

à	travers	across
	vers	towards

Location and distance

de l'	autre côté	on the other side
la	banlieue	suburbs
en	bas	below, downstairs
la	campagne	countryside
le	centre-ville	town centre
de	chaque côté	on each side
	chez	at, to (someone's house, home)
à	droite	right
l'	est (m)	east
à	gauche	left
en	haut	above, upstairs
	ici	here
un	kilomètre	kilometer
	là	there
	là-bas	down there
	loin de	far from
le	nord	north
l'	ouest (m)	west
	par	by
	partout	everywhere
	quelque part	somewhere
	situé(e)	situated
le	sud	south
	tout droit	straight on
	tout près	very near
	toutes directions	all routes
la	ville	town
le	village	village

V Various expressions to do with locations and distance have been summarised for you here. They will be useful with this and many other topics that you are going to study for your exam.

Stratégie

3.4 Les problèmes de l'environnement

1 **V** Match the English and French words. The French words are all very similar to the English words.

1	electricity	a	protéger
2	recycling	b	tempête
3	products	c	inondé
4	storm (or 'tempest')	d	environnement
5	bag (or 'sack')	e	gaz
6	environment	f	recyclage
7	bottles	g	planète
8	gas	h	tornade
9	planet	i	bouteilles
10	to protect	j	électricité
11	flooded (or 'inundated')	k	sac
12	tornado	l	produits

Planète en danger

A **On utilise trop de plastique, qui est très difficile à recycler.** Dans certains pays, il y a des montagnes de déchets. Avant, il y avait des sacs en plastique gratuits dans tous les supermarchés. Maintenant il y a des sacs en coton et des centres de recyclage.

B **Chaque année il y a de nouveaux records de températures.** Il y a de plus en plus de tempêtes et de tornades. Avant il y avait une grosse tornade par an, maintenant il y en a plusieurs! Dans certains pays il fait de plus en plus chaud. Les glaciers vont fondre, le niveau de l'eau va monter. Les villes et les villages près de la mer sont en danger.

C **Beaucoup d'espèces d'animaux sont en danger d'extinction.** Les usines sont responsables de la pollution de nos rivières avec leurs déchets. Les eaux polluées arrivent dans les mers et causent la mort de milliers de poissons. Notre industrie et notre agriculture causent la destruction de l'habitat des animaux, des oiseaux et des insectes.

2a Choose an English title for each paragraph (A–C).

1 Destruction of habitats   2 Recycling   3 Global warming

2b Below are five solutions. Say which of the three problems outlined above (A–C) each one is aimed at resolving.

Vous pouvez sauver la planète …

1 en achetant des produits qui ne polluent pas les rivières.
2 en recyclant les déchets.
3 en voyageant en train, pas en avion.
4 en utilisant des sacs en coton.
5 en protégeant le monde animal.

3a 🎧 🔊 Listen to Section A, and put these environmental issues into the order in which they are mentioned in the discussion.

climate change   river pollution

traffic fumes   pollution of the seas

destruction of the rain forest   extinction of wildlife

3b 🎧 🔊 Listen to Section B and answer the questions in English.

1   What does Sandrine see as the most serious environmental problem?
2   What is causing it, according to her?
3   Éric has a different cause to blame. What?
4   What problem does Adrien mention?
5   What do Sandrine and Adrien agree is the most serious problem?

🎧 While listening, you will notice that although many French and English words are similar to look at, they are often pronounced quite differently. As you carry out the listening task, check the pronunciation of *-ion* (in *pollution*), *i* (in *plastique*), *é* (in *pollué*) and *è* (in *problème*).

Stratégie

4 **G** Add the correct present participle to each sentence by choosing verbs from the box below.

1   Mon père pollue en _____ une grosse voiture.
2   En _____ mes courses à pied, je ne pollue pas.
3   Je protège l'environnement en _____ des pommes françaises.
4   Je protège l'environnement en _____ les produits emballés dans du plastique.
5   Sascha protège l'environnement en _____ des sacs en coton.
6   Et moi, je protège l'environnement en _____ mes déchets.

faire   refuser   conduire   utiliser   acheter   recycler

Present participle

The present participle in French ends in *-ant*, and it is used if you want to say 'by doing something'.

Je protège l'environnement en recyclant mes bouteilles en plastique.

I protect the environment by recycling my plastic bottles.

To form the present participle in French, take the *nous* form of the present tense, remove the *-ons*, and replace it with *-ant*.

Also learn about indefinite pronouns such as *tout le monde* and *personne*.

See page 112 ➡

Grammaire page 168

5 💬 Work in a small group. Take the various environmental problems mentioned on these two pages and agree on an order of importance. Then present them to the class: *le problème le plus grave, c'est… , puis c'est … , ensuite, c'est …* etc. For each one, suggest a way to improve the situation.

Le problème le plus grave est	le changement climatique.
	la pollution des rivières et de la mer (des mers).
	la pollution de l'air.
	la destruction de l'habitat des animaux.
On peut protéger l'environnement en	faisant des pistes cyclables / recyclant les déchets.
	faisant des économies d'eau / de gaz / d'électricité.
	se déplaçant à vélo / à pied.
	n'utilisant pas des sacs en plastique.
On ne doit pas	polluer la mer / les rivières.

You can suggest improvements by saying *on peut …* + infinitive (you can …) and by using the present participle (ending in *-ant*) with *en*.

Astuce

Objectifs

Local issues and action

Faire (present and perfect)

Recognising words from already known ones

Troyes: ville propre

Ici à Troyes on a fait beaucoup pour l'environnement …

1. Le centre-ville est une zone piétonne où les véhicules sont interdits.
2. On a introduit un système de pistes cyclables.
3. On a installé des poubelles dans les espaces verts.
4. Il y a des centres de recyclage dans les parkings.

 A
 B
 C
 D

Pour recycler vos déchets …

Il y a des centres de recyclage pour les bouteilles, le papier et pour toutes sortes de choses recyclables. Cette initiative a eu beaucoup de succès: il y a 3 ans, les habitants de Troyes recyclaient 10 pour cent de leurs déchets, aujourd'hui c'est 30 pour cent.

Pour avoir une ville propre …

On a installé des poubelles dans tous les espaces verts. Dans le quartier St-Julien, le club des jeunes a organisé l'opération «Nettoyage du jardin public». Ils l'ont vraiment transformé. Un grand merci à tous ces jeunes!

Pour pédaler sans polluer …

Une autre mesure qu'on a introduite dans la région est la construction de pistes cyclables. C'est surtout bon pour la santé des jeunes. On les encourage à prendre le vélo pour aller à l'école.

1a 📖 🎧 Decide which symbol (A–D) goes with each numbered point (1–4) in the first section.

1b 📖 🎧 Read the whole leaflet and say whether the following sentences are true (T), false (F) or not mentioned (?).

1. They have built recycling facilities.
2. Garden waste is collected from homes.
3. Young people are encouraged to cycle to school.
4. The city has done little to improve the environment.
5. There are initiatives for young people.
6. The park in St-Julien is dirty.

> 📖 You are often able to recognise new words from those you already know. For example, from the verb *recycler*, you recognise the noun *recyclage*. Find the verb from the noun *pollution* and the noun from the verb *nettoyer* in the leaflet.
>
> **Stratégie**

2a 🎧 Listen to the interviews. Match the pictures (A–C) to the right people (1–3).

1   Alex   2   Juliette   3   Zoé

2b 🎧 Who says what? Write Alex, Juliette or Zoé.

1   I refuse plastic bags.
2   I'm doing something good for my health.
3   We had to clear up after the party.
4   I use public transport.
5   Mum used to take me to school.
6   You have to pay for a plastic bag.
7   We recycled everything.

3   **G** Match the questions and answers below. Then start each question with *Hier* (Yesterday) and change all the verbs in the questions and the answers into the perfect tense.

1   Qu'est-ce que tu fais pour protéger l'environnement de ta ville?
2   Qu'est-ce que tu fais en ville?
3   Qu'est-ce que tu fais pour ton anniversaire?
4   Qu'est-ce que tu fais pour aider à la maison?

Faire (present and perfect)

It is important to be able to use the common verb *faire* (to do).

Je fais du nettoyage.   >   *J'ai fait du nettoyage.*

I am doing some cleaning.   >   I did some cleaning.

If you can't remember how to form the present tense or the past tense of *faire*, look it up in the verb tables (page 176).

Also learn about emphatic pronouns.

See page 113 ➡

Grammaire *page 169*

---

a   Je fais la fête avec mes copains.
b   Je fais des économies d'énergie.
c   Je fais mon lit.
d   Je fais les courses.

4   🖋 Your school magazine has asked you to write an article in French, describing environmental problems and solutions in your local area. Use the language box to help you.

You may need to offer advice and suggestions about what people should do.

Use *Il faut* … and *On doit* …

Both mean 'You should …'

Astuce

J'habite / on habite …	dans le nord / le sud / l'est / l'ouest etc.
Ma / Notre ville est …	historique / industrielle / touristique.
Le problème de l'environnement le plus grave est que / qu'	il y a trop de circulation.
	on ne recycle pas assez de déchets.
Moi, je … / Nous …	recycle / recyclons mes / nos déchets.
	utilise / utilisons la poubelle.
On ne doit pas …	mettre ses déchets par terre etc.
Il faut …	aller au centre de recyclage / utiliser les transports en commun etc.

Environment

Recycler, c'est bien!

Comment recycler – la collecte sélective

1 Les emballages

Bouteilles en plastique, boîtes en métal

Dans la poubelle jaune

2 Les déchets de cuisine

Déchets domestiques, textiles, objets et sacs en plastique

Dans la poubelle bleue

3 Le verre d'emballage

Bouteilles, pots

Mettez-les dans les conteneurs à déchets placés dans les parkings

4 Les journaux – et magazines

Prospectus, journaux, catalogues et magazines

Mettez les dans les conteneurs à déchets placés dans les parkings

5 Les déchets verts

Déchets de jardin, et de cuisine (légumes, fruits)

Dans la poubelle verte

Moins de déchets, moins de problèmes pour la planète

1 Votre centre de recyclage est près des magasins. Arrivez en ville avec vos déchets, partez avec vos achats!

2 On recycle déjà 40% des déchets de la ville. Merci! L'année prochaine, nous voulons en recycler 60%!

Les développements récents

3 Maintenant on peut recycler le carton en ville. C'est important car le carton peut être recyclé 10 fois. Il y a une poubelle spéciale dans tous les parkings des supermarchés.

4 Les vieux vêtements sont utiles, même les chaussures! Il y a trois poubelles en ville pour les textiles et les chaussures.

5 L'année prochaine, on va commencer à recycler les ordinateurs et les portables. On va installer un point de recyclage à côté de la mairie.

1a 📖📖🎧 Look at the instructions on how to dispose of your rubbish. For each picture note, in English, where you should place, or take, the item of rubbish.

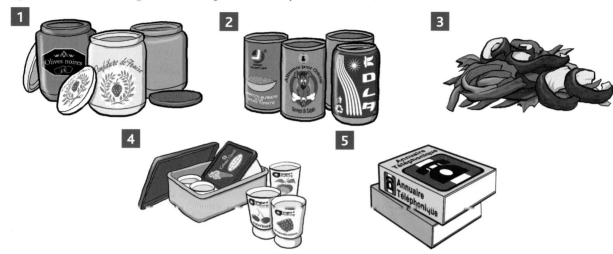

1b 📖📖🎧 Read the second part of the leaflet. Choose the correct English phrase to go with each point (1–5). Note that you won't need to use them all.

a   We want to recycle even more by next year!

b   Take your cardboard to the supermarket!

c   Combine your recycling activities with your shopping!

d   Compost your garden waste!

e   Your old computer can still be useful!

f   Bring your old clothes to the town hall!

g   We even want your old shoes!

2a 🎧 Listen to Section A (conversations between a mother and members of her family). Identify the correct person for the sentences below: Rémi (R), Bernard (B) or Danielle (D).

1   xxxxx grows vegetables.

2   xxxxx has left the fridge door open.

3   xxxxx has overheated a room.

4   xxxxx is asked to have a shower, rather than a bath.

5   xxxxx is reminded to switch off the television.

6   xxxxx intends to use low-energy light bulbs.

2b 🎧 Listen to the rest of the conversation. For each one explain a) why Danielle wants to do the activity, and b) why her mother disagrees.

1   leave a light on

2   take a taxi

3   wash jeans

Vocabulaire

avoir soif	to be thirsty
casser	to break
l'emballage (m)	packaging
éteindre	to switch off
penser	to think
utile	useful

AQA *Examiner's tip*

Some tasks may seem to expect you to know some unfamiliar words in French. However, you will hear linked words that you do know. For example, you may not know the word for 'overheat' in question 3, but you do know the word for 'hot'. Try to work out in advance what words might be used to lead you to the answers.

Present participles

🎧 Three of the speakers use a present participle in their conversations. Listen again, and try to pick them out. Who says in French:

'while working'

'when leaving'

'while playing'?

See page 112 for more examples of this form of the verb. ➡

Grammaire page 168

Ⓖ Environment

Present participles; *Tout le monde, personne*

1a 📖 Match the French and the English.

Je protège l'environnement …   I protect the environment …

1 … en prenant une douche.   a … by recycling rubbish.
2 … en utilisant un vélo.   b … by taking a shower.
3 … en recyclant les déchets   c … by using a bicycle.
4 … en économisant l'énergie.   d … by saving energy.

> ### Present participles
> The French equivalent of 'by + -ing' is *en* + *-ant*.
>
> *Je sauve la planète en prenant les transports en commun.*
>
> I save the planet by taking public transport.
>
> **Grammaire** page 168

1b ✏ Now translate the following sentences into English.

Je protège l'environnement …

1 en allant au collège à pied.
2 en refusant les sacs en plastique.
3 en utilisant des sacs en coton.
4 en respectant les rivières.

2a ✏ How can we save the planet? Choose between *personne ne / n'* and *tout le monde* to describe an environmentally friendly world.

Exemple: *Personne ne pollue les rivières.*

1 _____ a un vélo.   4 _____ prend des sacs en coton.
2 _____ va au collège en voiture.   5 _____ recycle le papier.
3 _____ utilise de sacs en plastique. 6 _____ économise l'eau.

2b 📖 Select sentences from Activity 2a as captions for these pictures.

> ### Tout le monde, personne
> The French for 'nobody' is *personne* and the French for 'everybody' is *tout le monde*. Both are followed by a verb in the singular. Note that in front of a verb *personne* is followed by *ne* (or *n'* before a vowel).
>
> *Tout le monde économise l'énergie.*
>
> Everyone saves energy.
>
> *Personne ne jette ses déchets ici.*
>
> Nobody throws their rubbish here.
>
> **Grammaire** page 165

Revision of *faire*; Time expressions; Emphatic pronouns

3 📖 Present or past? Which is the odd one out in each line?

	a		b		c		d	
1	a	**j'ai fait**	b	**tu as fait**	c	on fait	d	**elle a fait**
2	a	je fais	b	tu fais	c	il fait	d	**on a fait**
3	a	**j'ai fait**	b	elle fait	c	**tu as fait**	d	**ils ont fait**
4	a	**il a fait**	b	**tu as fait**	c	**j'ai fait**	d	elles font

4 📖 Present or past? Choose the correct form of *faire* to complete the following sentences.

1 Tu fais   as fait les devoirs hier?
2 Qu'est-ce qu'on fait   a fait aujourd'hui?
3 D'habitude, c'est mon père qui fait   a fait le ménage.
4 On fait   a fait les magasins le week-end dernier.
5 Je fais   J'ai fait des économies le mois dernier.
6 Qu'est-ce que tu fais   as fait normalement le samedi?

5 ✏️ Choose the correct pronoun from the box below to complete each sentence. Then translate into English.

1 _____, je fais mes courses avec des sacs en coton.
2 _____, tu utilises des sacs en plastique.
3 _____, il va à l'école en voiture.
4 _____, elle prend le bus.
5 _____, il jette ses déchets sur le trottoir.
6 _____, je mets mes déchets à la poubelle.

Elle	Lui	Lui	Moi	Moi	Toi

Revision of *faire*

Remember that you only need one word to make the present tense, but two for the perfect tense. Also remember that *faire* has two meanings.

Present tense

je fais	I do / make
elles font	they do / make

Perfect tense

j'ai fait	I did / made
elles ont fait	they did / made

Grammaire page 176

Time expressions

The following words help you decide whether the main verb needs to be in the present or the past.

Present

aujourd'hui	today
d'habitude	usually
normalement	normally

Past

la semaine dernière	last week
le mois dernier	last month
hier	yesterday

Grammaire page 163

Emphatic pronouns

In English, if you want to emphasise something you do, you just say it a bit more forcefully. French people put *moi* (me), *toi* (you), *lui* (him) or *elle* (her) at the beginning of the sentence.

Moi, je recycle.	I recycle.
Lui, il recycle toutes ses bouteilles.	He recycles all his bottles.
Elle, elle ne recycle rien.	She doesn't recycle anything.

The word for 'her' and 'she' is the same – *elle*!

Grammaire page 165

Environment

Les problèmes d'environnement ➡ *pages 106–107*

la	circulation	traffic
	conduire	to drive
les	déchets (m)	rubbish
se	déplacer	to move
l'	environnement (m)	environment
	fondre	to melt (down)
la	forêt	forest
	jeter	to throw
le	niveau	level
la	piste cyclable	cycle path
	pollué(e)	polluted
	protéger	to protect
le	sac en plastique	plastic bag
	sauver	to save

Ma ville ➡ *pages 108–109*

le	centre de recyclage	recycling centre
la	circulation	traffic
le	nettoyage	cleaning
la	piste cyclable	cycle path
le	problème	problem
	protéger	to protect
	recyclable	recyclable
les	transports en commun (m)	public transport
la	zone piétonne	pedestrian zone

1 **Ⓥ** Make a link between the words on the left and those on the right.

1	un sac		a	à pizza
2	une bouteille		b	piétonne
3	un carton		c	en coton
4	le centre		d	cyclable
5	les transports		e	en commun
6	une piste		f	en verre
7	la zone		g	de recyclage

Asking questions

À quelle heure?	At what time?
Ça s'écrit comment?	How do you spell that?
Ça va?	Is it OK?
C'est combien?	How much is it?
C'est quelle date?	What's the date?
C'est quel jour?	What day is it?
Combien de …?	How many …?
Comment?	How?
De quelle couleur?	What colour?
D'où?	Where from?
Est-ce que …?	Does …?
Où?	Where?
Où ça?	Where is that?
Où est?	Where is?
Pour combien de temps?	How long for?
Pourquoi?	Why?
Quand?	When?
Que?	What?
Quel(le) …?	What …?
Qu'est-ce qui?	Who?
Qu'est-ce que?	What?
Qu'est-ce que c'est?	What is it?
Que veut dire …?	What does … mean?
Quelle heure est il?	What time is it?
Qui?	Who?

Expressing opinions

à mon avis	in my opinion
absolument	absolutely
c'est affreux	it's horrible
c'est agréable	it's pleasant
j'aime …	I like …
c'est amusant	it's funny
c'est barbant	it's boring
c'est bien	it's good (experience)
bien entendu	of course
c'est bizarre	it's strange

c'est bon	it's good (food, objects)
ça m'énerve	it annoys me
ça me plaît	I like it
ça m'est égal	I don't mind
ça m'étonne	I'm surprised
ça m'intéresse	I'm interested in that
ça suffit	that's enough
c'est casse-pieds	it's a nuisance
cher(-ère)	expensive
c'est chouette	it's great
c'est comique	it's funny
comme ci comme ça	take it or leave it
compliqué(e)	complicated
content(e)	pleased
je crois …	I believe …
d'accord	agreed
je déteste …	I hate …
difficile	difficult
c'est drôle	it's funny
embêtant(e)	annoying
ennuyeux(-euse)	boring
j'espère …	I hope …
facile	easy
fantastique	fantastic
formidable	great
généralement	normally, usually
grave	serious
intéressant(e)	interesting
incroyable	unbelievable
marrant(e)	funny, amusing
j'en ai marre	I've had enough
mauvais(e)	bad
merveilleux(-euse)	marvellous
moche	horrid
negatif(-ive)	negative
c'est nul	it's rubbish
je suis optimiste	I am hopeful, optimistic
c'est passionnant	it's thrilling
je pense que …	I think that …
peut-être	perhaps

je préfère …	I prefer …
positif(-ive)	positive
c'est ridicule	it's daft
c'est rigolo	it's funny
c'est sensass	it's sensational
c'est stupide	it's stupid
c'est superbe	it's super
je veux …	I want …

Conjunctives or joining words

à cause de	because of
à part	apart from
alors	then
aussi	also
car	because
cependant	however
c'est à dire …	that means …
comme	like
d'une côté	on the one hand
de l'autre côté	on the other hand
donc	therefore
ensuite	next
et	and
mais	but
même si	even if
ou	or
parce que	because
par contre	in contrast
par example	for example
pourtant	however
puis	then
puisque	because
quand	when
sans doute	without doubt
y compris	including

3 ⬭ Chez moi

You are talking to your French friend about your house and your town. Your teacher will play the part of your friend and will ask you:

1 where you live and what your house is like
2 who lives in your house
3 what your room is like
4 about meal times
5 what you do to help round the house
6 what your nearest town is like
7 **!**

! Remember you will have to respond to something that you have not yet prepared.

1 **Where you live and what your house is like**
   ■ say where you live
   ■ say what your house is like
   ■ say how many rooms it has
   ■ talk about the garden and the garage

2 **Who lives in your house**
   ■ say who lives in your house
   ■ say what they are like
   ■ say who you get on with (or don't get on with)
   ■ talk about your pets

3 **What your room is like**
   ■ say what your room is like
   ■ say whether you share your room
   ■ say what is in your room
   ■ say what you like doing in your room

AQA Examiner's tips

Start with *J'habite* …
Use *est située dans le* + county or compass direction, e.g. *est située dans le sud-ouest de l'Angleterre,* to say where your house is located.
Use *au rez-de-chaussée* or *en bas* for downstairs and *au premier étage* or *en haut* for upstairs.
Use *chambres* for bedrooms and *pièces* for all other rooms.

AQA Examiner's tips

Now, start your plan. Write a maximum of six words for each of the seven sections that make up the task. Here are some suggested words for the first section:
exactement, description, pièces, jardin, garage, opinion
If the words you are using on your plan are not immediately understandable, e.g. *pièces*, make a point of learning them.

AQA Examiner's tips

Use *je m'entends bien avec…* to say who you get on with or *je ne m'entends pas bien avec …* to say who you don't get on with.
If you don't have a pet, start with *je n'ai pas d'animal à la maison* and say why not.
On your plan, use words that may not mean anything to someone else but suggest something specific to you, e.g. the name of your dog. That might not help you with vocabulary but it removes any possible ambiguity as to what you should be talking about.

AQA Examiner's tips

Show off your vocabulary. Talk about the walls, the curtains, the carpet and the furniture in your room, using adjectives to describe them.
Use *j'ai ma propre chambre* if you don't share your room. If you have to share, use *partager* for 'to share'.
Don't use words in your plan that are used in the task itself, e.g. *chambre*. It is a waste!

4 About meal times
   - say what times meals are
   - say whether you have your meals as a family
   - say what your favourite meal is
   - talk about the last time you went out for a meal

AQA Examiner's tips

Use *manger en famille* to say 'to eat as a family'. The last bullet point refers to an event in the past. See grammar section (page 167) for the use of the perfect tense, e.g. *je suis allé* (I went), *j'ai mangé* (I ate).
Add up to six words to your plan.

5 What you do to help round the house
   - say what you do to help round the house
   - say whether you get pocket money for helping
   - say what other members of the household do to help
   - say how you helped last weekend

AQA Examiner's tips

As the topic of helping round the house involves vocabulary hardly used in any other topic, you need to check how to say words like 'tidy', 'dishwasher', 'washing up', 'ironing', 'laying' or 'clearing the table' etc. Take care with the pronunciation of *vaisselle*.
Use *on me donne* or *je reçois …* to say what pocket money you get for helping.
Remember to use verbs on your plan. They will help you move from one idea to the next.

6 What your nearest town is like
   - say what the town centre is like
   - say what facilities there are for young people
   - say what you intend to do next time you go to town
   - talk about your ideal town

AQA Examiner's tips

Although you will inevitably use *il y a* and *c'est* in the first two sections, try to use other verbs too, e.g. *on peut faire / voir / aller …*
Start with *le week-end prochain, j'ai l'intention de …* to say what you intend to do in town next weekend. Use other phrases that refer to future events too, *je voudrais / j'aimerais / je vais* + infinitive.
On your plan, choose words that are immediately understandable, e.g. *centre*.

7 ! At this point, you may be asked
   - if there are problems in your town
   - if you like living in your town
   - if you prefer living in town or in the countryside
   - if you intend to continue living in the same town or if you would like to move to another area

AQA Examiner's tips

Choose which **two** options you think are the most likely, and for each of these, note down **three** different ideas. In your plan, write three words that illustrate each of the two most likely options. For the first option you might choose: *pollution, transports, jeunes* (the last one to remind you there is not enough for young people to do). Learn these two options using your reminder words.
Remember to check the total number of words you have used. It should be 40 or fewer.

You should now have completed your plan and prepared your answers. Compare your answers to the online sample version – you might find some useful hints to make yours even better.

3 ✏️ L'environnement

Your French friend Yannick has been asked to participate in a debate on the environment at school. As he is keen to have an international perspective, he has asked you the questions below.

1 What is your local town like?
2 Are there environmental problems there?
3 What do you think are the solutions to those problems?
4 What do you do that makes environmental problems worse?
5 What are the main problems of the environment in today's world?
6 What can we as individuals do about it?
7 Should we stop going on holiday by plane?

1 **What is your local town like?**
- say where it is situated
- describe it
- say what you think of it
- say whether you prefer to live in town or in the country

2 **Are there environmental problems there?**
- say whether the town is clean or dirty
- say whether there is a lot of pollution
- say how much traffic there is in town
- say whether there is enough room for pedestrians

3 **What do you think are the solutions to those problems?**
- say that litter should be taken home or put into bins
- say that there should be more bins and recycling centres
- say what can be done to reduce traffic in town
- say what can be done to help pedestrians

4 Work and education

School buildings; rooms and equipment

1a 📖🎧 Match each description (1–7) to the correct picture (A–G).

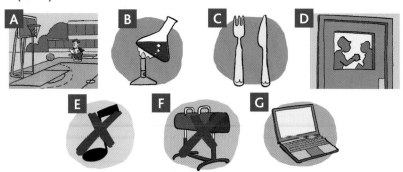

Dans mon collège ...

1 il y a une cantine.
2 il y a une cour de récréation.
3 il y a une salle des professeurs.
4 il y a deux laboratoires de chimie.
5 il y a trois salles d'informatique.
6 il n'y a pas de salle de musique.
7 il n'y a pas de gymnase.

Vocabulaire	
le CDI (centre de documentation et information)	school library
la cour de récréation	playground
le dictionnaire (bilingue)	(bilingual) dictionary
le laboratoire	laboratory
le livre	book
l'ordinateur (m)	computer
la salle de classe	classroom
la salle d'informatique	IT room
la salle des professeurs	staff room
le tableau interactif	interactive whiteboard

1b ✏️ Copy the sentences from Activity 1a that apply to your school. Adapt the others so they can also describe your school.

Dans mon collège, il y a _____ ...

Il n'y a pas de _____ ...

2a 📖🎧 Find the correct ending for each sentence. Then choose one of these sentences as a caption for this picture.

1 Il n'y a pas d'élèves ...
2 On peut jouer du piano ...
3 Il y a des dictionnaires bilingues ...
4 On peut lire des livres et faire des photocopies ...
5 Il y a des tables et des chaises pour manger ...
6 Il y a un ordinateur et un tableau interactif ...

a ... dans toutes les salles de classe.
b ... dans les salles de musique.
c ... dans les salles de langues.
d ... dans la salle des profs.
e ... à la cantine.
f ... au CDI.

2b 🗨️ Work in pairs. Partner A chooses one of the places from Activity 2a. Partner B asks yes/no questions to find which one it is. Then swap parts.

Exemple: B Il y a des élèves?
 A Oui.
 B Il y a un tableau interactif?

> **Using *de* after a negative**
>
> Remember to use *de* (or *d'* before a vowel or an 'h') after a negative.
>
> *Il n'y a pas de tableau interactif.*
> There is no interactive whiteboard.
>
> *Il n'y a pas d'ordinateur.*
> There is no computer.
>
> *Grammaire* page 168

School subjects; jobs

l'anglais (m)	English
la biologie	biology
la chimie	chemistry
le dessin	art
l'EPS (f)	PE
l'espagnol (m)	Spanish
le français	French
la géographie	geography
l'histoire (f)	history
l'informatique (f)	ICT
les math (ématique)s (f)	maths
la physique	physics
les sciences (f)	science
la technologie	D and T

1a 📖🎧 Choose a symbol (a–f) for each sentence. Then draw a smiley or grumpy face to indicate the opinion expressed.

1 J'aime l'EPS.
2 Je déteste l'anglais.
3 J'aime bien l'informatique.
4 J'aime beaucoup la chimie.
5 Je n'aime pas la géographie.
6 Ma matière préférée, c'est l'histoire.

1b 💬 Work in pairs and make up six dialogues following the instructions below.

Exemple: **A** Tu aimes le français?
  B Oui, j'aime bien le français.
  A Pourquoi?
  B Parce que c'est intéressant.

1 le français? ✓
2 les maths? ✗✗
3 l'EPS? ✓✓

4 le dessin? ✗
5 la biologie? ✓✓
6 l'anglais? ✓

Definite / indefinite articles

■ When talking about subjects you like and dislike, you need to use the definite article (*le, la, l', les*) before the noun.

  J'aime l'EPS mais je déteste le dessin.
  I like PE but I hate art.

■ Don't use the indefinite article (*un, une, des*) to introduce names of jobs in French.

  Mon père est plombier.
  My father is a plumber.

Grammaire *page 160*

2a 📖 Find the correct cartoon for the text below.

Mon père est fermier. Ma mère est professeur. Moi, je voudrais être chanteur.

2b ✎ Write a caption to match the other cartoon.

Mon père est _____ …   Ma mère _____ …   Moi, je _____ …

fermier / fermière	farmer
boucher / bouchère	butcher
boulanger / boulangère	baker
caissier / caissière	cashier
chanteur / chanteuse	singer
comptable	accountant
cuisinier / cuisinière	cook
électricien / électricienne	electrician
mécanicien / mécanicienne	mechanic
secrétaire	secretary
technicien / technicienne	technician
vendeur / vendeuse	sales assistant

Comment est ton collège?

1 Unjumble the French words and match them to English words.

1	miler street	a	to teach
2	emploiment u spud	b	a timetable
3	mistèr enoie	c	to pass
4	gala lune	d	former
5	rinse gene	e	the term
6	en inca	f	in year 10
7	sir rusé	g	the language

Collège Charlemagne

A Notre école

Le collège Charlemagne est un établissement moderne qui est situé au centre-ville de Troyes. Toutes les salles de classe sont équipées de tableaux blancs interactifs. Nous avons aussi un CDI moderne avec une bibliothèque et trois grandes salles d'informatique, chacune équipée de trente ordinateurs. Pour les demi-pensionnaires, il y a deux cantines.

B Nos élèves

Émilie Letort, élève de quatrième:

«Je suis élève ici depuis trois ans et je trouve que j'ai beaucoup appris. Les professeurs sont tous très gentils et ils font leur meilleur possible pour aider les élèves. Mon professeur principal m'enseigne le français.

En général, je travaille bien parce que j'aime bien être ici. J'étudie toutes sortes de matières mais ma matière préférée, c'est l'anglais.

L'année dernière, j'ai passé une dizaine de jours en Angleterre en voyage scolaire et on s'est tous bien amusé.

Cette année, je représente ma classe au Conseil des élèves et ça, c'est une grosse responsabilité, mais j'aime bien ça.»

2a Read Section A and choose the three statements that are true.

1 All classrooms have interactive whiteboards.
2 The school possesses 30 computers.
3 There is a library.
4 There is one canteen.
5 There are three ICT rooms.

2b Read Section B and answer the questions in English.

1 Approximately how old is Émilie?
2 What is her favourite subject?
3 Why does Émilie see her form tutor often?
4 What does Émilie tell us about school visits?
5 What position of responsibility does she have this year?

3a 🎧 🔊 Listen to Stéphanie talking about Collège Charlemagne (Section A) and correct the three statements that are wrong.

1 Stéphanie is 13 years old.
2 When one of the teachers talked in English, she found that funny.
3 She does not like languages.
4 She really enjoyed her visit.
5 She did not like some of the teachers she met.

3b 🎧 🔊 Listen to Florian (Section B) and correct the three statements that are wrong.

1 Florian stayed for five years at Collège Charlemagne.
2 He worked well and passed his exams.
3 He went on a school trip to Albania.
4 He thinks that his new school is better than Collège Charlemagne.

4 🇬 Fill in the gaps using the verbs below. Make sure you use the past participle form of each verb.

1 L'élève a _____ à la question du prof.
2 Quoi? Je n'ai pas _____.
3 Marc a _____ son vélo.
4 Claire a _____ une calculatrice.
5 Elle a _____ la rentrée avec impatience.
6 Nous avons _____ beaucoup de formules chimiques.

> apprendre   comprendre   attendre   vendre
>
> répondre   acheter

5 ✏️ Work in a group to design a website advertising an imaginary French secondary school (*collège*).

- ■ Student A describes the buildings and facilities.
- ■ Student B is a current student and talks about the school.
- ■ Student C is still at primary school and looking forward to moving on to secondary school.
- ■ Student D is at a sixth form college and looking back at secondary school days.

Mes professeurs sont / étaient	gentils / sympas etc.
Dans ce collège il y a / nous avons	des salles d'informatique etc.
Je suis en	quatrième / troisième / seconde.
Avant, j'étais	au collège …
L'année prochaine je vais aller	
Ma matière préférée est / était	l'anglais / le français etc.
J'aime / J'aimais	les profs / les matières.

🎧 Before you listen to a section, look carefully at the questions and work out what sort of answer you are expecting. For example, in reply to the first question in activity 3b, you are looking for a number, so listen specifically for that.

Stratégie

Perfect tense of *-re* verbs

The past participle of regular *-re* verbs ends in *-u: répondre* (*répondu*). Remove the *-re* ending and replace it with *-u*.

Tu as répondu.   You answered.

Note that there are two important exceptions: *apprendre* (*appris*) and *comprendre* (*compris*).

Il a appris.   He learnt.

Remember that the past participle of regular *-er* verbs ends in *-é*, e.g. *parlé* (*parler*).

Also practise saying 'this' and 'these'.   *See page 133* ➡️

Grammaire page 167

Take the opportunity to show that you can use a range of tenses (past, present, future).

Astuce

---

kerboodle!

1 🅥 Match the French and the English.

1 la rentrée   a a study period (when one of your teachers is away)
2 une heure d'étude   b a personal diary
3 un carnet de notes c a school book
4 la carte de sortie d a booklet for the marks / grades given to you by your teachers (school diary)
5 un journal intime   e a card you have to show to be allowed out of the school premises (exit pass)
6 un livre scolaire   f the first day of the school year

Manon, élève de sixième, écrit dans son journal intime

Mon journal intime

Lundi

Aujourd'hui, c'était la rentrée. Ma mère m'a accompagnée au collège et je n'ai pas aimé ça. Je ne suis plus un bébé! À huit heures, j'ai rencontré mon professeur principal et il est plutôt sévère. Puis, on a eu cours jusqu'à midi. Je suis allée à la cantine. Ce qu'on mange à la cantine, ce n'est jamais bon.

Mardi

Aujourd'hui, j'ai eu dessin, anglais et informatique. J'adore ces matières. J'ai aussi retrouvé trois de mes copines de l'école primaire qui sont aussi en sixième mais dans des classes différentes. On a beaucoup parlé à la récréation. Hier, elles n'étaient pas contentes non plus, mais aujourd'hui, ça va mieux.

Mercredi

Il n'y a pas de cours cet après-midi. Ça, c'est bien. Je dois sortir avec ma mère pour aller acheter mes livres scolaires et mes cahiers. Plus tard, Hélène va venir chez moi. C'est une nouvelle copine qui est dans ma classe. On va faire nos devoirs ensemble.

Jeudi

On n'a commencé les cours qu'à dix heures. C'est bien parce que je suis restée au lit jusqu'à neuf heures. Cet après-midi, entre trois heures et quatre heures, on a eu une heure d'étude parce qu'il n'y avait pas de professeur de science. Il était absent. L'étude, c'est une salle de classe où on fait ses devoirs si un professeur est absent.

Vendredi

J'ai trouvé la semaine plutôt longue. Je suis assez fatiguée parce qu'aujourd'hui, j'ai eu cours de huit heures à midi et de deux heures à cinq heures. Heureusement, c'est le week-end maintenant.

2a 📖🎧 Read Manon's diary and decide whether these statements are true (T), false (F) or not mentioned in the text (?).

1 Manon did not enjoy her first day in secondary school.
2 She is in the same class as three of her primary school friends.
3 She has to buy her own school books.
4 Hélène likes the same subjects as Manon.
5 On Thursday, Manon did her homework at lunch time.

2b 📖🎧 Read Manon's diary again and decide whether these statements are true (T), false (F) or not mentioned in the text (?).

1 Manon was unhappy on Monday because her mother took her to school, her tutor is strict and lunch was not nice.
2 She likes French and Geography.
3 She only had one lesson on Wednesday afternoon.
4 Manon had a study period when her science teacher was away.
5 She was tired on Friday as she had a lot of homework to complete over the week.

3a 🎧 Listen to the instructions given by Manon's tutor and match the topics below (1–4) to the four sections (A–D) you hear.

1   What you have to do in case of absence.
2   Students' timetable.
3   A card that says the time at which you are allowed to leave school.
4   A notebook in which students have to record the marks / grades they are given in all subjects.

3b 🎧 Listen again and answer the questions in English.

1   Why do pupils have to give their parents a copy of their timetable?
2   What is the purpose of the *carnet de notes*?
3   In case of absence, what do pupils have to do on their return to school?
4   How do pupils use their *carte de sortie*?

4 **G** Make these sentences negative in the way suggested. The ones marked * have an extra factor to think about, as you will need to use *de / d'*.

Exemple: Elle achète des livres scolaires. (never)
              Elle n'achète jamais de livres scolaires.

1   Je prends un repas à la cantine. (never)*
2   Manon a trois amis dans sa classe. (only)
3   Je suis contente de mes notes. (not)
4   Hélène a des devoirs à faire. (no more)*
5   Elle a une carte de sortie. (not)*
6   Elle a une heure d'étude. (never)*

> ### Negatives with *de*
> When you change a sentence from positive to negative, you must change *un, une* or *des* to *de* or *d'*. This must be remembered with all of the negative forms, e.g. *ne … plus, ne … jamais* as well as *ne … pas*.
>
> *J'ai des devoirs. > Je n'ai plus de devoirs.* (I haven't got any more homework.)
>
> Also learn to recognise the relative pronouns *qui* and *que*.
> *See page 132* ➡
>
> **Grammaire** page 168

5 🗨 🌐 Compare life in your school to that in a typical French school. Partner A plays the part of an interviewer from a French school. Partner B talks about life in a British school and makes comparisons. Below are some suggested questions.

■   Tu vas au collège quels jours de la semaine?
■   À quelle heure est-ce que tu es arrivé(e) au collège ce matin?
■   La pause déjeuner dure combien de temps?
■   À quelle heure est-ce que tu vas quitter le collège cet après-midi?
■   Est-ce que tu as acheté tes livres scolaires?

Tu vas au collège quels jours de la semaine?

Tous les jours, du lundi au vendredi. Je sais qu'en France, c'est différent. Vous ne travaillez pas le mercredi après-midi.

On va au collège	du lundi au vendredi.
J'ai acheté / je n'ai pas acheté	mes livres scolaires et mes cahiers.
Je trouve / J'ai trouvé la semaine	fatigante / longue.
La pause déjeuner dure	une heure / deux heures.
Les cours finissent à / Je vais quitter le collège à	trois heures et demie / cinq heures.
Je suis arrivé	à huit heures et demie.
À la récréation,	j'ai parlé à / retrouvé mes copines.

> 🗨 When speaking, try to make more complex sentences by joining up simpler ones. Useful words are *et* (and), *mais* (but), *parce que* (because) and *qui* (who).
>
> Think of some simple sentences about your school and join them together to make longer ones.
>
> **Stratégie**

4.3 Problèmes scolaires

Objectifs

Pressures, problems and improvements

How to say 'it' and 'them'

Correct spelling and accents

1 ⓥ Categorise these sentences into school work, school rules or facilities.

Il faut porter un uniforme.

Il faut arriver en cours à l'heure.

Les examens sont difficiles.

Il y a trop de devoirs.

Il n'y a pas assez d'ordinateurs.

Les bâtiments sont vieux.

Problèmes scolaires – Tante Hélène répond

Problèmes

1 Quand je vois des garçons ou des filles de ma classe qui portent des vêtements très chics, je suis jalouse. Moi aussi je voudrais porter des vêtements comme ça, mais ils sont trop chers! *Pascale, 14*

2 Beaucoup de cours sont barbants, je trouve. Je ne fais pas assez attention en classe, et donc, j'ai de mauvaises notes! *Laurence, 15.*

3 Comme il n'y a pas assez d'ordinateurs dans notre école, je voudrais bien travailler avec mon ordinateur portable, mais c'est interdit. *Sanja, 16*

4 On n'a pas le droit de porter de bijoux au collège et je trouve ça vraiment bête. Si je porte mon bracelet ou ma boucle d'oreille, quel problème est-ce que ça pose? *Marc, 14.*

Réponses

A Oui, moi aussi, je trouve que les profs devraient te permettre de l'utiliser. Mais tu peux quand même t'en servir pour faire tes devoirs et pour réviser.

B Je sais que c'est bien de porter des vêtements à la mode mais la mode, ce n'est pas vraiment important. Il ne faut pas être jalouse, ça ne change rien.

C Aucun problème. Je ne comprends pas pourquoi ils interdisent de les porter. Je te recommande cependant de respecter le réglement. Les bijoux, ce n'est pas très important.

D Je comprends que c'est difficile, mais il faut faire un effort. C'est ton avenir qui en dépend. Je suppose que plus tard, tu voudrais un travail intéressant? Penses-y, ça va te motiver.

2a 📖🎧 Match the students' problems (1–4) with Tante Hélène's replies (A–D).

2b 📖🎧 Choose the three sentences which are correct according to the text.

1. Tante Hélène says that laptops are not as good as school computers.
2. Fashion is an issue for Pascale.
3. Tante Hélène suggests thinking of a future career as a way to get more motivated.
4. Not being allowed to wear jewellery bothers Marc.
5. There is excellent IT provision in Sanja's school.

3a 🎬 🎧 Watch the video and / or listen to Section A of the conversation. The French Education minister is visiting a London comprehensive school, where he interviews a brother and sister. Their family moved from France a few years earlier and they are now fully integrated into British school life. Answer the questions in English.

1 What are the advantages of wearing a school uniform, according to Justine?
2 What does she not like about her uniform?
3 Which rules does she not agree with?

3b 🎬 🎧 Watch the video and / or listen to Section B. Answer the questions in English.

1 How much homework does Romain get each week?
2 How long does he take to complete it?
3 What does he complain about?
4 How does the Minister conclude the interview?

4 **G** Match these questions and answers.

1 Tu portes ton uniforme en voyage scolaire?
2 Tu fais tes devoirs au collège?
3 Tu aimes le chewing-gum?
4 Tu connais mon professeur principal?
5 Tu as acheté ton ordinateur récemment?

a Non, je ne l'ai jamais rencontré.
b Non, je le mets seulement au collège.
c On me l'a donné pour mon anniversaire.
d Non, je les fais chez moi.
e Non, je ne l'aime pas.

5 ✏ 🌐 Write an article about school pressures and problems, based on your school or an imaginary school. Don't forget to give your opinions and offer possible solutions wherever you can. Include your views on:

■ school uniform   ■ school rules   ■ homework

Illustrate your account with real examples of incidents that have happened in the school you are writing about.

Je pense que / qu'	certains cours sont barbants.
À mon avis	il y a trop de devoirs.
Je trouve que / qu'	les examens sont (trop) difficiles.
On n'a pas le droit de / il est interdit de	porter des bijoux / fumer au collège.
Les bâtiments sont vieux / modernes.	
On n'a pas assez de / d'	ordinateurs / tableaux interactifs.
Il faut / On doit	porter un uniforme scolaire.

Astuce

The passage contains several **near cognates**, or French words which are very similar to English ones, e.g. *discipliné* (well behaved).

Grammaire *page 165*

How to say 'it' and 'them'

The French words *le, la, l', les* (meaning 'the') have a different meaning when you see them immediately before a verb.

him	le, l'	Je le vois souvent.
her	la, l'	Je la connais.
it	le, la, l'	Le bus? Je le prends matin et soir.
them	les	Nos professeurs? Oui, je les aime bien.

Also revise the use of indirect object pronouns including *y*.

See page 133 ➡

Stratégie

✏ Although infinitives and past participles often sound the same, they need different endings, e.g. *on doit utiliser* (one must / has to use) but *j'ai utilisé* (I used).

Make sure you know the difference between *ou* (or) and *où* (where) – they also sound the same.

Check that you have remembered circumflexes (e.g. *hôpital*) and cedillas (e.g. *français*).

Astuce

When you are given a writing task like this one, there are normally bullet points for you to follow. However, the most important thing is to make sure that what you write is relevant to the title.

kerboodle!

School / college and future plans

L'école des parents en République centrafricaine

A

Il est 7h20 du matin, et il fait déjà du soleil. Les 104 enfants (64 garçons et 40 filles) sont déjà tous dans la cour de l'école. Achille joue au foot avec ses copains. Il porte un t-shirt et un short aux couleurs de son équipe de foot préférée. On ne peut pas avoir classe l'après-midi, car il fait trop chaud. Achille a 12 ans et il va bientôt quitter l'école, son éducation est presque finie.

B

En janvier 2006, Achille habitait un autre village et allait dans une autre école. Un jour des soldats ont attaqué le village et ont brûlé les maisons. Toute la famille a dû partir et a passé quelques mois dans la forêt, dans des conditions affreuses. Maintenant, son père a construit une nouvelle maison.

C

L'école est à 800 mètres de la nouvelle maison d'Achille. Les parents ont construit l'école pour leurs enfants. Les parents font aussi la classe mais ils n'ont pas beaucoup d'équipement. Ils veulent une vie normale pour leurs enfants après cette période difficile. *«Cette école est très différente. Avant, il y avait des cahiers, des crayons, des professeurs. Ici, on n'a rien»* dit Achille.

D

À 12h30, après quatre heures de classe, Achille rentre chez lui. L'après-midi il fait trop chaud pour travailler aux champs, mais le soir il aide son père à cultiver des légumes. L'ambition d'Achille? Être fermier comme son père? Non, il veut être médecin.

1a 📖🎧 Read the whole article and match the English paragraph headings to the paragraphs (A–D).

1 An abandoned village
2 A boy with ambition
3 An early morning start
4 A return to normal life

1b 📖🎧 Read the article in detail. Decide if the following statements are true (T), false (F) or not mentioned (?).

1 School starts early to avoid working in the heat.
2 Achille spent several months in the forest.
3 His mother teaches at the school.
4 Achille has all the basic equipment he needs for school.
5 He works with his father in the school holidays.
6 He wants to train for a different career from his father.

Vocabulaire

affreux(-euse)	awful
le bâtiment	building
brûler	to burn
le champ	field
construire	to build
cultiver	to grow
le soldat	soldier

2a 🎧 A reporter is visiting an African village school and interviews Madame Clara. Listen to Section A. Choose the correct word to complete each sentence.

1 Madame Clara is   a parent   a head teacher   an aid worker .
2 The villagers were afraid of   soldiers   animals   spirits .
3 They started to return after   six months   one year   two years .
4 The number of children at the school has reached   nearly 100   exactly 100   over 100 .
5 Conditions at the school are   easy   getting worse   difficult .

2b 🎧 Listen to Section B. Correct the mistakes in the statements.

1 There are enough teachers at the school.
2 The children say they need textbooks, pens, tables and chairs.
3 The children come to school to be safe and to be with other adults.
4 If they hear planes they are frightened.
5 The charity has given the school books and a computer.
6 The charity is training six parents to help rebuild the school.

Negative phrases

In the interview, the following negative phrases are used:

Il n'y avait personne.

Il n'y avait rien

What do they mean?

There are also two examples of the use of *ne … pas* in one sentence. Can you remember what they said?

Ⓖ*rammaire* page 168

G School / college and future plans

Sentences with *qui*; *Que* meaning 'that'

1 ✒ Use *qui* to turn each pair of sentences into one.

Exemple: J'étudie une matière. Elle est intéressante.
             J'étudie une matière qui est intéressante.

1   Il y a des élèves. Ils m'énervent.
2   Il y a des matières. Elles sont difficiles.
3   Elle a une prof de maths. Elle explique bien.
4   Il y a des professeurs. Ils encouragent beaucoup leurs élèves.
5   Nous avons une pause-déjeuner. Elle dure une heure et demie.
6   J'ai compris l'exemple. Il est au tableau.

2 📖 Match the sentences (1–4) to the cartoons (A–D).

1   J'étudie des matières que j'adore.
2   Elle porte un uniforme qu'elle déteste.
3   Il y a des professeurs que je n'aime pas.
4   Elle utilise des mots que je ne comprends pas.

C'est une anomalie incompréhensible

> ### Sentences with *qui*
> *Grammaire* page 171
>
> ▩ *Qui* (meaning 'who' or 'that') can refer to either people or objects, and is used to link phrases together.
> *Tu as un prof. Il est gentil.*
> *Tu as un prof qui est gentil.*
> You have a teacher who is kind.
> *Il y a un livre. Il est intéressant.*
> *Il y a un livre qui est intéressant.*
> There is a book that is interesting.
>
> ▩ Remember you will score higher marks (in Speaking and Writing) if you use longer sentences that have linking words like *qui*.

> ### *Que* meaning 'that'
> *Grammaire* page 171
>
> ▩ *Que* (or *qu'* before a vowel) is also used to link phrases together. Whereas *qui* usually comes immediately before the verb, *que* comes before the subject.
> *le prof que j'adore*
> the teacher (that) I love
> *la matière que j'étudie*
> the subject (that) I am studying
>
> ▩ *Que* means 'that'. It is often left out in English, but not in French.

How to say 'this' and 'these'; Indirect object pronouns; Understanding *y*

3 🖊 Complete these sentences with *ce, cet, cette* or *ces*.

1 _____ élèves préparent le bac.
2 _____ matière est assez facile.
3 Je vais acheter _____ ordinateur.
4 Il y a 1200 élèves dans _____ lycée.
5 _____ examen n'est pas très difficile.
6 Je peux utiliser _____ calculatrice?
7 _____ professeurs m'ont encouragé.
8 Dans _____ collège, les élèves sont travailleurs.

4 📖 Choose the correct translation for each sentence, a or b.

1 Je ne lui réponds jamais.
   a I never answer him.   b I never answer you.
2 Il te pose une question.
   a He is asking me a question.   b He is asking you a question.
3 Est-ce que tu leur as demandé?
   a Did you ask them?   b Did you ask her?
4 Mes parents m'ont acheté un dictionnaire.
   a My parents bought me a dictionary.   b My parents bought us a dictionary.
5 Elle nous a dit qu'on ne travaillait pas assez.
   a She told them that we didn't work enough.   b She told us that we didn't work enough.
6 Le professeur vous donne de bonnes notes.
   a The teacher gives them good grades.   b The teacher gives you good grades.

5 📖 Match the questions and answers. Then note down what *y* stands for in each case.

Exemple: Tu vas à l'université?
            Oui, j'y vais. (y = à l'université)

1 Tu prépares le bac dans ce lycée?
2 Ils vont souvent à la bibliothèque?
3 Son père travaille dans ce collège?
4 Ton frère étudie l'espagnol à l'université?
5 Tu ne fais jamais tes devoirs dans la cour?
6 Sa sœur apprend le piano dans cette école?

a Non, je n'y fais jamais mes devoirs.
b Non, elle n'y apprend pas le piano.
c Non, il n'y étudie pas l'espagnol.
d Oui, ils y vont souvent.
e Oui, j'y prépare le bac.
f Oui, il y travaille.

Grammaire (page 162)

How to say 'this' and 'these'
The French for 'this' and 'that' is *ce, cet* or *cette*. Use:

- *ce* before a masculine noun
- *cet* before a masculine noun that begins with a vowel or a silent 'h'
  ce professeur this teacher
  cet étudiant this student
- *cette* before a feminine noun
  cette université this university

The French for 'these' and 'those' is *ces*.
ces stylos these / those pens

Grammaire (page 165)

Indirect object pronouns
These expressions (to me, to you etc.) come before the verb in French.

- Singular: *me* (to me), *te* (to you), *lui* (to him / her / it).
  Elle me donne un stylo. She gives a pen to me. (She gives me a pen.)
- Plural: *nous* (to us), *vous* (to you), *leur* (to them)
  Elle leur donne un livre. She gives a book to them. (She gives them a book.)

Grammaire (page 165)

Understanding *y*
The word *y* is used to avoid repeating the name of a place. It usually means 'there'.
Tu vas au laboratoire?
Are you going to the laboratory?
Oui, j'y vais.
Yes, I am going there.

School / college and future plans

Comment est ton collège? ➡ *pages 124–125*

	ancien(ne)	old
	apprendre	to learn
	attendre	to wait for
	comprendre	to understand
l'	*emploi du temps (m)*	timetable
	enseigner	to teach
	étudier	to study
	gentil(le)	nice
la	*langue*	language
la	*matière*	subject
	parler	to talk
	passer	to take (an exam)
	penser	to think
	réussir	to succeed
	répondre	to answer
le	*trimestre*	term
	en sixième	in year 7
	en cinquième	in year 8
	en quatrième	in year 9
	en troisième	in year 10
	en seconde	in year 11
	en première	in year 12
	en terminale	in year 13

La vie au collège en France ➡ *pages 126–127*

le	*cahier*	exercise book
le	*carnet*	notebook
le	*carnet de notes*	school report book
la	*carte de sortie*	exit pass
le	*cours*	lesson
l'	*heure d'étude (f)*	study period
le	*journal intime*	diary
le	*livre scolaire*	school book, textbook
	montrer	to show
la	*note*	mark, grade
la	*récréation*	playtime, break
la	*rentrée*	the start of the new school year
	savoir	to know (a fact)
	vérifier	to check, verify

Les problèmes scolaires ➡ *pages 128–129*

	avoir le droit de	to have the right to
	barbant(e)	boring, dull
les	*bijoux (m)*	jewellery
la	*boucle d'oreille*	earring
	démodé(e)	oldfashioned, out-of-date
les	*devoirs (m)*	homework
l'	*examen (m)*	exam
	faire attention	to pay attention
	interdit	forbidden
	mâcher	to chew
le	*maquillage*	make-up
l'	*ordinateur (m)*	computer
	porter	to wear
le	*règlement*	rules, regulations
l'	*uniforme (m)*	uniform

Time expressions

d'	abord	first
un	an	year
une	année	year
	après	after
l'	après-midi (m)	afternoon
	aujourd'hui	today
en	avance	in advance
	avant	before
à l'	avenir	in the future
	bientôt	soon
de	bonne heure	early
	déjà	already, still
	demain	tomorrow
	encore une fois	once more
	enfin	at last, finally
la	fin	end
d'	habitude	normally
à l'	heure	on time
	hier	yesterday
le	jour	day
la	journée	day
le	lendemain	next day
	longtemps	a long time
	maintenant	now
le	matin	morning
en	même temps	at the same time
la	minute	minute
le	mois	month
en ce	moment	at the moment, currently
	normalement	normally, usually
la	nuit	night
	parfois	sometimes
	pendant	during
	plus tard	later
	prochain(e)	next
	quelquefois	sometimes
	rarement	rarely

	récemment	recently
en	retard	late
la	semaine	week
le	siècle	century
	soudain	suddenly
	souvent	often
de	temps en temps	sometimes
	tôt	early
	toujours	always
	tous les jours	every day
	tout de suite	straightaway
	vite	quickly
le	week-end	weekend

Expressing the negative

ne … jamais	never
ne … pas	not
ne … personne	nobody
ne … plus	not any more
ne … que	only
ne … rien	nothing
ni … ni	neither … nor

1 **V** Choose a speech bubble for each job.

1 checkout worker
2 worker in a school
3 waiter
4 postal worker
5 factory worker
6 office worker

A J'ai livré des paquets.

B J'ai travaillé à la caisse.

C J'ai travaillé dans une école primaire.

Je sers les clients. **D**

J'ai travaillé dans une usine. **E**

Je fais des photocopies. **F**

Quatre jeunes qui travaillent

Pendant les vacances scolaires, Juliette travaille toujours comme caissière dans un magasin. Elle travaille bien et elle est assez bien payée, mais elle dit que c'est un peu ennuyeux.

Comme Jérome fait un stage, il n'est pas payé. Il est dans l'entreprise d'un électricien au centre-ville. Il voudrait être électricien un jour parce qu'il veut gagner un bon salaire.

Xavier voudrait travailler comme mécanicien à la fin de ses études. Mais pour son stage, il n'a pas trouvé de place de mécanicien, alors il a travaillé comme technicien dans une entreprise d'informatique. Il a bien travaillé parce qu'il adore les ordinateurs.

Zoé travaille tous les samedis comme vendeuse chez un boucher. C'est mal payé mais malheureusement elle n'a pas pu trouver autre chose. Elle espère bientôt trouver quelque chose de plus intéressant et surtout de mieux payé.

2a 📖🎧 Read the article and decide which picture goes with which person. Write the names.

1

2

3

4

2b 📖🎧 Name the person being referred to in each case.

1 The job xxxxx wants is well paid.
2 xxxxx always has the same holiday job.
3 xxxxx worked for an IT company.
4 xxxxx has a Saturday job.
5 xxxxx is doing this job because it's the only one she could get.

3a 🎧 🔊 Listen to Section A and choose the correct answers.

1   Nicolas works in   **a bakery   a butcher's   an office** .

2   He works   **every Sunday   every Saturday   in the holidays** .

3   Émilie   **works in a shop   works in an office   delivers the post** .

4   She   **writes   sends   opens** letters.

3b 🎧 🔊 Listen to Section B and choose the correct answers.

1   Mehmet   **has done   is doing   is going to do**   his work experience.

2   He found the work   **easy   hard   boring** .

3   Dominique worked   **with horses   for a firm   on a farm** .

4   One day she wants to   **go on the stage   work in agriculture   race horses** .

🎧 Sometimes a listening passage has a section in the present tense and another in the past tense. Listen for auxiliaries (*avoir / être*) and past participles (*sorti, travaillé*). This tells you that that section is in the past tense. Which section is in the present / past tense here?

Stratégie

4 🅖 Complete these sentences with an adverb.

1   J'ai travaillé _____. (quickly)

2   On ne peut pas trouver de travail _____ dans notre ville. (easily)

3   _____, j'ai gagné beaucoup d'argent. (luckily)

4   _____ je reste chez moi le dimanche. (normally)

5   J'étais _____ payé. (well)

6   Et moi, j'étais _____ payé! (badly)

Forming adverbs

French adverbs normally end in -*ement*, which is the equivalent of the English ending -*ly*.

Normalement, heureusement, malheureusement, facilement have been used in either the reading or the listening activities on these pages. What do you think they mean?

There are four common exceptions: *vite* (quickly), *dur* (hard), *bien* (well), *mal* (badly).

Also learn to recognise the passive form.

See page 144 ➡

Grammaire page 163

5 🗨 Work in pairs. Pretend to be a teacher carrying out a de-brief with a pupil after work experience.

■ Où as-tu fait ton stage?

■ Qu'est-ce que tu as fait?

■ C'était comment?

■ Est-ce que tu as aussi un petit job (emploi) le soir ou le week-end?

■ Est-ce que tu voudrais un emploi permanent comme ça plus tard?

Où as-tu fait ton stage?

Dans une école primaire, près de chez moi.

Pour mon stage, j'ai travaillé	dans un bureau / un magasin / une usine / une école.
Le (samedi), je travaille	
Je fais / J'ai fait	des photocopies.
Je sers / J'ai servi	les clients.
C'est / C'était / J'ai trouvé le travail	barbant / dur / fatigant / pas mal / amusant parce que …
Un jour, je voudrais travailler	dans un bureau etc.

Don't forget to include an adverb to say HOW you worked.

Astuce

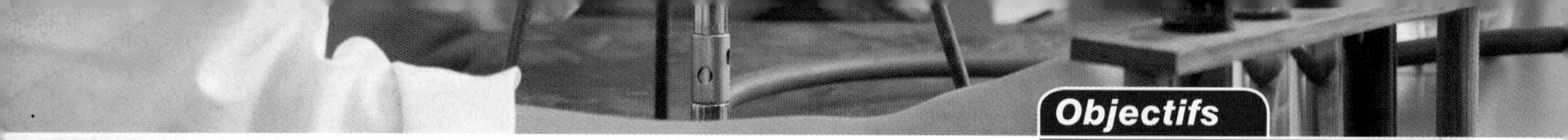

Objectifs

Job search and application

Using *vous* (polite form)

Masculine and feminine forms of jobs

1 ⓥ Unjumble these French words for jobs and translate them into English. Add accents where they are needed.

1. fire in mire
2. nice musi
3. rut face
4. i erase trec
5. i reli cop

■ Offres d'emploi

Le supermarché du
CAMPING DE L'OCEAN
cherche
vendeur / vendeuse
pour travailler à la caisse
tous les après-midi de 14 à
16 heures.
Salaire à discuter.
Expérience préférable.
Présentez-vous au chef du
personnel.

Halte-garderie
ST-JACQUES
24, rue des Pins,
cherche
un(e) assistant(e) pour
travailler pendant les grandes
vacances avec des petits
enfants du lundi au vendredi,
tous les matins de 8h à
12h30.
Écrivez à l'adresse ci-dessus.

Restaurant marocain
LE CASBAH
avenue de la Forêt,
Jard-sur-Mer,
tél. 02-44-63-91-45.
Nous cherchons quelqu'un
pour travailler comme
serveur / serveuse le
week-end de 9 à 17 heures.
Formation: pas nécessaire.

C'est exactement ce que
je cherche. Je n'ai pas le temps
de travailler en semaine, mais
le samedi et le dimanche, c'est
différent. Je n'ai jamais travaillé
avant mais ils disent que ce n'est
pas essentiel. Je vais
leur téléphoner ce soir.

Clara

En ce moment,
je travaille le samedi dans
un petit magasin mais ce que
je voudrais, c'est un travail en
semaine après l'école. Je ne veux
pas finir trop tard parce que j'ai
toujours beaucoup de devoirs à
faire. Je vais y
aller cet après-midi.

Yasmina

J'avais demandé à faire
ce travail il y a deux ans, mais j'étais
trop jeune à cette époque. Cette
année, pas de problème, je pense.
J'ai dix-sept ans maintenant. C'est
bien comme travail saisonnier parce
que je vais avoir mes après-midi
de libre. Je vais leur
envoyer une lettre.

Antoine

2a 📖 🎧 🌐 Read the job adverts and also what the three applicants are thinking. Who is best suited to each job?

1. Restaurant Le Casbah
2. Halte-garderie St-Jacques
3. Supermarché Océan

📖 Most words for jobs have a masculine and a feminine version:

employé / employée
caissier / caissière
vendeur / vendeuse

However, *professeur* (teacher), and *médecin* (doctor) don't change. See page 160.

Make a list of jobs with their male and female versions. Use a dictionary if you like.

Stratégie

2b 📖🎧🔵 Choose three sentences which are true according to the adverts and thought clouds.

1 No experience is necessary if you want to work at Le Casbah.
2 The job at St-Jacques crèche is for afternoons only.
3 To work at the supermarket, they'd rather you had experience.
4 Antoine worked at St-Jacques crèche two years ago.
5 Yasmina wants to finish work early so as to have enough time to do her homework.

3a 🎧 Listen to Yasmina's interview (Section A) and choose the correct answers.

1 Yasmina is   15   16   17   years old.
2 Her family name is   Farik   Fariq   Feriq   .
3 She is offered a salary of   7   8   9   euros an hour.
4 She can start work next   Monday   Tuesday   Wednesday   .

3b 🎧 Listen to Antoine's interview (Section B) and choose the correct answers.

1 Antoine's age is   16   a problem   no longer a problem   .
2 He has   two brothers and one sister   two brothers and two sisters   one brother and two sisters   .
3 He is offered a salary of   five   one hundred   one hundred and five   euros a week.
4 He can start work on   1 July   1 June   1 August   .

4 🅖 Interview a partner. Imagine he or she is a stranger and change the questions into the *vous* form.

1 Tu t'appelles comment?
2 Tu as quel âge?
3 Tu as de l'expérience?
4 Quel est ton salaire?
5 Quand peux-tu commencer?
6 Le travail que nous offrons t'intéresse?

> **Using *vous* (polite form)** 🅖 *Grammaire*
>
> In English there is only one word for 'you', but in French you use *tu* when talking to a friend or family member, and *vous* for an adult you don't know well or when talking to more than one person. When using *vous*, remember to use *votre, vos* instead of *ton, ta, tes.*
>
> *Avez-vous de l'expérience? Quand pouvez-vous commencer?*
>
> Also learn to recognise the pluperfect tense.
>
> *See page 144* ➡️
>
> *page 164*

5 🗨️ One partner asks the questions, as in a job interview, and the other makes up the answers. The interviewer notes down the answers. Then carry out the conversation again with different details. Ask and answer questions about the following:

- the type of job being applied for
- name and age, including spelling
- experience
- salary
- when you can start work

Bonjour monsieur. C'est à propos de la place de serveuse dans votre restaurant.

Oui, vous vous appelez comment?

> Look at activity 4 to get help with forming the questions.
>
> **Astuce**

C'est à propos du poste / de la place	d'assistant(e) / de vendeur(-euse).
J'ai / Je n'ai pas	d'expérience.
J'ai déjà travaillé	avec les enfants / dans un bureau.
Je gagne	sept / huit euros de l'heure / par semaine.
Je peux commencer	lundi / mardi etc.
J'ai déjà travaillé	dans un supermarché / dans une école etc.

4.6 La vie professionnelle

Objectifs

Comparing jobs, careers and post-16 choices

Recognising the future tense

Checking work

1 ⓥ Choose the correct endings for the following sentences from the list below:

1 Je voudrais devenir acteur. Je travaillerai …
2 Je veux être professeur. Je travaillerai …
3 Je serai hôtesse de l'air. Je travaillerai …
4 Je deviendrai secrétaire. Je travaillerai …
5 Je veux être fermier. Je travaillerai …
6 J'ai décidé que je serai policier. Je travaillerai …

<blockquote>
avec des adolescents   dans un théâtre   en plein air

dans le tourisme   dans un bureau   avec le public
</blockquote>

Qu'est-ce que tu feras dans la vie?

A Fabrice ira passer une année aux États-Unis. Il travaillera peut-être dans le tourisme, comme guide. Comme ça il apprendra l'anglais. À son avis, c'est essentiel pour la carrière qu'il veut faire.

Catherine a déjà commencé son boulot. Elle travaille comme hôtesse de l'air. C'est un travail très dur. Elle doit toujours dormir dans un hôtel à l'étranger.

B Tina ira à l'université l'année prochaine. Pour le moment, elle est toujours au lycée et elle passera son bac au mois de juin. Après ça, elle dit qu'elle voudrait devenir ingénieur, parce qu'elle pense que c'est un travail plus varié que d'autres professions. Elle a déjà fait un stage chez un ingénieur et elle a bien aimé ça.

Roger a décidé de devenir plombier. Il a choisi ça parce qu'il trouve que c'est un métier très pratique. «Tout le monde a besoin d'un plombier de temps en temps» dit-il. «En plus, on peut gagner beaucoup d'argent si on travaille bien. J'ai passé six mois en Irlande, où j'ai fait un stage de plombier. C'était vraiment intéressant.»

2a 📖🎧 Read Section A and decide whether Fabrice or Catherine is being referred to. Write F or C.

1 xxxxx va aller en Amérique.
2 xxxxx passe beaucoup de temps en avion.
3 xxxxx n'est pas souvent à la maison.
4 xxxxx pense que les langues sont importantes.

2b 📖🎧 Read Section B and decide whether Tina or Roger is being referred to. Write T or R.

1 xxxxx veut être étudiante.
2 xxxxx a travaillé à l'étranger.
3 xxxxx aimerait avoir un travail pratique.
4 xxxxx n'a pas de travail en ce moment.
5 xxxxx sera ingénieur un jour.

3a 🎧 Listen to Section A and write down the letter of the job each person would like.

 A    B    C    D

1 Nicolas
2 Mehmet
3 Olivier
4 Émilie

3b 🎧 Listen to Section B and join up the sentences.

1 Jérémy wants to be …	a … the open air.
2 He thinks it is …	b … well paid.
3 He likes the idea of working in …	c … an office.
4 Charlotte wants to be …	d … a PE teacher.
5 She thinks it is …	e … a programmer.
6 She likes the idea of working in …	f … not well paid.

4 Ⓖ Complete these sentences using a future tense verb below.

1 Après les examens, Éric _____ dans un magasin.
2 Je _____ au bureau jusqu'à 6 heures.
3 Nicolas _____ au Canada.
4 J' _____ dix-sept ans en juin.
5 Après le travail, je _____ le bus pour aller à la maison.
6 Papa _____ à la maison à cinq heures.

    arrivera   ira   aurai

   prendrai   travaillera   resterai

> ### Recognising the future tense
>
> *Je gagnerai* (I will earn) is in the future tense. It is similar to *Je vais gagner*.
>
> You need to recognise the future tense. Start with the infinitive and add these endings in the singular: *-ai, -as, -a.*
>
> Exceptions:
>
> | | | | |
> |---|---|---|---|
> | *je ferai* | I will make / do | *j'aurai* | I will have |
> | *j'irai* | I will go | *je prendrai* | I will take |
>
> Also practise when to use *le* and *la* and when to leave them out.   *See page 145* ➡️

Ⓖ **Grammaire** *page 168*

5 ✏️ 🌐 Write an e-mail to your French penfriend, explaining your future plans.

- Say what you will do as soon as you leave school.
- Say what career you hope to follow later.
- Add any details you can.
- Say what's good about this career.
- Mention one or two of its disadvantages.

Je vais travailler / Je travaillerai	à l'étranger / en plein air.
	avec les enfants / adolescents.
	dans le tourisme / un bureau / l'informatique.

Je voudrais travailler comme / être / devenir	professeur / infirmier(-ière) / chauffeur / caissier(-ière) etc.	
J'ai choisi ce métier	parce que c'est	intéressant / bien payé / varié etc.
Je ne veux pas être …		dur / ennuyeux / mal payé etc.

> ✏️ Before handing in written work, always make sure you have checked it carefully. Think about accents (for example *-é* on a past participle), plural endings on nouns (*les parents*) and correct verb endings (*ils regardent*).

🌐 **Stratégie**

> Get better marks in your exam by including past, present and future tense verbs. You could say what jobs you have done (past) and will do (future), plus give your opinions (present).

Astuce

Current and future jobs

Un four marocain, ouvert à tout le monde!

Nadège Gahinet, une étudiante française de Rouen, passe une année sabbatique au Maroc. Elle a dix-neuf ans et étudie la cuisine. Elle travaille pendant six mois dans un restaurant marocain. Son père est boulanger en France, alors, elle sait bien comment préparer le pain français.

Un jour, elle a visité une boulangerie marocaine. Voilà sa description de la visite:

«J'étais à Assilah, une petite ville, à 30 kilomètres de la mer. Un dimanche matin, j'ai vu un groupe de femmes. Chaque personne portait une grande assiette sur la tête. Elles portaient leurs morceaux de pâte à pain chez le boulanger. Elles sont entrées dans le petit bâtiment, le boulanger a mis la pâte dans un grand four. Il m'a invitée à passer quelques heures avec lui.

Il a continué à faire cuire le pain de ses clients. Un peu plus tard les clients sont revenus chercher leur pain. Beaucoup ont aussi acheté des gâteaux traditionnels, préparés par la femme du boulanger.

J'ai comparé son système avec la boulangerie en France. Mon père utilise des machines pour préparer la pâte. Le pain aussi est différent. On ne voit pas de baguettes françaises au Maroc, mais un pain rond et plat. C'est très bon!»

1a 📖🎧 Read the introduction to the article. Note, in English, the details that Nadège needs to include in the form below. One has been done for you.

First name	
Surname	
Age	
Subject studied	
Time she will spend working in Morocco	
Place of work	restaurant
Father's profession	

1b 📖🎧 Which three of the following pictures could correctly illustrate the scene at the Moroccan bakery (1–3)?

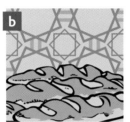

2a 🎧 Nadège is on the phone to the owner of the restaurant in Morocco, before she arrives to start work. Listen to Section A and answer the questions in English.

1 When will she start work?
2 What hours will she work?
3 How far is the restaurant from her accommodation?
4 What clothes should she wear to work?
5 When will she have days off?

2b 🎧 Listen to Section B. In what order are the following topics discussed (1–5)?

a cooking fish
b eating with the owner
c working as a waitress
d visiting the market
e her experience of working in a café

Vocabulaire

une année sabbatique	gap year
faire cuire	to cook
le four	oven
le Maroc	Morocco
la pâte	dough
les provisions (f)	groceries

Imperfect tense

In the first part of the article (page 142), the imperfect tense is used to describe what people **were doing**. There is also an example in the conversation in activity 2b, describing what Nadège **used to do**. Can you pick them out?

Grammaire *page 167*

(G) Current and future jobs

Understanding the passive: The pluperfect tense

1 In the paragraph below, find phrases that mean:

1   are bought
2   are sent
3   are done
4   are served
5   is forgotten
6   are delivered
7   is prepared

Grammaire page 168

> **Understanding the passive**
>
> The passive is used to say what is done to someone or something. It is formed from *être* followed by a past participle.
>
> | active form | passive form |
> |---|---|
> | *Elle écrit la lettre.* | *La lettre est écrite.* |
> | She writes the letter. | The letter is written |
> | *Il prépare le thé.* | *Le thé est préparé.* |
> | He prepares tea. | Tea is prepared. |

Je suis bien payée et mon assistante est super. Quand j'arrive au bureau, le café est préparé et les croissants sont achetés. Ensuite les clients sont servis rapidement, les photocopies sont faites et les paquets sont envoyés et sont livrés sans problème. Rien n'est oublié. C'est fantastique!

2 ✏ Each of the sentences below contains an example of the pluperfect tense. Each one is made up of two words – copy them. Then match four of these sentences with the pictures below.

1   Il savait que j'avais oublié le paquet.
2   Je pensais que tu n'avais pas trouvé de travail.
3   Elle était arrivée au bureau à huit heures ce matin-là.
4   Elle était très contente parce que j'avais préparé du bon café.
5   On m'a dit que tu n'avais pas aimé ton stage l'année dernière.
6   Elle m'a dit qu'elle avait travaillé dans un hôtel pendant trois ans.

Grammaire page 168

> **The pluperfect tense**
>
> The pluperfect tense is used to refer to something further back in the past than the perfect or the imperfect – to say what someone had done or had been doing. It is made with the imperfect of *avoir* or *être* followed by a past participle.
>
> *Je savais qu'il avait travaillé chez un boulanger.*
> I knew he had worked in a bakery.

A

B

C

D

'Our', 'your' and 'their'; Nouns with and without 'a'

3 🖊 Replace the English with *notre, nos, votre, vos, leur* or *leurs*.

1 (Their) _____ travail est varié.
2 Voici (our) _____ numéro de téléphone.
3 Le facteur a distribué (your) _____ lettres.
4 Donnez-moi (your) _____ nom, s'il vous plaît.
5 Ils s'entendent bien avec (their) _____ collègues?
6 (Our) _____ salaires sont ridicules, nous sommes mal payés.

4 📖 Match the captions and the pictures. Complete the captions using names of jobs from the word snake. You need to decide which ones need the indefinite article (*un / une*) and which ones don't.

1 J'adore la musique et je voudrais être _____!
2 Ma grand-mère était _____ dans un café.
3 C'est _____ qui fait du bon pain.
4 Je vais appeler _____ pour réparer la douche.
5 Il adore les voitures et il a trouvé un stage chez _____.
6 Ma mère adore voyager, elle est _____.

Grammaire *page 163*

'Our', 'your' and 'their'

When using the French for 'our', 'your' and 'their', make the word you choose agree with the noun that comes after it.

▪ our: *notre* (singular) and *nos* (plural)
▪ your: *votre* (singular) and *vos* (plural)
▪ their: *leur* (singular) and *leurs* (plural)

Nous avons aimé notre stage. — We liked our work experience.

Nos collègues étaient très sympas. — Our colleagues were very friendly.

Grammaire *page 160*

Nouns with and without 'a'

Remember not to use the indefinite article (*un / une*) when saying what someone's job is, or what they want it to be, in French.

Mon frère est infirmier et ma sœur est architecte. — My brother is a nurse and my sister is an architect.

It is needed in all other cases.

C'est une très bonne actrice. — She is a very good actress.

Va voir un médecin! — Go and see a doctor!

a

b

c

d

e

f

boulangerhôtessedel'airmécanicienmusicienplombierserveuse

Current and future jobs

Stages et petits jobs ➡ *pages 136–137*

le	bois	wood
en	bois	(made) of wood
le	boulot	work
le	bureau	office
la	caisse	till, cash register
la	caissière (f)	cashier
le	client	client, customer
	dur(e)	hard
l'	emploi (m)	job
l'	entreprise (f)	firm
	fabriquer	to make
	faire un stage (en entreprise)	to do training, an apprenticeship (in a firm)
	gagner	to earn
	livrer	to deliver
le	meuble	item of furniture
la	place	job, position
l'	usine (f)	factory
la	vache	cow
	vite	quickly

La vie professionnelle ➡ *pages 140–141*

l'	acteur (m)	actor
l'	avenir (m)	the future
la	carrière	career
	décider	to decide
	devenir	to become
	en plein air	in the open air, outdoors
à l'	étranger	abroad
l'	étudiant (m)	student
l'	étudiante (f)	student
le	fermier	farmer
l'	hôtesse de l'air (f)	air stewardess, flight attendant
l'	ingénieur (m)	engineer
	quitter	to leave
	varié(e)	varied

Je cherche un emploi ➡ *pages 138–139*

l'	employé (m)	employee
le	facteur	postman
la	halte-garderie	day nursery
l'	infirmier (m)	nurse
le	médecin	doctor
le	musicien	musician
le	policier	policeman
le	poste	job, post
le	professeur	teacher
le	salaire	salary
le	serveur	waiter
la	serveuse	waitress
le	travail saisonnier	seasonal work

1 **V** Read the clues 1–8. Complete the gapped French words a–h to do with jobs and future plans and match each one to its clue.

1 the money paid to an employee each month
2 the girl who brings a meal to your table
3 the person who delivers your letters
4 girl studying at a college
5 the opposite of *le passé* (the past)
6 a place where objects are made
7 a person who gets up early and works outdoors
8 a person who enforces the law

a l __ __ __ __ __ __ __ u __ __
b le __ __ l __ __ __ e
c __ __ __ __ __ i __ __ e __
d __ ' __ __ __ __ __ i __
e __ __ __ __ __ m __ __ r
f l' __ __ __ __ e
g l' __ __ u __ __ __ __ t __
h __ __ __ __ c __ __ u __

2 **V** Find the 11 words about jobs and occupations in the wordsearch.

Q	I	F	E	R	M	I	E	R	P
S	F	É	G	J	U	H	S	S	J
H	Ô	T	E	S	S	E	A	E	P
B	X	U	G	V	I	K	L	R	O
F	M	D	A	N	C	E	A	V	L
U	S	I	N	E	I	O	I	E	I
Q	F	A	C	T	E	U	R	U	C
W	Z	N	D	H	N	U	E	R	I
A	C	T	E	U	R	L	E	E	E
C	I	E	M	P	L	O	Y	É	R

4 ⬭ Au travail

You are talking to your French friend about part-time jobs, work experience, future careers and your free time. Your teacher will play the part of your friend and will ask you:

1 what part-time job you do and when
2 further details about your part-time job
3 details about your work experience
4 what the possibilities are when you leave school
5 what career you envisage for yourself
6 what you do with your leisure time
7 **!**

! Remember you will have to respond to something that you have not yet prepared.

> **AQA Examiner's tips**
>
> Start with *je travaille* …
> Use *le* + day to say you work for instance *le samedi*.
> If you don't have a job, feel free to make one up. If your job is too complicated to talk about, you don't have to tell the truth!

1 What part-time job you do and when
- say what job you do
- say how long you have had your job for
- mention your hours of work
- say which days you work

> **AQA Examiner's tips**
>
> Now, start your plan. Write a maximum of six words for each of the seven sections that make up the task. Here are some suggested words for the first section.
> *travailler, depuis, commencer, finir, jours*
> Using verbs in your plan is helpful. However, remember that you have to write them in the infinitive or the past participle. If you can manage with five words here, you will have more available for later.

2 Further details about your part-time job
- say where you work
- say how you get to work
- say how much you earn
- say what you think of the job

> **AQA Examiner's tips**
>
> Use *est situé* to say where your place of work is.
> Use *livres de l'heure / par semaine / par mois* to say how much you earn an hour / a week / a month.
> When you say what you think of your job, try to give a reason as well.
> Add up to six words to your plan.

3 Details about your work experience
- say when it took place
- say what work you did
- say what you enjoyed about your work experience
- compare a day at work with a day at school

> **AQA Examiner's tips**
>
> Use *faire un stage* for saying 'to go on work experience'.
> As this section is about something that has happened in the past, check how to use the perfect tense. See grammar section page 167.
> In your plan include a reference to the fact that your work experience has already happened, e.g. *l'année dernière*. It will remind you that you should be using the perfect tense.

4 What the possibilities are when you leave school
- say you can take up an apprenticeship
- say you can continue with your education then go to university
- say you can go straight into a job
- talk about your own intentions

Use *on peut* when you want to talk about possibilities for people in general.

Use *faire un apprentissage* for 'to take up an apprenticeship'.

To talk about your own intentions, you have to refer to the future. Use *je vais / je voudrais / j'aimerais / j'espère / j'ai l'intention de* ... All of these are followed by a verb in the infinitive.

In your plan, you are allowed to use visuals as well as words.

5 What career you envisage for yourself
- say what career you envisage for yourself
- explain one of the advantages of that job
- state one of the disadvantages
- say what you will do if that proves impossible

Use *je voudrais* (or another phrase that refers to a future event) + *devenir / être* + job title (without *un / une*) to say what you would like to be.

Start with *si ce n'est pas possible, je* ... to introduce the last point.

In your plan, use words that suggest more than one sentence to you, e.g. *pilote* might suggest that it is your choice of career or that you love flying.

6 What you do with your leisure time
- say how much leisure time you have now
- say what you do when you stay at home
- say what you do when you go out
- say what you think you will do with your leisure time when you also have to work

Use *heures de loisirs* or *temps libre* for 'leisure time'. Start with *quand je vais travailler* ... to introduce the last point. Unlike in English, you have to use *je vais* or another phrase that indicates the future after *quand* in French.

Test how good your plan is. By looking at it and the task box only, you should be able to say what is in all the bullet points.

7 ! At this point, you may be asked
- if you are prepared to move to another area
- what the members of your family do for a living
- whether you have started your career, or whether you will settle down, get married and have children
- whether you are planning to have a gap year

Choose which **two** options you think are the most likely, and for each of these, note down **three** different ideas. In your plan, write three words that illustrate each of the two most likely options. For the third option you might choose: *s'installer, mariage, enfants*. Learn these two options using your reminder words. The expression to use for gap year is *une année sabbatique*.

Remember to check the total number of words you have used. It should be 40 or fewer.

You should now have completed your plan and prepared your answers. Give your plan to your teacher for feedback. Compare your answers to the online sample version – you might find some useful hints to make yours even better.

kerboodle!

4 ✏ Mon collège

Your French friend Jean-Luc has asked you to write an article in French for his school magazine. The article is entitled 'A life in the day of a pupil in Britain'. You could include:

1 the facilities in your school
2 your school routine
3 your subjects and teachers
4 your friends
5 extra-curricular activities
6 your school uniform
7 your ambitions for the future

1 The facilities in your school
   ■ introduce your school, giving its name and location
   ■ mention the size of the school, giving numbers of students and teachers
   ■ say a little about its organisation, e.g. mixed or single sex, age range
   ■ mention the various buildings and say what the facilities are

2 Your school routine
   ■ say at what time you arrive, when lessons start and the number of lessons you have each day
   ■ mention break and what you do then
   ■ say what you do at lunchtime
   ■ say at what time school finishes and how you get back home

3 Your subjects and teachers
   ■ mention compulsory subjects and options
   ■ say which subject is your favourite and give a reason
   ■ say which subject is your least favourite, again with a reason
   ■ write about your favourite teacher, saying why you like him / her

AQA Examiner's tips

Start off by giving your name and giving the name of your school.
Je m'appelle … is for saying your name. When naming someone or something else, use *s'appelle* …
Use *il y a* (there is, there are) and *nous avons* (we have) to describe the school.
As well as saying what there is, you can make your work more interesting by describing the facilities, e.g. *les bâtiments sont modernes*.

AQA Examiner's tips

Now, start your plan. Write a maximum of six words for each of the seven sections that make up the task. Here are some suggested words for the first section.
se trouver, mixte, élèves, professeurs, bâtiments, équipement
Remember that if you use words in your plan that are not immediately understandable, you have to make a point of learning them.

AQA Examiner's tips

Don't mention subjects and teachers in this section as this information is required in the next section.
When referring to what you normally do, use the present tense, e.g. *normalement, j'arrive à* …
Use the past tense to refer to what you did yesterday, e.g. *hier, j'ai mangé* … (extra marks are awarded for correct examples of the past tense).
Add up to six more words to your plan.

AQA Examiner's tips

Use *les matières obligatoires* for 'compulsory subjects'.
Use *il faut* + infinitive to say that you have to do something.
You could use *j'ai choisi* followed by your options.
Use various ways of expressing your opinion, e.g. *je pense que / je trouve que / ce que je préfère, c'est / j'aime* etc.
Link your sentences using *et, mais, car* or *parce que*.
This time, your plan may contain a few adjectives to indicate your opinions.

4 Your friends
- give some information about your friends at school
- choose one and describe him / her (physically and also character)
- say when and where you meet
- say what you did with him / her yesterday

Use *on* for 'we', e.g. *on se retrouve* (we meet). The verb which follows *on* has the same ending as it would if you were using *il* or *elle*. See grammar section page 164.

Use the perfect tense to express what you did yesterday. See grammar section page 167.

5 Extra-curricular activities
- mention which extra-curricular activities are on offer at your school
- say which activity you are involved in
- say what you think of it and give a reason for your opinion
- say where and when the activity takes place

Use *on peut* + verb to list what is on offer. See grammar section on useful verbs, page 169. You could use *ça se passe* to introduce where and when the activity takes place.

If you are not involved in extra-curricular activities, be creative and make up some information!

Use words in your plan that illustrate what you intend to say, whether you are telling the truth or not.

6 Your school uniform
- say what you wear at school
- say what you think of it and give a reason
- say when the next non-uniform day will be and what you will wear
- say what you think of the fact that French students do not wear a school uniform

Adjectives (e.g. colours) are usually placed after the noun they describe and have to be made feminine and / or plural as necessary. See grammar section page 161.

Vary the ways in which you express your opinion, e.g. *je pense que / je trouve que*.

When you talk about your non-uniform day (*une journée sans uniforme*), you can say whether it is for a trip (*une excursion*) or for charity (*une bonne cause*). Use the future tense (*je vais* + infinitive) to explain this.

7 Your ambitions for the future
- say what you are intending to do next September
- mention the subjects you would like to study and give reasons for your choices
- say what career you hope to have in the future
- say whether you would like to stay In your area or live elsewhere / abroad and give a reason

Show that you know different ways of referring to things that you hope or intend to do. Use *je voudrais / j'aimerais / j'espère / j'ai l'intention de* – all are followed by an infinitive.

Use the future tense if you are sure: *je vais* + infinitive or *j'irai* (I will go), *je ferai* (I will do).

Now you should have a complete set of 40 words on your plan, in seven groups with either five or six words in each. You can give this plan to your teacher for feedback.

Now, compare your answer with the online sample version – you might find some useful hints to make yours even better.

4

Le sais-tu? ???????

Pendant les trois années que les jeunes Français passent au lycée pour préparer au bac, le règlement est moins strict. Par exemple, pendant la pause déjeuner, les élèves ont souvent la possibilité de sortir du lycée. Ils peuvent aller au café ou en ville avec leurs amis. Ces moments de relaxation sont importants!

Le sais-tu? ???????

Si on veut trouver un emploi après le collège, une bonne possibilité est l'apprentissage. Pendant un mois typique, le jeune passe trois semaines en entreprise et une semaine en CFA (centre de formation d'apprentis). 80% des apprentis français trouvent rapidement un emploi à la fin de l'apprentissage.

1 Choose the correct form of the verb to fill the gap.

J'ai _____ aux questions du professeur.
a répondant   b répondre
c répondait   d répondu

2 Choose the correct translation for this English sentence.

We don't have any lessons on Saturdays.
a Nous n'allons pas en ville le samedi.
b Nous n'avons pas de cours le samedi.
c Nous n'avons pas de cours d'histoire le samedi.
d Nous ne faisons pas les courses le samedi.

3 Choose the correct answer to this question.

Voilà quatre aspects d'un collège britannique. Lequel n'existe pas dans les collèges français?
a les devoirs   b le règlement
c l'uniforme   d les matières

4 Choose the correct ending for this sentence.

J'aimerais travailler en plein air. Je voudrais devenir …
a secrétaire   b professeur de maths
c fermier   d médecin

5 Choose the correct ending for this sentence.

Un facteur …
a vend des livres.
b distribue les lettres.
c travaille dans une usine.
d travaille dans un café.

6 Choose the correct form of the verb to fill the gap.

À l'avenir, je _____ dans un bureau.
a travaille   b travaillé
c travaillerai   d travaillais

Frequently asked questions: Speaking

This general guidance is in the form of answers to 'frequently asked questions' (FAQs).

1 How many tasks do I have to complete for the Speaking part of my GCSE French?

There are two tasks, both of a similar kind. Your teacher will ask you the questions and listen to your answers. One of your tasks will be recorded as it may have to be submitted to the AQA Examination Board. Each task lasts between four and six minutes. The Speaking test counts for 30 per cent of the whole GCSE French – so, each of the two Speaking tasks is worth 15 per cent.

2 When do the tasks have to be done?

There is no specified time for the completion of the tasks. When your teacher thinks that you have been taught the language you need and feels that you are ready, you will be given the task to prepare. It could be a task designed by the AQA Examination Board or a task designed by French teachers in your school. Your teacher will decide how long you are allowed to prepare for the task (it cannot be more than six hours).

3 Who will mark my work?

Your teacher will mark your work. A Moderator (i.e. an examiner) will sample the work of your school and check that it has been marked correctly. A Team Leader will check the work of the Moderator. The Principal Moderator will check the work of the Team Leader. The Chief Examiner will check the work of the Principal Moderator. This complicated but secure system ensures that candidates are given the correct mark.

4 What am I allowed to write on my plan?

You are allowed to write a maximum of 40 words on your plan. Those words can be in French or English. Choose them carefully so that your plan works well as an *aide-mémoire*. Remember that you are not allowed to use conjugated verbs (i.e. verbs with an ending other than the infinitive or the past participle) on your plan. Codes, letters or initialled words, e.g. *j … s … a …* as being *je suis allé*, are not allowed. There is no limit to the number of visuals you can use, and you can mix visuals and words if you wish.

5 What help is allowed from the moment I am given the task to prepare?

Your teacher is allowed to discuss the task in English with you, including the kind of language you may need and how to use your preparatory work. You can have access to a dictionary, your French books and Internet resources. This is the stage when you will prepare your plan using the Task Planning Form. You will then give this to your teacher who will give you feedback on how you have met the requirements of the task. When you actually perform the task, you will only have access to your plan and your teacher's comments (i.e. the Task Planning Form).

6 How can I prepare for the unpredictable element (the exclamation mark)?

Ask yourself: What question would logically follow the questions I have already answered? Practise guessing what the unpredictable bullet point might be about. You are likely to come up with two or three possibilities. Prepare answers to cover those possibilities. Practise your possible responses. When you are asked the question, focus on the meaning of the question itself to make sure you understand it and then give it your full answer.

7 How best can I practise for the test?

Treat each bullet point as a mini task. Practise your answer to one bullet point at a time. Say your answer aloud for what is illustrated by one word on your plan. Repeat the process for each word on your plan. Next, try to account for two words, then for three words, etc. Time your answer for one whole bullet point. Repeat the process for each bullet point. Practise saying things aloud. Record yourself if possible.

8 Does it matter that my verbs are wrong as long as I can get myself understood?

Communication can break down because of poor grammatical accuracy. If that happens, you will lose marks in Communication and also in Accuracy. If you give the correct message but grammatical accuracy is poor, you will only lose marks in Accuracy. Communication is of primary importance, of course, but the quality of that communication matters too and is enhanced by grammatical accuracy.

Frequently asked questions: Speaking

9 How do I make sure I get the best possible marks for my answers?

You will score well in the Speaking test if:

- you say a lot that is relevant to the question.
- you have a good range of vocabulary.
- you can include complex structures.
- you can refer to present, past and future events.
- your French accent is good.
- you can speak fluently.
- you can show initiative.
- you can speak with grammatical accuracy.

10 How will my mark be affected if my French accent is not very good?

You will receive a mark for Pronunciation. However, as long as your spoken French is understandable, your Communication mark will not suffer.

11 What will I gain by giving long answers?

Consider the task as an opportunity for you to show off what you can do in French. Offer long answers whenever possible, develop the points you are trying to make, give your opinion and justify that opinion as appropriate etc. As a general rule, the more French you speak, the more credit you will be given (provided that what you say is relevant and understandable).

12 What does speaking with fluency mean?

Fluency is your ability to speak without hesitation. Try and speak with fluency but not too fast. If you are likely to be nervous when performing the task, practise it and practise it again. Time your whole response. Make a point of slowing down if you feel that you are speaking too fast. Practise with your plan in front of you so that you know what you are going to say next and therefore do not hesitate when delivering your contribution to the dialogue.

13 What does showing initiative mean?

Showing initiative does not mean that you suddenly ask your teacher 'What about you, where did you go on holiday?' (although you could do that!). You are generally expected to answer questions. For instance, if you are asked the question *Tu aimes le foot?*, you should first answer it directly and then try to develop your answer, e.g. *Oui, j'aime le foot. J'y joue trois fois par semaine avec mes copains.*

Showing initiative means that you take the conversation elsewhere in a way that is connected to your answer and still relevant to the original question, e.g. *J'aime aussi jouer au basket. En fait, c'est mon sport préféré*. You were not asked about basketball, but you decided to add it to your response. It is relevant, linked to what you were asked and follows your developed answer quite naturally. That is showing initiative. Use it to extend your answers and therefore show off extra knowledge of French.

14 Why is it important to refer to present, past and future events?

If you are aiming at a grade C, you will need to use a variety of structures, and you will need to include different time frames and make reference to past and future events in your spoken language. To achieve grade A, you will be expected to use a variety of verb tenses.

15 How many bullet points are there in each task?

There are typically between five and eight bullet points. One of the bullet points will be the unpredictable element and will appear on your task as an exclamation mark. All bullet points will be written in English.

16 Will I be asked questions which are not written in the task?

That is possible. Although you will have prepared the task thoroughly and will have a lot to say, your teacher may want you to expand or give further details on particular points you have made. You must listen to your teacher's questions attentively, as you will have to understand his/her questions in the first place.

Frequently asked questions: Writing

This general guidance is in the form of answers to 'frequently asked questions' (FAQs).

1 How many Writing tasks do I have to complete and what proportion of my French GCSE is the Writing test?

You have to complete two Writing tasks. The tasks can be those provided by the AQA Examination Board, although your French teachers have the option of devising their own tasks if they so wish. As in the Speaking test, the two tasks count for 30 per cent of your grade (15 per cent for each Writing task).

2 How much time do I have to complete the final version of a task?

You will be given 60 minutes to complete the final version of a task. It will be done under the direct supervision of your teacher. You will not be allowed to interact with others.

3 What resources will I be able to use on the day?

You can have access to a dictionary. You will also have the task itself, your plan and your teacher's feedback on your plan. These will be on the AQA Task Planning Form. That is all. You cannot use your exercise book, textbook or any drafts you may have written to help you practise.

4 What am I allowed to write on my plan?

Much the same as you are allowed in your plan for Speaking – a maximum of 40 words and no conjugated verbs or codes. You also have the option of using visuals instead of or as well as words in your Task Planning Form. Your teacher will comment on your plan, using the AQA Task Planning Form. Make sure you take that information on board before you write the final version.

5 How many words am I expected to write for each task?

Students aiming at grades G–D should produce 200–350 words across the two tasks (i.e. 100–175 words per task).

Students aiming at grades C–A* should produce 400–600 words across the two tasks (i.e. 200–300 words per task).

6 Can I write a draft?

You may produce a draft, but this is for your use only. Your teacher cannot comment on it and you cannot have access to any draft when you write the final version.

7 What do I have to do to gain the best possible mark?

You will score well if:

- you communicate a lot of relevant information clearly.
- you can explain ideas and points of view.
- you have a good range of vocabulary.
- you can include complex structures.
- you can write long sentences.
- you can refer to past, present and future events.
- you can write with grammatical accuracy.
- you organise your ideas well.

You will have noticed that there are similarities between the ways Writing and Speaking are assessed. As most of the points above are discussed in the FAQs for Speaking, you are advised to read the answers again, before you embark on your first task.

8 When will I do the tasks?

When your teacher has taught you the necessary language for you to complete a task, you will be given the task to prepare. You may be asked to do a plan using the Task Planning Form. You will get some feedback on your plan from your teacher at that point on how you have met the requirements of the task. The final version will be done after that, under the direct supervision of your teacher.

9 Who will mark my work?

AQA Examiners will mark your work. A Team Leader will check the work of the Examiner. The Principal Examiner will check the work of the Team Leader. The Chief Examiner will check the work of the Principal Examiner. This is a complicated but secure system to ensure that candidates are given the correct mark for their work.

On fait du camping

You are camping in France. You meet Jessica who asks you details about:

1 yourself
2 your holidays
3 your family
4 your last holiday
5 your free time
6 your friends
7 !

! Remember you will have to respond to something that you have not yet prepared.

1 Yourself
- say your name and age
- say where you live in Britain
- say whether you like living in Britain
- say how long you have been learning French for

2 Your holidays
- say what you think of your holiday so far
- say whether you like the campsite
- say where you normally go on holiday.
- say where you would like to go next year

3 Your family
- say how many people there are in your family
- say whether you like your brothers and sisters
- say what your parents are like
- say who you get on well with in your family

4 Your last holiday
- say where you went
- say who you went with
- say what you did
- say whether you enjoyed your holiday

5 Your free time
- say how much free time you have
- say what you do with your free time at home
- say what you do when you go out
- say what you did last weekend

6 Your friends
- say who your friends are
- say who your best friend is
- say how well you get on
- say what you do together

7 ! At this point, you may be asked
- if you would like to be friends with Jessica for the rest of the holiday
- whether you prefer going on holiday in France or in Britain
- to talk about your school
- to talk about your home town

Now, compare your first draft with the online sample version – you might find some useful hints to make yours even better.

À propos de moi!

You have been asked to send a letter of introduction to Ahmed, a pupil in a French school. You should include information about:

1 yourself
2 your house
3 your local town
4 your school
5 your daily routine
6 what you do to stay healthy
7 your work experience

1 Yourself
- say your name, your age and the name of the school you go to
- give a physical description of yourself
- say something about your character
- say what you like doing

2 Your house
- say whether you live in a house or a flat
- say whether you like your house / flat
- say whether you share a room
- say whether there is a garage and / or a garden

3 Your local town
- say where your local town is situated
- say what sort of town it is
- say what there is for young people to do
- say how clean your town is

4 Your school
- say how big your school is
- say how many subjects you study and which one is your favourite
- say whether you like your school
- say how much homework you get

5 Your daily routine
- say what you do before breakfast
- say what you have for breakfast
- say when you do your homework
- say whether you watch television in the evening

6 What you do to stay healthy
- say whether you like sports
- say whether you walk to and from school
- say what you eat that is healthy
- say what else you do to keep healthy

7 Your work experience
- say where you went for work experience
- say when it was
- say what you did
- say what you thought of it

Now, compare your first draft with the online sample version – you might find some useful hints to make yours even better.

G Grammaire

Contents

■ Glossary of terms

Adjectives *les adjectifs*

Words that describe somebody or something.

petit	small
timide	shy

Adverbs *les adverbes*

Words that complement verbs, adjectives or other adverbs.

très	very
lentement	slowly

Articles *les articles*

Short words used with nouns.

un / une	a, an
le / la / les	the
des	some, any

The infinitive *l'infinitif*

The verb form given in the dictionary.

aller	to go
avoir	to have

Nouns *les noms*

Words that identify a person, a place or a thing.

mère	mother
maison	house

Prepositions *les prépositions*

Words used in front of nouns to give information about when, how, where etc.

à	at
avec	with
de	of, from
en	in

Pronouns *les pronoms*

Short words used to replace nouns.

je	I
tu	you
elle	she
il	he

Verbs *les verbes*

Words used to express an action or a state.

je **parle**	I *speak*
il **est**	he *is*

A Nouns

Masculine and feminine nouns

All French nouns are either masculine or feminine.

In the singular, masculine nouns are introduced with *le, l'* or *un*.

le père	**the** father
*l'*hôtel	**the** hotel
un livre	**a** book

Feminine nouns are introduced with *la, l'* or *une*.

la mère	**the** mother
*l'*eau	**the** water
une table	**a** table

Some nouns have a masculine and a feminine form.

le prof	**the** (male) teacher
la prof	**the** (female) teacher

Some other nouns have two different forms.

un copain	a male friend
une copine	a female friend
un coiffeur	a male hairdresser
une coiffeuse	a female hairdresser
un acteur	an actor
une actrice	an actress

Singular and plural forms

As in English, French nouns can either be singular (one) or plural (more than one).

Most plural nouns end in -*s*. Unlike English, the added -*s* is usually not pronounced.

un chat > deux chats   one cat > two cats

As in English, there are some exceptions.

- Most nouns ending in -*al* change to -*aux*.
  un animal > des animaux   animals
- Many nouns ending in -*au* and -*eu* add an -*x*.
  un gâteau > des gâteaux   cakes
  un jeu > des jeux   games
- Words already ending in -*s*, -*x* or -*z* do not change.
  le bras > les bras   arms
  le nez > les nez   noses
- A few nouns change completely.
  un œil > des yeux   eyes

B Articles

le, la, les (the)

The word for 'the' depends on whether the noun it goes with is masculine, feminine, singular or plural.

masculine singular	feminine singular	masculine and feminine plural
le	*la*	*les*
le grand-père	*la* grand-mère	*les* grands-parents
the grandfather	**the** grandmother	**the** grandparents

When a singular noun starts with a vowel or a silent h, *le* and *la* are shortened to *l'*.

*l'*ami	the friend
*l'*histoire	the story

Le, la and *les* are often used when we don't say 'the' in English.

*J'adore **les** frites.*	I love chips.
*Elle déteste **les** maths.*	She hates maths.
*Il rentre à **la** maison.*	He goes home.

un, une, des (a, some)

Like the words for 'the' (*le / la / les*), the words for 'a' or 'an' and 'some' depend on whether the noun they go with is masculine or feminine, singular or plural.

masculine singular	feminine singular	masculine and feminine plural
un	*une*	*des*
un vélo	*une* moto	*des* voitures
a bike	**a** motorbike	(**some**) cars

When talking about jobs, *un* and *une* are not used in French where 'a' or 'an' is used in English.

Il est professeur.	He is **a** teacher.

de

- *De* replaces *un, une* or *des* after *pas*.
  *J'ai un frère. > Je n'ai **pas de** frère.*
  I don't have **any** brothers.

  Il y a une piscine. > Il n'y a pas de piscine.
  There is **no** swimming pool.

  *J'ai des sœurs. > Je n'ai **pas de** sœur.*
  I don't have **any** sisters.
- *De* changes to *d'* in front of a vowel or a silent h.
  *Je n'ai pas **d'**animaux.*   I don't have **any** pets.

du, de la, de l', des (some / any)

■ *Du, de la, de l', des* are used to mean 'some' or 'any'.

masculine	feminine	words beginning with a vowel or silent h	plural
de + le = du	de + la = de la	de + l' = de l'	de + les = des
du *café*	**de la** *limonade*	**de l'***aspirine*	**des** *chocolats*
(**some**) coffee	(**some**) lemonade	(**some**) aspirin	(**some**) chocolates

*Je voudrais **du** poulet.*	I'd like **some** chicken.
*Elle prend **de la** limonade.*	She's having (**some**) lemonade.
*Elle boit **de l'**eau.*	She's drinking (**some**) water.
*Avez-vous **des** croissants?*	Do you have **any** croissants?

■ *Du, de la, de l', des* are also used to talk about activities someone is doing or musical instruments someone is playing.

*Je fais **du** judo.*	I do judo.
*Elle joue **de la** guitare.*	She is playing the guitar.
*Il fait **de l'**équitation.*	He goes horseriding.
*Ils font **des** excursions.*	They go on trips.

C Adjectives

Feminine, masculine, singular and plural adjectives

In French, adjectives have different endings depending on whether they describe masculine, feminine, singular or plural nouns.

■ The masculine form has no extra ending.
Mon frère est petit. My brother is small.

■ Add *-e* if the noun is feminine singular.
Ma sœur est petite. My sister is small.

■ Add *-s* if the noun is masculine plural.
Mes frères sont petits. My brothers are small.

■ Add *-es* if the noun is feminine plural.
Mes sœurs sont petites. My sisters are small.

There are exceptions.

■ Adjectives that already end in *-e* don't add a second *-e* in the feminine.
un vélo rouge a red bike
une moto rouge a red motorbike

■ Adjectives that end in *-é* add a second *-e* in the feminine.
mon film préféré my favourite film
ma chanson préférée my favourite song

■ Some adjectives double the final consonant before the *-e*.
Il est italien. He is Italian.
Elle est italienne. She is Italian.

■ Adjectives that end in *-eux* or *-eur* change to *-euse* in the feminine.
un garçon paresseux a lazy boy
une fille paresseuse a lazy girl
un garçon travailleur a hardworking boy
une fille travailleuse a hardworking girl

■ Adjectives that end in *-eau* change to *-elle*.
un beau vélo a beautiful bike
une belle voiture a beautiful car

■ Adjectives that end in *-if* change to *-ive* in the feminine.
un copain sportif a sporty (boy)friend
une copine sportive a sporty (girl)friend

■ The feminine form of *blanc* is *blanche*.
Elle porte une robe blanche.
She is wearing a white dress.

■ The feminine form of *frais* is *fraîche*.
Je voudrais une boisson fraîche.
I would like a cool drink.

■ The feminine form of *gentil* is *gentille*.
Ma grand-mère est gentille. My grandmother is kind.

■ The feminine form of *sympa* is *sympa*.
Ma mère est sympa. My mother is nice.

■ Adjectives that end in *-al* change to *-aux* in the masculine plural.
J'ai des poissons tropicaux. I have got some tropical fish.

■ A few adjectives, like *marron* and *super*, do not change at all.
Elle porte des bottes marron. She's wearing brown boots.

- When an adjective describes a group that includes both masculine and feminine nouns, use the masculine plural form of the adjective.

*Mes parents sont grand**s**.*   My parents are tall.

The position of adjectives

Most adjectives follow the noun they describe.

*un prof **sympa***	a nice teacher
*une copine **intelligente***	an intelligent friend
*des idées **intéressantes***	interesting ideas

However, a few adjectives, such as *petit, grand, bon, mauvais, joli, beau, jeune, vieux* and *nouveau,* usually come in front of the noun, as in English.

*un **petit** garçon*	a small boy
*une **jolie** ville*	a pretty town

Adjectives of nationality

Adjectives of nationality do not begin with a capital letter.

*Nicolas est **français**.*	Nicolas is French.
*Laura est **galloise**.*	Laura is Welsh.

Like other adjectives, feminine adjectives of nationality take an *-e* at the end, unless there is one there already.

*Sophie est **française**.*	Sophie is French.
*Juliette est **suisse**.*	Juliette is Swiss.

Three irregular adjectives

Three common adjectives come before the noun: *vieux, nouveau, beau.*

*un **vieux** musée*	an old museum
*un **nouveau** centre commercial*	a new shopping centre
*un **beau** cheval*	a beautiful horse

Their feminine forms are *vieille, nouvelle* and *belle.*

*une **nouvelle** piscine*	a new swimming pool

They also have a special form which is used before a vowel or a silent h.

*un **vieil** homme*	an old man
*un **nouvel** aéroport*	a new airport
*un **bel** endroit*	a beautiful place

Comparatives and superlatives

To make comparisons, use:

- *plus … que* = more… than / […]er than.

*La Loire est **plus** longue **que** la Tamise.*
The Loire is **longer than** the Thames.

- *moins … que* = less … than

*Les vélos sont **moins** rapides **que** les trains.*
Bikes are **less** fast **than** trains.

- *aussi … que* = as … as

*Les tomates sont **aussi** chères **que** les pêches.*
Tomatoes are **as** dear **as** peaches.

To say 'the most', 'the […]est', use *le / la / les plus*:

*C'est la chambre **la plus** chère.*
It is **the most** expensive room.

*C'est **le plus petit** vélo.*
It is **the smallest** bike.

To say 'the least', use *le / la / les moins*:

*C'est le film **le moins** intéressant.*
It is **the least** interesting film.

The French for 'better' is *meilleur* or *mieux* and for 'worse' is *pire*.

*Internet est **mieux que** la télé.*
The Internet is **better than** television.

*Le football est **pire que** le rugby.*
Football is **worse than** rugby.

ce, cet, cette, ces (this, that, these, those)

The French for 'this' / 'that' is *ce, cet* or *cette*. The French for 'these' / 'those' is *ces*.

masculine	feminine	masculine and feminine plural
ce	*cette*	*ces*
***ce** magasin*	***cette** chemise*	***ces** baskets*
this / that shop	**this / that** shirt	**these / those** trainers

Note that the masculine form changes to *cet* when the noun that follows begins with a vowel or a silent h.

***cet** ami*	**this / that** friend
***cet** hôtel*	**this / that** hotel

chaque (each); quelques (a few)

The French for 'each' is *chaque*.

*Il y a une télévision dans **chaque** chambre.*
There is a television in **each** room.

The French for 'a few' is *quelques*.

*J'ai acheté **quelques** gâteaux.*
I bought **a few** cakes.

mon / ma / mes (my); *ton / ta / tes* (your); *son / sa / ses* (his / her / its)

■ There are three different ways of saying 'my' in French, as it depends on whether the noun it goes with is masculine or feminine, singular or plural. The words for 'your', 'his', 'her' and 'its' also change depending on whether the noun is masculine or feminine, singular or plural.

masculine singular	feminine singular	masculine and feminine plural
mon, ton, son	*ma, ta, sa*	*mes, tes, ses*

mon père	**my** father
ton père	**your** father (to someone you normally say *tu* to)
son pied	**his / her / its** foot
ma mère	**my** mother
ta mère	**your** mother
sa porte	**his / her / its** door
mes parents	**my** parents
tes parents	**your** parents
ses fenêtres	**his / her / its** windows

French doesn't have different words for 'his', 'her' and 'its'. What counts is whether the accompanying noun is masculine, feminine, singular or plural.

notre / nos (our); *votre / vos* (your); *leur / leurs* (their)

masculine and feminine singular	masculine and feminine plural
notre, votre, leur	*nos, vos, leurs*

notre père	**our** father
notre mère	**our** mother
votre père	**your** father
votre mère	**your** mother
leur frère	**their** brother
leur sœur	**their** sister
nos parents	**our** parents
vos copains	**your** friends
leurs profs	**their** teachers

D Adverbs

Most French adverbs end in *-ment* and their English equivalents end in '-ly'.

franche**ment**	frank**ly**
générale**ment**	general**ly**
lente**ment**	slow**ly**
normale**ment**	normal**ly**

Other common adverbs are:

■ *très* (very)

*Elle est **très** gentille.* She is **very** nice.

■ *assez* (fairly, quite)

*Je suis **assez** bonne en maths.*
I am **quite** good at maths.

■ *beaucoup* (a lot)

*Il mange **beaucoup**.* He eats **a lot**.

■ *trop* (too)

*C'est **trop** cher.* It is **too** expensive.

■ *bien* (well)

*Elle joue **bien**.* She plays **well**.

■ *mal* (badly)

*Il mange **mal**.* He eats **badly**.

■ *vite* (quickly)

*Tu parles **vite**.* You speak **quickly**.

As with adjectives, you can sometimes make comparisons by using *plus / moins / aussi … que.*

*Tu parles **plus** lentement **que** moi.*
You speak **more** slowly **than** me.

*Je mange **moins** vite que ma sœur.*
I eat **less** quickly **than** my sister.

*Elle joue **aussi** bien que Paul.*
She plays **as** well **as** Paul.

You can also use superlatives.

*Marc travaille **le plus** lentement.* — Marc works **the slowest**.

*Carole travaille **le plus** vite.* — Carole works **the fastest**.

Adverbs of time

hier	yesterday
aujourd'hui	today
demain	tomorrow

Adverbs of place

ici	here
là-bas	(over) there

Adverbs of frequency

quelquefois	sometimes
souvent	often
toujours	always

Adverbs of sequencing

d'abord	firstly
après	afterwards
ensuite	next
enfin	finally
puis	then

Adverbs of quantity

très	very
assez	enough
trop	too (much)
beaucoup	a lot
un peu	a little
peu	little

Adverbs of quantity can be used with *de* + noun.

*On a **trop de** devoirs.*	We have **too much** homework.
*Je n'ai pas **assez d'**argent.*	I don't have **enough** money.

E Pronouns

Subject pronouns: *je, tu, il, elle, on, nous, vous, ils, elles*

- ■ *je* (I)

Je parle français.	I speak French.

- ■ *tu* (you)

Tu as quel âge?	How old are **you**?

- ■ *il* (he / it)

Il s'appelle Théo.	**He** is called Théo.

- ■ *elle* (she / it)

Elle s'appelle Aïcha.	**She** is called Aïcha.

- ■ *on* (we / you / they)

On se retrouve où?	Where shall **we** meet?

- ■ *nous* (we)

Nous habitons en ville.	**We** live in town.

- ■ *vous* (you)

Vous avez une chambre?	Do **you** have a room?

- ■ *ils* (they) (masculine)

  J'ai deux chiens, (m) ***ils** s'appellent Do et Mi.*
  I have two dogs, **they**'re called Do and Mi.

- ■ *elles* (they) (feminine)

  J'adore mes sœurs, (f) ***elles** sont marrantes.*
  I love my sisters, **they** are fun.

Je is shortened to *j'* if the word that follows begins with a silent h or a vowel.

J'aime les pommes.	I like apples.
J'habite en Écosse.	I live in Scotland.

There are two French words for 'you': *tu* and *vous*.

- ■ Use *tu* when talking to someone (one person) of your own age or someone in the family.

- ■ Use *vous* when talking to an adult not in your family (e.g. your teacher). The following phrases are useful to remember:

*Avez-**vous** … ?*	Have **you** got… ?
*Voulez-**vous** … ?*	Do **you** want… ?
*Désirez-**vous** … ?*	Would **you** like… ?

- ■ Also use *vous* when talking to more than one person – whatever their age, and whether you know them well or not.

Il and *elle* can both also mean 'it'.

*L'hôtel est bien? – Oui, **il** est très confortable.*
Is the hotel good? – Yes, **it** is very comfortable.

*Je déteste ma chambre: **elle** est trop petite.*
I hate my bedroom: **it**'s too small.

On can mean 'we', 'you' or 'they'.

On s'entend bien.
We get on well.

Comment dit-on "pencil" en français?
How do **you** say 'pencil' in French?

On parle français au Canada.
They speak French in Canada.

There are two French words for 'they': *ils* and *elles*.

- ■ *ils* = they (all male or mixed group of males and females)

  J'ai un frère et une sœur: ils s'appellent Nicolas et Aurélie.
  I have a brother and a sister: **they** are called Nicolas and Aurélie.

- ■ *elles* = they (all female)

  *J'ai deux copines espagnoles; **elles** habitent à Madrid.*
  I have two Spanish (girl)friends: **they** live in Madrid.

Direct object pronouns: *me, te, le, la, nous, vous, les*

You need to be able to recognise these pronouns:

singular		plural	
me	me	*nous*	us
te	you	*vous*	you
le / l'	him / it (masculine)	*les*	them
la / l'	her / it (feminine)		

Direct object pronouns come in front of the verb.

*Je **le** prends.*   I take **it**.

*Je peux **vous** aider?*   Can I help **you**?

Le and *la* are shortened to *l'* in front of a vowel or a silent h.

*Mon petit frère a deux ans. Je **l'**adore!*
My little brother is two. I love **him**!

Indirect object pronouns: *me, te, lui, nous, vous, leur*

You need to be able to recognise these pronouns:

singular		plural	
me	(to) me	*nous*	(to) us
te	(to) you	*vous*	(to) you
lui	(to) him / her / it	*leur*	(to) them

*Je donne du café à mon père. > Je **lui** donne du café.*
I give **him** some coffee.

Je parle à ma mère. >   *Je **lui** parle.*
I speak to **her**.

*J'écris à mes grands-parents. > Je **leur** écris.*
I write to **them**.

You will sometimes see two pronouns in the same sentence.

*Je **te les** donne.*   I give **them** to **you**.

*Il **nous en** a parlé.*   He has talked to **us** about **it**.

When you use two object pronouns together, they must be in the right order. Indirect object pronouns *me* and *te*, *nous* and *vous* come before direct object pronouns *le, la, les*.

J'adore ce CD.   I love this CD.

*Martine **me l'**a donné.*   Martine gave **it** to **me**.

Indirect object pronouns: *en* and *y*

The French way to say 'of it' or 'of them' is *en*. Use it to avoid repeating a noun introduced with *du / de la / de l' / des*.

Tu as des chiens?   *Oui, j'**en** ai trois.*
Have you got dogs?   Yes, I have got three (**of them**).

Tu manges de la viande?   *Oui, j'**en** mange.*
Do you eat meat?   Yes, I do (**eat it**).

Another useful pronoun is *y*, which usually means 'there'. You can use *y* to avoid repeating the name of a place.

Tu vas à Glasgow?   Are you going to Glasgow?
*Oui, j'**y** vais demain.*   Yes, I'm going **there** tomorrow.

Disjunctive pronouns: *moi, toi, lui, elle, nous, vous, eux, elles*

Use *moi, toi, lui, elle, nous, vous, eux, elles* after a preposition.

*avec **moi***	with **me**	*avec **nous***	with **us**
*pour **toi***	for **you**	*pour **vous***	for **you**
*chez **lui***	at **his** house	*chez **eux***	at **their** house
*à côté d'**elle***	next to **her**	*à côté d'**elles***	next to **them**

You can also use these pronouns for emphasis.

***Moi**, j'adore les fraises.*   **I** love strawberries.

***Toi**, tu as quel âge?*   How old are **you**?

Indefinite pronouns (*quelqu'un, tout le monde, personne*)

The French for 'nobody' is *personne* and the French for 'everybody' is *tout le monde*. The French for 'somebody' is *quelqu'un*. If these pronouns come at the beginning of a sentence, they are followed by a verb in the singular. Note that *ne* must also be used with *personne*.

***Tout le monde** économise l'énergie.*   **Everyone** saves energy.

***Personne ne** jette ses déchets ici.*   **Nobody** throws their rubbish here.

*Il **n'y a personne** au centre de recyclage.*   There is **nobody** at the recycling centre

***Quelqu'un** est à la porte.*   **Somebody** is at the door.

*Il y a **quelqu'un** à la maison.*   There is **somebody** at home.

Demonstrative pronouns: *ce, cela, ça* (it / this / that)

Ce is usually followed by a form of *être*. It is shortened to *c'* before a vowel.

C'est vrai.	**It**'s true.
C'est facile.	**It**'s easy.

Cela is often shortened to *ça*.

Ça va?	Are **you** okay?
Tu aimes ça?	Do you like **it**?

F Verbs

French verbs have different endings depending on who is doing the action and whether the action takes place in the past, the present or the future. Turn to the verb tables on page 174 for further details.

When using a name or a noun instead of a pronoun, use the same form of the verb as for *ils / elles*.

*Martin **parle** espagnol.*   Martin **speaks** Spanish.

When using two names or a plural noun, use the same form of the verb as for *ils / elles*.

*Thomas et Lola **jouent** au basket.*
Thomas and Lola **are playing** basketball.

*Mes frères **écoutent** de la musique.*
My brothers **are listening** to music.

The infinitive

The infinitive is the form of the verb you find in a dictionary, e.g. *jouer, finir, être*. The infinitive never changes.

When two verbs follow each other, the second one is always in the infinitive. That's what happens in the following sentences:

*J'aime **jouer** de la guitare.*	I like **playing** the guitar.
*Je préfère **écouter** des CD.*	I prefer **listening** to CDs.
*Je dois **faire** mes devoirs.*	I must **do** my homework.
*Tu veux **aller** au cinéma?*	Do you want **to go** to the cinema?
*On peut **faire** du shopping.*	You can **go** shopping.
*Je voudrais **aller** en Italie.*	I'd like **to go** to Italy.
*Je déteste **laver** la voiture.*	I hate **washing** the car.

Sometimes you will see a preposition between the first verb and the infinitive.

*J'ai l'intention **de** voyager en Italie.*
I intend to travel around Italy.

*Il apprend **à** nager.*
He is learning to swim.

Reflexive verbs

Reflexive verbs have an extra pronoun in front of them.

*je **me** réveille*	**I** wake up
*tu **te** lèves*	**you** get up
*il / elle **s'**appelle*	**he / she** is called
*on **s'**amuse bien*	**we** have a good time
*nous **nous** lavons*	**we** have a wash
*vous **vous** couchez*	**you** go to bed
*ils / elles **s'**entendent bien*	**they** get on well

Note that *me / te / se* are shortened to *m' / t' / s'* in front of a vowel or a silent h.

G Verb tenses

The present

Use the present tense to describe:

■ something that is taking place now

*J'**écoute** un CD.*   I **am listening** to a CD.

■ something that happens regularly

*J'**ai** les maths le lundi.*   I **have** maths on Mondays.

Turn to the verb tables on page 174 for details of verb endings in the present tense.

There are three groups of regular verbs: *-er, -ir, -re* verbs.

To form their present tense, take the ending from the infinitive and add these endings to the stem.

	-er verbs e.g. *parler*	*-ir* verbs e.g. *finir*	*-re* verbs e.g. *vendre*
je	*parl**e***	*fin**is***	*vend**s***
tu	*parl**es***	*fin**is***	*vend**s***
il / elle / on	*parl**e***	*fin**it***	*vend*
nous	*parl**ons***	*fin**issons***	*vend**ons***
vous	*parl**ez***	*fin**issez***	*vend**ez***
ils / elles	*parl**ent***	*fin**issent***	*vend**ent***

The perfect

Use the perfect tense to talk about what somebody did or has done.

*J'**ai parlé** au professeur.*   I **spoke** to the teacher.

To make the perfect tense of most verbs, use *avoir* + past participle.

*Il **a mangé** un sandwich.*   He **ate** a sandwich.

The following verbs use *être,* instead of *avoir.*

aller	to go
arriver	to arrive
descendre	to go down
entrer	to enter, to go in
monter	to go up
partir	to leave
rentrer	to come back, to return
rester	to stay
sortir	to go out
tomber	to fall
venir	to come

*Je **suis allé** au cinéma.*   I **went** to the cinema.

Reflexive verbs all use *être,* instead of *avoir.*

*Il **s'est levé** à 11 heures.*   He **got up** at 11 o'clock.

When using *être:*

- add *-e* to the past participle, if the subject is female
  *Elle est parti**e** en Écosse.*   She **went** off to Scotland.

- add *-s* to the past participle, if the subject is plural
  *Ils sont arrivé**s** en retard.*   They **arrived** late.
  *Elles sont parti**es**.*   They (have) **left**.

When making a negative statement, *ne* comes before *avoir / être* and *pas* comes after.

*Je **n'**ai **pas** mangé.*   I **haven't** eaten.

*Elle **n'**est **pas** sortie.*   She **didn't** go out.

Past participles

The past participle of *-er* verbs ends in *-é.*

*all**er** – all**é***		gone
*donn**er** – donn**é***		given
*parl**er** – parl**é***		spoken

The past participle of many *-ir* verbs ends in *-i.*

*chois**ir** – chois**i***		chosen
*fin**ir** – fin**i***		finished

The past participle of many *-re* verbs ends in *-u.*

*atten**dre** – atten**du***		waited
*ven**dre** – ven**du***		sold

The past participle of many common verbs is irregular.

*avoir – **eu***	had		*lire – **lu***	read
*boire – **bu***	drunk		*mettre – **mis***	put
*devoir – **dû***	had to		*pouvoir – **pu***	able to
*dire – **dit***	said		*prendre – **pris***	taken
*écrire – **écrit***	written		*venir – **venu***	come
*être – **été***	been		*voir – **vu***	seen
*faire – **fait***	done, made		*vouloir – **voulu***	wanted

See the verb tables on page 174.

The imperfect

The imperfect tense is used to describe a place, an activity or an event that took place in the past, and to give your opinion. You are expected to be able to use the verbs *avoir, être, faire* in the imperfect tense.

*Il y **avait** une grande piscine.*	There **was** a big pool.
*C'**était** délicieux.*	It **was** delicious.
*Il **faisait** du soleil.*	It **was** sunny.

You will also need to recognise the imperfect tense when it is used with other verbs.

*Il **regardait** un film quand je suis arrivé.*
He **was watching** a film, when I arrived.

You can also use the imperfect after *si* to make a suggestion.

*Si on **allait** au cinéma?*   **Shall we go** to the cinema?

For the full pattern, see the verb tables on page 174.

The immediate future

Use *aller* followed by a verb in the infinitive to say what you're going to do or what's going to happen.

*Je **vais continuer** mes études.*	I'm **going to go on** studying.
*Il **va neiger**.*	It's **going to snow**.
*On **va décider** demain.*	We are **going to decide** tomorrow.
*Nous **allons jouer** au tennis.*	We are **going to play** tennis.

The simple future

You will need to recognise this form of the future tense. The future tense is often used for predictions, such as weather forecasts, or for long-term plans.

> *Il **fera** beau / froid / chaud etc.*
> It **will be** fine / cold / hot etc.

> *Le temps **sera** pluvieux / nuageux etc.*
> The weather **will be** rainy / cloudy etc.

> *Il **neigera**.*   It **will snow**.

> *Je **resterai** en France.*   I **will stay** in France.

> *Je **voyagerai** en Afrique.*   I **will travel** around Africa.

> *Qu'est-ce que **vous ferez** après l'école?*
> What **will you do** after school?

> ***Vous travaillerez** dans l'informatique?*
> **Will you work** in computing?

The pluperfect

You need to recognise this form of the past tense. It is used to describe what someone had done or had been doing. It uses the imperfect of *avoir* or *être* plus the past participle.

> *J'**avais parlé**.*   I **had spoken**.

> *Il **était parti**.*   He **had left**.

The passive

You need to recognise this form of the verb. It is used to say what is done to someone or something. It is formed from *être* and a past participle.

> *Je **suis invité(e)**.*   I **am invited**.

> *Les glaces **sont vendues**.*   Ice creams **are sold**.

This form of the passive is often avoided by using *on*.

> ***On parle français** au Québec.*   **French is spoken** in Quebec.

En + present participle

The English present participle ends in '-ing' and the French present participle ends in -*ant*. You will need to recognise this form of the verb. It is often used with *en* to mean 'while' or 'by' doing something.

> *Il fait ses devoirs **en** écoutant de la musique.*
> He does his homework while **listening** to music.

> ***En** travaillant le soir, je gagne de l'argent.*
> By **working** in the evening, I earn money.

The imperative

Use the imperative when giving orders or instructions.

Use the *tu* form with people your own age or people you know very well.

> ***Continue** tout droit.*   **Go** straight on.

> ***Prends** la première rue.*   **Take** the first street.

> ***Tourne** à gauche.*   **Turn** left.

Use the *vous* form to people you don't know very well or to more than one person.

> ***Continuez** tout droit.*   **Go** straight on.

> ***Prenez** la première rue.*   **Take** the first street.

> ***Tournez** à gauche.*   **Turn** left.

H Negative sentences

To make a sentence negative, you normally put *ne* before the verb and *pas* after it.

> *Je parle espagnol.* > *Je **ne** parle **pas** espagnol.*
> I **don't** speak Spanish.

Shorten *ne* to *n'* if the word that follows begins with h or a vowel.

> *C'est difficile.* > *Ce **n'est pas** difficile.*
> It's **not** difficult.

In negative sentences, use *de* instead of *un, une* or *des*.

> *Il y a un cinéma.* > *Il n'y a pas **de** cinéma.*
> There is **no** cinema.

> *J'achète une pizza.* > *Je n'achète pas **de** pizza.*
> I am not buying **a** pizza.

> *J'ai des frères.* > *Je n'ai pas **de** frère.*
> I don't have **any** brothers.

Other common negative phrases:

- ◼ *ne … plus* (no more)
  > *Je **ne** fume **plus**.*   I don't smoke any more.

- ◼ *ne … jamais* (never)
  > *Je **ne** fume **jamais**.*   I **never** smoke.

- ◼ *ne … personne* (nobody)
  > *Les fumeurs **ne** respectent **personne**.*   Smokers don't respect anyone.

- ◼ *ne … rien* (nothing)
  > *Ça **ne** me dit **rien**.*   That does not interest me. (Literally: That says nothing to me).

- ◼ *ne … que* (only)
  > *Je n'ai qu'une sœur*   I only have one sister.

I Questions

Forming questions

You can turn statements into questions by adding a question mark and making your voice go up at the end.

Tu joues au tennis. > **Tu joues au tennis?**
Do you play tennis?

You can also add *est-ce que … ?* at the beginning.

Je peux vous aider. > **Est-ce que** *je peux vous aider?*
Can I help you?

In more formal situations, you can change the word order so that the verb comes first.

Vous pouvez m'aider. > **Pouvez-vous m'aider?**
Can you help me?

Many questions start with *qu'est-ce que …*

Qu'est-ce que c'est?	**What** is it?
Qu'est-ce qu'il y a à manger?	**What** is there to eat?
Qu'est-ce que vous avez comme journaux? **What** (kind of) papers have you got?	

Question words

Other questions use the following words:

- *combien (de)* (how much / how many)

*Tu as **combien** de frères?* How many brothers have you got?

- *comment* (how)

Comment *vas-tu?* **How** are you?

- *où* (where)

Où habites-tu? **Where** do you live?

- *pourquoi* (why)

Pourquoi *est-ce que tu n'aimes pas ça?* **Why** don't you like it?

- *quand* (when)

*Il vient **quand**?* **When** is he coming?

- *quel / quelle* (which, what)

*Ça commence à **quelle** heure?* **What** time does it start?

- *que / qu'* (what)

Que *veux-tu?* **What** do you want?

- *qui* (who)

*C'est **qui**?* **Who** is it?

- *quoi* (what)

*Elle fait **quoi**?* **What** is she doing?

J Useful verbs

avoir (to have)

Use *avoir mal* to talk about a pain or an ache.

*J'ai **mal** à la tête.*	I **have** a headache.
*J'ai **mal** au ventre.*	I **have** a stomach ache.
*J'ai **mal** aux dents.*	I **have** toothache.

Use the verb *avoir* to say how old people are.

J'ai 15 ans. I **am** 15 years old.

Il y a means both 'there is' and 'there are'.

Il y a une banque.	**There is** a bank.
Il y a beaucoup de cafés.	**There are** lots of cafés.

The negative form is *il n'y a pas de*.

Il n'y a pas de piscine. **There is no** swimming pool.

faire (to do)

This verb has a range of meanings depending on the context.

*Je **fais** de la natation.*	I **go** swimming.
*Ils **font** du judo.*	They **do** judo.
faire du jardinage	**to do** some gardening
faire la vaisselle	**to do** the washing-up
faire le lit	**to make** the bed
*Il **fait** chaud.*	It **is** hot.
*Il **fait** beau.*	The weather **is** lovely.

When talking about other sports or pastimes, use *faire + du / de la / de l' / des*:

*Je fais **du** karaté.*	I do karate.
*Je fais **de l'**equitation.*	I go horse-riding.
*Je fais **de la** voile.*	I go sailing.

devoir (to have to)

Use *devoir + infinitive* to say what you must and mustn't do.

*Je **dois** porter un uniforme.*
I **have to** wear a uniform.

*On **ne doit pas** jeter de papiers par terre.*
You **mustn't** drop litter.

pouvoir (to be able to)

Use *pouvoir + infinitive* to say what you can and can't do.

*On **peut** faire des randonnées.*
You **can** go hiking.

*Elle **ne peut pas** sortir pendant la semaine.*
She **can't** go out during the week.

vouloir (to want to)

Use *vouloir* + infinitive to say what you want and don't want to do.

*Je **veux** partir.*　　　I **want** to leave.

The conditional form of *vouloir*, *je voudrais*, is used to mean 'I would like'.

***Je voudrais** partir en vacances.*
I would like to go on holiday.

Note that *j'aimerais*, the conditional form of *aimer*, means the same as *je voudrais*.

***J'aimerais** faire de la planche à voile.*
I would like to go windsurfing.

jouer (to play)

When talking about games, use *jouer* + *au / à la / à l' / aux*:

*Je joue **au** tennis.*　　　I play tennis.

*Je joue **à la** pétanque.*　　I play pétanque.

*Je joue **aux** cartes.*　　　I play cards.

When talking about musical instruments, use *jouer* + *du / de la / de l' / des*:

*Je joue **au** violon.*　　　I play the violin.

*Je joue **de la** batterie.*　　I play the drums.

*Je joue **des** percussions.*　　I play percussion.

il faut (to be necessary to)

Use *il faut* + infinitive to say what it is necessary to do.

Il faut partir.　　　We have to leave.

In general, with verbs of liking and disliking, when there are two verbs in a row, the second verb is in the infinitive.

J'aime porter une robe.　　I like wearing dresses.

Je déteste faire les magasins.　I hate shopping.

Je préfère aller à la patinoire.　I'd rather go ice skating.

K　Prepositions

à, au, à l', à la, aux

Use *à* to mean 'in', 'at' or 'to'.

in	*J'habite **à** Nice.*	I live **in** Nice.
at	*Je me lève **à** sept heures.*	I get up **at** seven.
to	*Je vais **à** l'école.*	I go **to** school.

Some special expressions with *à*:

à pied	**on** foot
à vélo	**by** bike
à gauche	**on** the left
à droite	**on** the right
*Je vais **à la** pêche.*	I go **fishing**.

Use *à* also with names of towns.

*Il habite **à** Grenoble.*　　He lives **in** Grenoble

*Je vais **à** Paris.*　　　I'm going **to** Paris.

à + le / la / les

masculine	feminine	words beginning with a vowel or silent h	plural
à + le = au	*à + la = à la*	*à + l' = à l'*	*à + les = aux*
***au** théâtre*	***à la** piscine*	***à l'**hôtel*	***aux** États-Unis*
at / to the theatre	**at / to the** pool	**at / to the** hotel	**to the** USA

Note that the word order can be different from English.

*un sandwich **au jambon***　　**a ham** sandwich

*une glace **à la vanille***　　**a vanille** ice cream

de

De is shortened to *d'* before a vowel or a silent h.

De can mean 'of'.

*la mère **de** ma copine* (= the mother of my friend)
my friend's mother

*le prof **d'**histoire* (= the teacher of history)
the history teacher

Note that the word order can be different from English.

*un jus **d'**orange*	an orange juice
*un match **de** foot*	a football match
*la maison **de** mes grands-parents*	my grandparents' house

De can also mean 'from'.

*Elle vient **d'**Écosse.*　　She comes **from** Scotland.

De is sometimes part of an expression.

■ *près de* (near)

*Il habite **près de** Lyon.*　　He lives **near** Lyon.

■ *beaucoup de* (many, a lot of)

| *Elle a **beaucoup de** copains.* | She has **a lot of** friends. |

■ *de … à …* (from … to …)

| *de neuf heures*
 à cinq heures | **from** nine **to** five |

en, au

En is used to introduce most names of countries – it means both 'to' and 'in'.

*Je vais **en** Allemagne.*	I am going **to** Germany.
*Il habite **en** France.*	He lives **in** France.
*Elle part **en** Angleterre.*	She's off **to** England.

A few names of countries are masculine. Those are introduced with *au* or *aux*.

*Il va **au** Portugal.*
He's going **to** Portugal.

*Elle habite **au** pays de Galles.*
She lives **in** Wales.

*Nous partons **aux** États-Unis.*
We're off **to the** United States.

More prepositions

■ *à côté de* (next to)

à côté de *la salle de bains*
next to the bathroom

■ *avec* (with)

*Je me dispute **avec** ma sœur.*
I have an argument **with** my sister.

■ *chez* (at / to [someone's house])

*Je suis **chez ma copine**.*
I am at **my friend's house**.

*Je vais **chez mon copain**.*
I'm going to **my friend's house**.

■ *dans* (in)

*Il est **dans** sa chambre.*
He is **in** his bedroom.

■ *derrière* (behind)

derrière *l'hôtel*
behind the hotel

■ *devant* (in front of)

*On se retrouve **devant** le théâtre?*
Shall we meet **in front of** the theatre?

■ *en face de* (opposite)

en face du *parking*
opposite the car park

■ *entre* (between)

entre *la salle à manger et l'ascenseur*
between the dining room and the lift

■ *pendant* (during)

*Qu'est-ce que tu fais **pendant** les vacances?*
What are you doing **during** the holidays?

■ *près de* (near)

*Mon chien est **près de** moi.*
My dog is **near** me.

■ *pour* (for)

*C'est super **pour** les jeunes.*
It's great **for** young people.

■ *sous* (under)

*Le chat est **sous** le lit.*
The cat is **under** the bed.

■ *sur* (on)

*Il y a des livres **sur** les étagères.*
There are books **on** the shelves.

■ *depuis* (for / since)

To say how long someone has been doing something, use the present tense with *depuis*.

J'apprends *le français **depuis** quatre ans.*
I have been learning French **for** four years.

J'ai *mal à la gorge **depuis** hier.*
I have had a sore throat **since** yesterday.

L Linking words

Relative pronouns (*qui*, *que* and *où*)

qui	who, that
que	that
où	where

Qui and *que* are used to link phrases together.

*le copain **qui** habite à Lyon*	the friend **who** lives in Lyon
*le livre **qui** est sur la chaise*	the book **that** is on the chair
*le copain **que** j'ai vu*	the friend (**that**) I saw
*le livre **que** j'ai acheté*	the book (**that**) I bought

Note that *qui* and *que* are not optional. You cannot leave them out in French.

You can use *où* in the same way.

| *La région **où** j'habite.* | The area **where** I live. |

Conjunctions

The following words are used to link parts of sentences together:

■ *et* (and)

*J'ai 15 ans **et** j'habite en France.*

I am 15 years old **and** I live in France.

■ *et puis* (and then)

*Je me lève **et puis** je prends mon petit déjeuner.*

I get up **and then** I have breakfast.

■ *mais* (but)

*J'ai deux frères **mais** je n'ai pas de sœur.*

I have two brothers **but** I don't have any sisters.

■ *ou* (or)

*Je joue au foot **ou** je vais à la patinoire.*

I play football **or** I go to the ice rink.

■ *parce que* (because)

*J'aime la géographie **parce que** c'est intéressant.*

I like geographie **because** it is interesting.

■ *car* (because)

*Je vais au collège à pied **car** j'habite tout près.*

I walk to college **because** I live very near.

M Numbers, dates and time

Numbers 1–2002

1 un	*16 seize*
2 deux	*17 dix-sept*
3 trois	*18 dix-huit*
4 quatre	*19 dix-neuf*
5 cinq	*20 vingt*
6 six	*21 vingt et un*
7 sept	*22 vingt-deux*
8 huit	*23 vingt-trois*
9 neuf	*24 vingt-quatre*
10 dix	*25 vingt-cinq*
11 onze	*26 vingt-six*
12 douze	*27 vingt-sept*
13 treize	*28 vingt-huit*
14 quatorze	*29 vingt-neuf*
15 quinze	*30 trente*

40 quarante	*100 cent*
41 quarante et un	*101 cent un*
42 quarante-deux	*102 cent deux*
50 cinquante	*200 deux cents*
51 cinquante et un	*201 deux cent un*
52 cinquante-deux	*202 deux cent deux*
60 soixante	*300 trois cents*
61 soixante et un	*301 trois cent un*
62 soixante-deux	*302 trois cent deux*
70 soixante-dix	*1000 mille*
71 soixante et onze	*1001 mille un*
72 soixante-douze	*1002 mille deux*
80 quatre-vingts	*2000 deux mille*
81 quatre-vingt-un	*2001 deux mille un*
82 quatre-vingt-deux	*2002 deux mille deux*
90 quatre-vingt-dix	
91 quatre-vingt-onze	
92 quatre-vingt-douze	

Ordinal numbers: *premier, deuxième* etc.

The French for 'first' is *premier* in the masculine and *première* in the feminine.

mon **premier** cours	my **first** lesson
mes **premières** vacances	my **first** holiday

To say 'second', 'third' etc., simply add *-ième* to the original number.

deuxième	second
troisième	third

To say 'fifth', add a *u*.

> *cinquième*   fifth

To say 'ninth', change the *f* of *neuf* to a *v*.

> *neuvième*   ninth

If the original number ends with an *-e*, drop the *-e* before adding *-ième*.

> *quatrième*   fourth
> *onzième*   eleventh

Days and dates

lundi	Monday
mardi	Tuesday
mercredi	Wednesday
jeudi	Thursday
vendredi	Friday
samedi	Saturday
dimanche	Sunday

janvier	January
février	February
mars	March
avril	April
mai	May
juin	June
juillet	July
août	August
septembre	September
octobre	October
novembre	November
décembre	December

Use normal numbers for dates and note that there is no word for 'of'.

> *Son anniversaire est le 27 décembre.*
> His birthday is on **the 27th of December**.

The only exception is the first of the month, when you use le premier.

> **le premier** *janvier*   **the first of** January

Days of the week and months don't have a capital letter in French (unless they are at the beginning of a sentence).

> *Son anniversaire est en* **avril.**
> His / Her birthday is in **April**.

Use *le* + *lundi* / *mardi* etc. to mean 'on Mondays' / 'on Tuesdays' etc.

> *Je ne vais pas à l'école* **le dimanche**.
> I don't go to school **on Sundays**.

Use *lundi* / *mardi*, etc. (without *le*) to mean 'on Monday' / 'on Tuesday' etc.

> *Je vais chez le dentiste* **jeudi**.
> I'm going to the dentist **on Thursday**.

Time

The 12-hour clock goes as follows:

Il est deux heures cinq.	It's five past two.
Il est deux heures dix.	It's ten past two.
Il est deux heures et quart.	It's a quarter past two.
Il est deux heures vingt.	It's twenty past two.
Il est deux heures vingt-cinq.	It's twenty-five past two.
Il est deux heures et demie.	It's half past two.
Il est trois heures moins vingt-cinq.	It's twenty-five to three.
Il est trois heures moins vingt.	It's twenty to three.
Il est trois heures moins le quart.	It's a quarter to three.
Il est trois heures moins dix.	It's ten to three.
Il est trois heures moins cinq.	It's five to three.
Il est trois heures.	It's three o'clock.
Il est midi.	It's midday.
Il est minuit.	It's midnight.

When using the 24-hour clock, use the word *heures* to separate the minutes from the hours.

> *Il est treize* **heures** *vingt.*   It's 13.20.
> *À douze* **heures** *quarante-cinq.* At 12.45.

When written down, times are often shortened.

> *8h30*
> *14h15*

As in English, when using the 24-hour clock, use numbers such as *quinze*, *trente* etc. instead of *et quart*, *et demie* etc.

> *quatorze heures* **quinze**   14.**15**
> *seize heures* **trente**   16.**30**

There are three ways to ask the time.

- ■ The most correct and formal is:
  > *Quelle heure est-il?*   What time is it?
- ■ In more casual contexts, you can say:
  > *Il est quelle heure?*
  > *Quelle heure il est?*

Verb tables

Regular verbs

infinitive	present	perfect	imperfect	future
parler to speak	je parle	j'ai parlé	je parlais	je parlerai
	tu parles	tu as parlé	tu parlais	tu parleras
	il / elle / on parle	il / elle / on a parlé	il / elle / on parlait	il / elle / on parlera
	nous parlons	nous avons parlé	nous parlions	nous parlerons
	vous parlez	vous avez parlé	vous parliez	vous parlerez
	ils / elles parlent	ils / elles ont parlé	ils / elles parlaient	ils / elles parleront
se laver to have a wash	je me lave	je me suis lavé(e)	je me lavais	je me laverai
	tu te laves	tu t'es lavé(e)	tu te lavais	tu te laveras
	il se lave	il s'est lavé	il se lavait	il se lavera
	elle se lave	elle s'est lavée	elle se lavait	elle se lavera
	on se lave	on s'est lavé(e)(s)	on se lavait	on se lavera
	nous nous lavons	nous nous sommes lavé(e)s	nous nous lavions	nous nous laverons
	vous vous lavez	vous vous êtes lavé(e)(s)	vous vous laviez	vous vous laverez
	ils se lavent	ils se sont lavés	ils se lavaient	ils se laveront
	elles se lavent	elles se sont lavées	elles se lavaient	elles se laveront
finir to finish	je finis	j'ai fini	je finissais	je finirai
	tu finis	tu as fini	tu finissais	tu finiras
	il / elle / on finit	il / elle / on a fini	il / elle / on finissait	il / elle / on finira
	nous finissons	nous avons fini	nous finissions	nous finirons
	vous finissez	vous avez fini	vous finissiez	vous finirez
	ils / elles finissent	ils / elles ont fini	ils / elles finissaient	ils / elles finiront
vendre to sell	je vends	j'ai vendu	je vendais	je vendrai
	tu vends	tu as vendu	tu vendais	tu vendras
	il / elle / on vend	il / elle / on a vendu	il / elle / on vendait	il / elle / on vendra
	nous vendons	nous avons vendu	nous vendions	nous vendrons
	vous vendez	vous avez vendu	vous vendiez	vous vendrez
	ils / elles vendent	ils / elles ont vendu	ils / elles vendaient	ils / elles vendront

Common irregular verbs

infinitive	present	perfect	imperfect	future
avoir to have	j'ai tu as il / elle / on a nous avons vous avez ils / elles ont	j'ai eu tu as eu il / elle / on a eu nous avons eu vous avez eu ils / elles ont eu	j'avais tu avais il / elle / on avait nous avions vous aviez ils / elles avaient	j' aurai tu auras il / elle / on aura nous aurons vous aurez ils / elles auront
être to be	je suis tu es il / elle / on est nous sommes vous êtes ils / elles sont	j'ai été tu as été il / elle / on a été nous avons été vous avez été ils / elles ont été	j'étais tu étais il / elle / on était nous étions vous étiez ils / elles étaient	je serai tu seras il / elle / on sera nous serons vous serez ils / elles seront
aller to go	je vais tu vas il va elle va on va nous allons vous allez ils vont elles vont	je suis allé(e) tu es allé(e) il est allé elle est allée on est allé(e)(s) nous sommes allé(e)s vous êtes allé(e)(s) ils sont allés elles sont allées	j'allais tu allais il allait elle allait on allait nous allions vous alliez ils allaient elles allaient	j' irai tu iras il ira elle ira on ira nous irons vous irez ils iront elles iront
boire to drink	je bois tu bois il / elle / on boit nous buvons vous buvez ils / elles boivent	j'ai bu tu as bu il / elle / on a bu nous avons bu vous avez bu ils / elles ont bu	je buvais tu buvais il / elle / on buvait nous buvions vous buviez ils / elles buvaient	je boirai tu boiras il / elle / on boira nous boirons vous boirez ils / elles boiront
devoir to have to	je dois tu dois il / elle / on doit nous devons vous devez ils / elles doivent	j'ai dû tu as dû il / elle / on a dû nous avons dû vous avez dû ils / elles ont dû	je devais tu devais il / elle / on devait nous devions vous deviez ils / elles devaient	je devrai tu devras il / elle / on devra nous devrons vous devrez ils / elles devront

infinitive	present	perfect	imperfect	future
dire to say	je dis tu dis il / elle / on dit nous disons vous dites ils / elles disent	j'ai dit tu as dit il / elle / on a dit nous avons dit vous avez dit ils / elles ont dit	je disais tu disais il / elle / on disait nous disions vous disiez ils / elles disaient	je dirai tu diras il / elle / on dira nous dirons vous direz ils / elles diront
dormir to sleep	je dors tu dors il / elle / on dort nous dormons vous dormez ils / elles dorment	j'ai dormi tu as dormi il / elle / on a dormi nous avons dormi vous avez dormi ils / elles ont dormi	je dormais tu dormais il / elle / on dormait nous dormions vous dormiez ils / elles dormaient	je dormirai tu dormiras il / elle / on dormira nous dormirons vous dormirez ils / elles dormiront
écrire to write	j'écris tu écris il / elle / on écrit nous écrivons vous écrivez ils / elles écrivent	j'ai écrit tu as écrit il / elle / on a écrit nous avons écrit vous avez écrit ils / elles ont écrit	j'écrivais tu écrivais il / elle / on écrivait nous écrivions vous écriviez ils / elles écrivaient	j' écrirai tu écriras il / elle / on écrira nous écrirons vous écrirez ils / elles écriront
faire to do	je fais tu fais il / elle / on fait nous faisons vous faites ils / elles font	j'ai fait tu as fait il / elle / on a fait nous avons fait vous avez fait ils / elles ont fait	je faisais tu faisais il / elle / on faisait nous faisions vous faisiez ils / elles faisaient	je ferais tu feras il / elle / on fera nous ferons vous ferez ils / elles feront
lire to read	je lis tu lis il / elle / on lit nous lisons vous lisez ils / elles lisent	j'ai lu tu as lu il / elle / on a lu nous avons lu vous avez lu ils / elles ont lu	je lisais tu lisais il / elle / on lisait nous lisions vous lisiez ils / elles lisaient	je lirai tu liras il / elle / on lira nous lirons vous lirez ils / elles liront
mettre to put	je mets tu mets il / elle / on met nous mettons vous mettez ils / elles mettent	j'ai mis tu as mis il / elle / on a mis nous avons mis vous avez mis ils / elles ont mis	je mettais tu mettais il / elle / on mettait nous mettions vous mettiez ils / elles mettaient	je mettrai tu mettras il / elle / on mettra nous mettrons vous mettrez ils / elles mettront

infinitive	present	perfect	imperfect	future
pouvoir to be able to	je peux	j'ai pu	je pouvais	je pourrai
	tu peux	tu as pu	tu pouvais	tu pourras
	il / elle / on peut	il / elle / on a pu	il / elle / on pouvait	il / elle / on pourra
	nous pouvons	nous avons	nous pouvions	nous pourrons
	vous pouvez	vous avez pu	vous pouviez	vous pourrez
	ils / elles peuvent	ils / elles ont pu	ils / elles pouvaient	ils / elles pourront
prendre to take	je prends	j'ai pris	je prenais	je prendrai
	tu prends	tu as pris	tu prenais	tu prendras
	il / elle / on prend	il / elle / on a pris	il / elle / on prenait	il / elle / on prendra
	nous prenons	nous avons pris	nous prenions	nous prendrons
	vous prenez	vous avez pris	vous preniez	vous prendrez
	ils / elles prennent	ils / elles ont pris	ils / elles prenaient	ils / elles prendront
venir to come	je viens	je suis venu(e)	je venais	je viendrai
	tu viens	tu es venu(e)	tu venais	tu viendras
	il vient	il est venu	il venait	il viendra
	elle vient	elle est venue	elle venait	elle viendra
	on vient	on est venu(e)(s)	on venait	on viendra
	nous venons	nous sommes venu(e)s	nous venions	nous viendrons
	vous venez	vous êtes venu(e)(s)	vous veniez	vous viendrez
	ils viennent	ils sont venus	ils venaient	ils viendront
	elles viennent	elles sont venues	elles venaient	elles viendront
voir to see	je vois	j'ai vu	je voyais	je verrai
	tu vois	tu as vu	tu voyais	tu verras
	il / elle / on voit	il / elle / on a vu	il / elle / on voyait	il / elle / on verra
	nous voyons	nous avons vu	nous voyions	nous verrons
	vous voyez	vous avez vu	vous voyiez	vous verrez
	ils / elles voient	ils / elles ont vu	ils / elles voyaient	ils / elles verront
vouloir to want	je veux	j'ai voulu	je voulais	je voudrai
	tu veux	tu as voulu	tu voulais	tu voudras
	il / elle / on veut	il / elle / on a voulu	il / elle / on voulait	Il / elle / on voudra
	nous voulons	nous avons voulu	nous voulions	nous voudrons
	vous voulez	vous avez voulu	vous vouliez	vous voudrez
	ils / elles veulent	ils / elles ont voulu	ils / elles voulaient	ils / elles voudront

Glossaire

A

à   in, at, to
d' abord   first
absolument   absolutely
d' accord   agreed
acheter   to buy
l' acteur (m)   actor
l' activité physique(f)
   physical activity
les actualités (f)   the news
l' addition (f)   bill
l' aéroport (m)   airport
affreux(-euse)   hideous,
   horrible
l' agence de voyages (f)   travel
   agent
agréable   pleasant
l' Aïd (m)   Eid
aider   to help
j' aime …   I like …
aîné(e)   older
une alimentation saine (f)
   healthy eating
aller   to go
aller à la pêche   to go fishing
aller à la piscine   to go
   swimming
l' aller retour (m)   return ticket
l' aller simple (m)   single,
   one-way ticket
aller sur un site   to go to a
   website
alors   so, then
l' alpinisme (m)
   mountaineering
l' alto (m)   viola
l' amour (m)   love
amusant(e)   funny
l' an (m)   a year
ancien(ne)   old
l' anglais (m)   English
animé(e)   lively, busy
l' année (f)   a year
l' anniversaire (m)   birthday
août   August
l' appareil-photo (m)   camera
l' appartement (m)
   apartment, flat
apprendre   to learn
après   after
l' après-midi (m)   afternoon
l' argent de poche (m)   pocket
   money

l' armoire (f)   wardrobe
l' arrêt (m)   stop
arrêter   to stop
l' artisan (m)   craftsman
l' ascenseur (m)   lift
l' aspirine (f)   aspirin
assez   quite, enough
l' athléthisme (m)   athletics
attendre   to wait (for)
au-dessous de   above
au-dessus de   below
aujourd'hui   today
aussi   also
en automne   in autumn
l' automne (m)   autumn
l' autoroute (f)   motorway
autour de   around
de l' autre côté   on the other side
en avance   in advance
avant   before
l' avantage (m)   advantage
avec   with
à l' avenir   in the future
l' avenir (m)   future
l' avion (m)   plane
en avion   by plane
à mon avis   in my opinion
avoir de la chance   to be
   lucky
avoir le droit de   to have the
   right to
avril   April

B

le badminton   badminton
les bagages (m)   baggage
le balcon   balcony
la bande dessinée   cartoon
   strip, comic book
la banlieue   suburbs
barbant(e)   dull, boring
en bas   below, downstairs
bas(se)   low
le basket   basketball
les baskets (f)   trainers
le bateau   boat
en bateau   by boat
la batterie   drums
bavarder   to chat, talk
beaucoup   a lot, lots
beaucoup de   a lot of
le beau-père   stepfather
la belle vue   fine view

belle/beau   beautiful, nice
la belle-mère   stepmother
le beurre   butter
la bibliothèque   library
bien   good
bien entendu   of course
le bien-être   well-being
bientôt   soon
bienvenue   welcome
la bière   beer
le bifteck   steak
les bijoux (m)   jewellery
la biologie   biology
bizarre   strange
blanc(he)   white
bleu(e)   blue
boire   to drink
le bois   wood
en bois   (made of) wood
la boisson   drink
la boîte   box, tin
la boîte de nuit   nightclub
bon anniversaire!   happy
   birthday!
bon(ne)   good
la bonne cause   good cause
en bonne forme   in good shape
de bonne heure   early
au bord de   by, at
le bord de la mer   seaside
la bouche   mouth
le boucher   butcher (m)
la bouchère   butcher (f)
la boucherie   butcher's shop
la boucle d'oreille   earring
le boulanger   baker (m)
la boulangère   baker (f)
la boulangerie   bakery
le boulot   work
au bout de   at the end of
la bouteille   bottle
la boutique   boutique
le bras   arm
bronzer   to sunbathe
le brouillard   fog
le bureau   office
le bureau de renseignements
   information office
en bus   by bus

C

le cadeau   present
le cahier   notebook

la caisse till, cash register
le caissier cashier (m)
la caissière cashier (f)
la calculatrice calculator
calme calm, peaceful
la campagne countryside
le camping camping
le Canada Canada
le cannabis cannabis
car because
en car by coach
le car a coach
les Caraïbes (f) the Carribbean
la caravane caravan
caritative charitable
le carnet notebook, ticket
le carnet de notes school report
la carrière career
les cartes (f) cards
la carte de sortie exit pass
la carte postale postcard
casse-pieds annoying
à cause de because of
la cave cellar
le CDI (Centre de documentation et information) school library
le centimètre centimetre
le centre commercial shopping centre
le centre de recyclage recycling centre
le centre-ville town centre
cependant however
la chambre bedroom
la chambre familiale family room
le champ field
le champignon mushroom
chanter to sing
le chanteur singer (m)
la chanteuse singer (f)
le chapeau hat
de chaque côté on each side
la charcuterie pork butcher's shop and delicatessen
le chat cat
chatter sur MSN to chat on instant messenger
chaud(e) hot
les chausettes (f) socks
les chaussures (f) shoes
la chemise shirt
cher(-ère) expensive
les cheveux (m) hair
chez at, to (someone's house, home)

chic stylish
le chien dog
la chimie chemistry
la Chine China
les chips (f) crisps
le chocolat chocolate
choisir to choose
le choix choice
le chômage unemployment
la chorale choir
les choses en commun (f) things in common
chouette great
le chou-fleur cauliflower
le cinéma cinema
en cinquième in year 8
la circulation traffic
le citron lemon
le clavier keyboard
le client client, customer
le club des jeunes youth club
la cocaïne cocaine
le cœur heart
le collant tights
la colonie de vacances holiday camp
comique funny
comme like
comme ci comme ça so-so
comment? how?
la commode chest of drawers
compliqué(e) complicated
composter to stamp
compréhensif(-ive) understanding
comprendre to understand
le comprimé tablet
y compris including
compris(e) included
le comptable accountant
conduire to drive
construire to build, construct
content(e) pleased
contre against
le copain friend (m)
les copains (m) friends
la copine friend (f)
à côté de by the side of, next to
en coton (made of) cotton
se coucher to go to bed
la couleur colour
la cour de récréation playground
courir to run
le cours class, lesson
les courses (f) shopping

la cravate tie
le crayon pencil
critiquer to criticise
en cuir (made of) leather
la cuisine kitchen, cooking
la cuisinier cook (m)
la cuisinière cooker, cook (f)
le cyclisme cycling

D

dangereux(-euse) dangerous
dans in
danser to dance
la date date
de of, from
le dealer drug dealer
décembre December
les déchets (m) rubbish
decider to decide
les défilés de mode (m) fashion show
en dehors de outside of
déjà already, still
demain tomorrow
demi(e) half
le demi-frère stepbrother / half-brother
la demi-pension half board
démodé(e) old-fashioned, out-of-date
le dentiste dentist
les dents (f) teeth
le départ departure
dépenser to spend
se déplacer to move
déprimé(e) depressed
depuis since, for
derrière behind
le désavantage disadvantage
le dessin art
se détendre to relax, calm down
devant in front of
devenir to become
les devoirs (m) homework
le dictionnaire dictionary
difficile difficult
dimanche Sunday
se disputer to quarrel, argue
le divorce divorce
divorcé(e) divorced
divorcer to divorce
donc therefore
dormir to sleep
le dortoir dormitory
le dos back
se droguer to take drugs

les *drogues douces (f)*   soft drugs
les *drogues dures (f)*   hard drugs
à *droite*   right
drôle   funny
dur(e)   hard
durer   to last

E

l' *eau (f)*   water
écouter   to listen (to)
écouter de la musique   to listen to music
l' *éducation (f)*   education
l' *église (f)*   church
égoïste   selfish
l' *électricien*   electrician (m)
l' *électricienne*   electrician (f)
embêtant(e)   annoying
l' *émission (f)*   programme
l' *emploi (m)*   job
l' *emploi du temps (m)*   timetable
l' *employé (m)*   employee
en   in, to
j' *en ai marre*   I've had enough
en ligne   online
encore (de)   more (of)
encore une fois   once more
enfin   at last, finally
ennuyeux(-euse)   boring
enseigner   to teach
ensemble   together
ensuite   next, then
s' *entendre bien avec …*   to get on well with …
s' *entraîner*   to train
entre   between
l' *entrée (f)*   starter
l' *entreprise (f)*   firm
l' *environnement (m)*   environment
envoyer   to send
épicé(e)   spicy
l' *épicerie (f)*   greengrocer's shop
l' *époque (f)*   era, period of time
l' *EPS (f)*   PE
équilibré(e)   well-balanced
l' *équitation (f)*   horse riding
l' *escalade (f)*   climbing
l' *Espagne (f)*   Spain
l' *espagnol (m)*   Spanish
j' *espère …*   I hope …
essayer   to try
l' *essence (f)*   petrol
l' *est (m)*   east

est   is
est-ce que …?   does …?
et   and
l' *étage (m)*   floor, level
l' *étagère (f)*   shelf
les *États-Unis (m)*   United States
en *été*   in summer
l' *été (m)*   summer
à l' *étranger*   abroad
l' *étranger (m)*   foreigner
étranger(-ère)   foreign
l' *étudiant (m)*   student
l' *étudiante (f)*   student
étudier   to study
éviter   to avoid
l' *examen (m)*   exam

F

fabriquer   to make
en *face de*   opposite
fâché(e)   angry, cross
facile   easy
le *facteur*   postman
faire   to do / to make
faire attention   to pay attention
faire de la lecture   to read, do some reading
faire de la planche à voile   to go windsurfing
faire de la voile   to go sailing
faire des économies   to save up (money)
faire des promenades   to go for walks
faire des randonnées   to go hiking
faire du camping   to go camping
faire du cheval   to go horse riding
faire du jardinage   to garden
faire du judo   to do judo
faire du patinage sur glace   to go ice skating
faire du ski   to go skiing
faire la cuisine   to cook
faire la fête   to have a party
faire la grasse matinée   to have a lie-in
faire les devoirs   to do homework
faire les magasins   to go shopping
faire un stage (en entreprise)   to do training, an apprenticeship (in a firm)

faire une promenade   to go for a walk
la *famille monoparentale*   single-parent family
fantastique   fantastic
la *femme*   woman, wife
la *fenêtre*   window
le *fermier*   farmer (m)
la *fermière*   farmer (f)
la *fête*   party, festival
le *feuilleton*   series, soap opera
les *feux rouges*   traffic lights
février   February
fidèle   faithful, loyal
les *films d'horreur (m)*   horror films
les *films de guerre (m)*   war films
les *films de science-fiction (m)*   science fiction films
les *films policiers (m)*   detective films
les *films romantiques (m)*   romantic films
la *fin*   end
finir   to finish
fleuri(e)   in bloom, decorated with flowers
la *flute*   flute
le *foie*   liver
au *fond de*   at the bottom of
fonder   to set up, found, to melt down
le *football*   football
la *forêt*   forest
formidable   great
fort(e)   strong
les *forums sur Internet*   internet chatrooms
le *four à micro-ondes*   microwave oven
la *fraise*   strawberry
le *français*   French
le *frère*   brother
le *frère aîné*   older brother
le *frigo*   fridge
les *frites (f)*   chips
froid(e)   cold
le *fromage*   cheese
fumer   to smoke
le *fumeur*   smoker (m)
la *fumeuse*   smoker (f)
au *futur*   in the future

G

gagner   to earn
garder la forme   to keep in shape
la *gare routière*   coach station

la *gare SNCF* train station
à *gauche* left
généralement normally, usually
le *genou* knee
gentil(le) kind, nice
la *géographie* geography
le *gîte* gite
la *glace à la vanille* vanilla ice cream
la *gomme* eraser
la *gorge* throat
le *goût* taste
le *gramme* gramme
grand(e) big, tall, large
la *grand-mère* grandmother
le *grand-père* grandfather
gratuit(e) free
grave serious
la *grippe* flu
gris(e) grey
gros(se) fat
la *guerre* war
la *guitare* guitar
le *gymnase* gym

H

l' *habitant (m)* occupant, inhabitant
d' *habitude* normally, usually
l' *habitude (f)* habit
la *halte-garderie* day nursery
les *haricots verts (m)* green beans
en *haut* above, upstairs
à l' *heure* on time
l' *heure d'étude (f)* study period
hier yesterday
l' *histoire (f)* history
historique historical
en *hiver* in winter
l' *hiver (m)* winter
l' *horaire (m)* timetable
l' *hôtel de ville (m)* town hall
l' *hôtesse de l'air (f)* air stewardess

I

ici here
l' *immeuble (m)* block of flats
les *inconvenients (m)* disadvantages
incroyable unbelievable
industriel(le) industrial
l' *infirmier (m)* nurse
l' *infirmière (f)* nurse
l' *informatique (f)* ICT

l' *ingénieur (m)* engineer
interdit(e) forbidden
intéressant(e) interesting
s' *intéresser à* to be interested in
l' *Italie (f)* Italy

J

jaloux(-ouse) jealous
jamais never
la *jambe* leg
le *jambon* ham
janvier January
le *jardin* garden
le *jardin public* park
le *jardinage* gardening
jaune yellow
le *jean* jeans
jeter to throw
le *jeu* game
le *jeu de société* board game
le *jeu vidéo* video game
jeudi Thursday
jouer to play
jouer au ping-pong to play table-tennis
jouer de la clarinette to play the clarinet
les *jouets (m)* toys
le *jour* day
le *journal* newspaper
le *journal intime* diary
la *journée* day
le *judo* judo
juillet July
juin June
la *jupe* skirt
jusqu'à as far as

K

le *kilo* kilo
le *kilomètre* kilometer

L

là there
là-bas down there
le *laboratoire* laboratory
en *laine* (made of) wool
la *langue* language
large wide, broad
le *lave-vaisselle* dishwasher
le *vent* wind
le *lecteur DVD* DVD player
le *lecteur mp3* mp3 player
la *lecture* reading
le *légume* vegetable
le *lendemain* next day

se *lever* to get up
au *lieu de* instead of
la *limonade* lemonade
lire to read
le *lit* bed
le *litre* litre
le *livre* book
le *livre scolaire* schoolbook, textbook
livrer to deliver
la *location* hire
la *location de voitures* car hire
le *logement* housing
loger to live
loin de far from
longtemps a long time
louer to hire
louer un gîte to hire a gite
lundi Monday
le *lycée* upper secondary school

M

mâcher to chew
la *machine à laver* washing machine
les *magasins (m)* shops
mai May
maigre thin
le *maillot de bain* swimming costume
la *main* hand
maintenant now
la *mairie* town hall
mais but
la *maison individuelle* detached house
la *maison jumelée* semi-detached house
malade ill, sick, unwell
la *maladie* illness
les *maladies cardiaques (f)* heart diseases
malgré despite
malheureux(-euse) unfortunate
manger équilibré to eat a well-balanced diet
manquer to miss
le *manteau* coat
le *maquillage* make-up
le *marché* market
mardi Tuesday
le *mari* husband
le *mariage* marriage
marié(e) married
se *marier* to marry

marrant(e) funny, amusing
mars March
les *mathématiques (f)* maths
la *matière* subject
le *matin* morning
mauvais(e) bad
les *mauvaises nouvelles (f)* bad news
le *mécanicien* mechanic (m)
la *mécanicienne* mechanic (f)
méchant(e) naughty, wicked
le *médecin* doctor
le *meilleur ami* best friend (m)
la *meilleure amie* best friend (f)
même si even if
en *même temps* at the same time
le *ménage* housework
le *menu* menu
mercredi Wednesday
la *mer* sea
la *mère* mother
merveilleux(-euse) marvellous
les *messages électroniques* electronic messages
le *mètre* metre
en *métro* by underground
le *métro* underground (train)
le *meuble* item of furniture
midi midday
mignon(ne) sweet, cute, pretty
au *milieu de* in the middle of
mince thin
minuit midnight
la *minute* minute
moche horrid
la *mode* fashion
moderne modern
le *mois* month
la *montagne* mountain
montrer to show
les *monuments historiques (m)* historic monuments
le *morceau* piece
la *mort* death
mort(e) dead
le *moyen* average
le *musée* museum
le *musicien* musician
musulman(e) Muslim

nager to swim
la *natation* swimming

negatif(-ive) negative
le *nettoyage* cleaning
le *nez* nose
ni ... ni neither ... nor
le *niveau* level
Noël Christmas
noir(e) black
nombreux(-euse) numerous
le *non-fumeur* non-smoker
le *nord* north
normalement normally, usually
la *note* mark, grade
la *nourriture* food
novembre November
les *nuages* clouds
la *nuit* night
nul(le) rubbish

l' *obésité (f)* obesity
octobre October
l' *odeur (f)* odour
l' *œil (m)* eye
l' *office de tourisme (m)* tourist information office
onze eleven
optimiste optimistic
l' *ordinateur (m)* computer
les *ordinateurs portables (m)* laptops
l' *oreille (f)* ear
ou or
où? where?
oublier to forget
l' *ouest (m)* west

le *pantalon* trousers
Pâques Easter
le *paquet* packet
par by
par contre in contrast
par exemple for example
parce que because
les *parents (m)* parents
paresseux(-euse) lazy
parfois sometimes
parler to talk
parmi among
à *part* apart from
le / la *partenaire* partner
partout everywhere
le *passager* passenger
passer to take (an exam)
passionnant(e) thrilling
la *pastille* pastille, lozenge

les *pâtes (f)* pasta
la *patinoire* skating rink
la *pâtisserie* cake and pastry shop
pauvre poor
le *pays* the country
le *pays de Galles* Wales
la *pêche* fishing
pendant during
pénible hard, tiresome
penser to think
la *pension complète* full board
perdre to lose
le *père* father
le *permis* permit, licence
le *petit ami* boyfriend
petit(e) small, little
la *petite amie* girlfriend
les *petits pois (m)* peas
peu de a little of
peut-être perhaps
la *pharmacie* pharmacy
la *physique* physics
le *piano* piano
la *pièce* room
à *pied* on foot
le *pied* foot
le *pique-nique* picnic
la *piscine* swimming pool
la *piste cyclable* cycle path
pittoreqsue picturesque
la *place* job, position
la *plage* the beach
la *planche à voile* windsurfing
le *plat du jour* dish of the day
le *plat principal* main course
les *plats (m)* dishes
les *plats traditionnels (m)* traditional food
en *plein air* in the open air
plein de lots of, full of
la *pluie* rain
plus tard later
la *pointure* size
le *poisson* fish
le *poisson rouge* goldfish
le *policier* policeman
pollué(e) polluted
la *pomme de terre* potato
le *porc* pork
le *porc gras* fatty pork
le *port* port, harbour
la *porte* door
porter to wear, carry
positif(-ive) positive

le poste job
le poulet chicken
les poumons (m) lungs
pour for
pourquoi? why?
pourtant however
en première in year 12
prendre to take
prendre des photos to take photos
près de near to
la presse écrite the press
la pression pressure
prévenir to prevent, warn
au printemps in the spring
le printemps spring
les prix (m) prices
le problème problem
prochain(e) next
les produits de beauté (m) beauty products
le professeur teacher
la promenade walk
promener le chien to walk the dog
propre clean, tidy, own
protéger to protect
la publicité publicity
puis then
puisque because
le pull jumper
le pyjama pyjamas

Q

quand? when?
le quartier district, area
en quatrième in year 9
que? what?
quel(le)? what?
quelque part somewhere
quelquefois sometimes
qui? who?
quitter to leave

R

la radio radio
les randonnées (f) walks, hikes
ranger sa chambre to clean one's room
les rapports (m) relationships
rarement rarely
récemment recently
recevoir to receive
la récréation playtime, break
recyclable recyclable
recycler to recycle
redevenir to become again

refuser to refuse
regarder to look, watch
regarder des DVD to watch DVDs
regarder la télé to watch telly
le régime diet
la règle ruler
le règlement rules, regulations
régulièrement regularly
se relaxer to relax
se remarier to remarry
remplir to fill
les renseignements (m) information
la rentrée the start of the new school year
le repas meal
répondre to answer
réservé(e) reserved, shy
réserver to reserve
respirer to breathe
la responsabilité responsibility
en retard late
le retard delay
réussir to succeed
se réveiller to wake up
réveillonner to celebrate Christmas or New Year's Eve
revenir to come back
revisiter to revisit
le rez-de-chaussée ground floor
le rhume cold
riche rich
ridicule ridiculous
rien nothing
rigolo funny
rire to laugh
la rivière river
la robe dress
le rond-point roundabout
rose pink
rouge red
la rue street
le rugby rugby

S

le sac à main handbag
le sac de couchage sleeping bag
le sac en plastique plastic bag
sain et sauf safe and sound
le salaire salary
sale dirty
la salle à manger dining room
la salle d'attente waiting room
la salle de bains bathroom

la salle de classe classroom
la salle d'informatique IT room
la salle des professeurs staff room
la salle de séjour living room
le salon lounge, living room
samedi Saturday
sans without
sans doute without doubt, probably
sans travail without work, unemployed
la santé health
sauf except
sauver to save
savoir to know (a fact)
le savon soap
les sciences (f) science
SDF (sans domicile fixe) homeless
en seconde in year 11
la secrétaire secretary
le séjour stay
selon according to
la semaine week
le sens de l'humour sense of humour
sensass sensational
se sentir to feel
se sentir bien to feel well
la séparation separation
séparé(e) separated
septembre September
le serveur waiter (m)
la serveuse waitress (f)
le service (compris) service charge (included)
seul(e) alone, lonely
sévère strict, severe
le shampooing shampoo
le short shorts
le siècle century
le sirop (cough) syrup
situé(e) situated
en sixième in year 7
le skate skateboard
le ski nautique water skiing
la sœur sister
les soldes (m) the sales
le soleil sun
le sommeil sleep
la sonnerie des téléphones portables the ringing of mobile phones
sortir to go out, leave
soudain suddenly

la *soupe aux légumes* vegetable soup

sous under

le *sous-sol* basement

souvent often

les *spécialités de la region (f)* the specialities of the region

sportif(-ive) sporty

les *sports d'hiver (m)* winter sports

des *sports nautiques (m)* watersports

le *stade* stadium

la *station thermale* thermal spa

stationner to park

la *station-service* service-station

stressant(e) stressful

stupide stupid

le *stylo* pen

le *sucre* sugar

sucré(e) sweet

le *sud* south

suffisamment plenty

ça *suffit* that's enough

superbe super

sur on

surfer to surf

le *sweat* sweatshirt

sympa nice

le *syndicat d'initiative* tourist information office

T

le *tabac* tobacco

le *tableau interactif* interactive whiteboard

la *taille* size

le *tarif réduit* reduced price

la *tasse* cup

le *technicien* technician (m)

la *technicienne* technician (f)

la *technologie* D and T

la *télé par satellite* satellite television

le *(téléphone) portable* mobile (phone)

le *tennis* tennis

en *terminale* in year 13

le *terrain de camping* campsite

le *terrain de jeux* playground

le *terrain de sport* sports field

la *terrasse* terrace

la *tête* head

les *textos (m)* texts

en *TGV (train à grand vitesse)* by high-speed train

le *théâtre* theatre

le *timide* shy

les *toilettes (f)* toilet

la *tomate* tomato

tomber to fall

tôt early

toujours always

le *tourisme* tourism

touristique tourist

tourner to turn

tous les jours everyday

tousser to cough

tout de suite immediately

tout droit straight on

tout près very near

toutes directions all routes

en *train* by train

la *tranche* slice

tranquil(le) calm

les *transports en commun (m)* public transport

le *travail saisonnier* seasonal work

travailler to work

à *travers* across

traverser to cross

très very

le *trimester* term

triste sad

en *troisième* in year 10

trop (too) much

trop de monde too many people

le *trottoir* pavement

la *trousse* pencil case

U

l' *uniforme (m)* uniform

l' *usine (f)* factory

utiliser to use

V

les *vacances (f)* holidays

la *vache* cow

la *vaisselle* washing-up

la *valise* suitcase

varié(e) varied

les *vedettes de cinéma (f)* cinema stars

végétarien(ne) vegetarian

à *vélo* by bike

le *vendeur* shop assistant (m)

le *vendeuse* shop assistant (f)

vendre to sell

vendredi Friday

le *ventre* stomach

verifier to check, verify

la *vérité* truth

vers towards

vert(e) green

la *veste* jacket

les *vêtements (m)* clothes

la *viande* meat

vieux/vieil(le) old

le *village* village

la *ville* town

le *vin* wine

violet(tte) purple

le *violon* violin

la *visite guidée* guided tour

visiter to visit

vite quickly

vivre to live

vivre en concubinage to co-habit

la *voie* track, road

la *voile* sailing

le *voisin* neighbour

en *voiture* by car

le *vol* flight

voler to fly

le *VTT (vélo tout terrain)* mountain bike

W

le *week-end* weekend

Y

le *yaourt* yoghurt

les *yeux (m)* eyes

Z

la *zone piétonne* pedestrian zone

Glossary

A

above au-dessous de, en haut
abroad à l'étranger
absolutely absolument
according to selon
accountant le comptable
across à travers
actor l'acteur (m)
in advance en avance
advantage l'avantage (m)
aeroplane l'avion (m)
after après
afternoon l'après-midi (m)
against contre
agreed d'accord
air stewardess l'hôtesse de l'air (f)
airport l'aéroport (m)
alone seul(e)
already déjà
also aussi
always toujours
among parmi
amusing marrant(e)
and et
angry fâché(e)
annoying casse-pieds, embêtant(e)
to answer répondre
apartment l'appartement
apart from à part
April avril
to argue se disputer
arm le bras
around autour de
art le dessin
as far as jusqu'à
aspirin l'aspirine (f)
at à
at, to (someone's house, home) chez
athletics l'athléthisme (m)
August août
autumn l'automne (m)
in autumn en automne
average le moyen
to avoid éviter

B

back le dos
bad mauvais(e)
bad news les mauvaises nouvelles (f)
badminton le badminton
baggage les bagages (m)
baker le boulanger (m), la boulangère (f)
bakery la boulangerie
balcony le balcon
basement le sous-sol
basketball le basket
bathroom la salle de bains
beach la plage
beautiful belle/beau
beauty products les produits de beauté (m)
because car, parce que, puisque
because of à cause de
to become devenir
to become again redevenir
bed le lit
to go to bed se coucher
bedroom la chambre
beer la bière
before avant
behind derrière
below au-dessus de, en bas
best friend le meilleur ami (m), la meilleure amie (f)
between entre
big grand(e)
by bike à vélo
bill l'addition (f)
biology la biologie
birthday l'anniversaire (m)
black noir(e)
block of flats l'immeuble (m)
blue bleu(e)
board game le jeu de société
boat le bateau
by boat en bateau
book le livre
boring ennuyeux(-euse)
bottle la bouteille
at the bottom of au fond de
boutique la boutique
box la boîte
boyfriend le petit ami
break (school day) la récréation
to breathe respirer
broad large
brother le frère
to build, construct construire

by bus en bus
busy animé(e)
but mais
butcher le boucher (m), la bouchère (f)
butcher's shop la boucherie
butter le beurre
to buy acheter
by par
by, at au bord de

C

cake and pastry shop la pâtisserie
calm calme
camera l'appareil-photo (m)
camping le camping
to go camping faire du camping
campsite le terrain de camping
Canada le Canada
cannabis le cannabis
by car en voiture
car hire la location de voitures
caravan la caravane
cards les cartes (f)
career la carrière
Carribbean les Caraïbes (f)
to carry porter
cartoon strip, comic book la bande dessinée
cash register, till la caisse
cashier le caissier (m), la caissière (f)
cat le chat
cauliflower le chou-fleur
to celebrate Christmas or New Year's Eve réveillonner
cellar la cave
centimetre le centimètre
century le siècle
charitable caritative
to chat bavarder
to chat on instant messenger chatter sur MSN
to check verifier
cheese le fromage
chemistry la chimie
chest of drawers la commode
to chew mâcher
chicken le poulet
China la Chine
chips les frites (f)

chocolate   le chocolat
choice   le choix
choir   la chorale
to choose   choisir
Christmas   Noël
church   l'église (f)
cinema   le cinéma
cinema stars   les vedettes de cinéma (f)
classroom   la salle de classe
to clean one's room   ranger sa chambre
clean, tidy   propre
cleaning   le nettoyage
client   le client
climbing   l'escalade (f)
clothes   les vêtements (m)
clouds   les nuages
coach   le car
by coach   en car
coach station   la gare routière
coat   le manteau
cocaïne   la cocaine
to co-habit   vivre en concubinage
cold   froid(e)
cold   le rhume
colour   la couleur
to come back   revenir
complicated   compliqué(e)
computer   l'ordinateur (m)
in contrast   par contre
to cook   faire la cuisine
cooker   la cuisinière
cotton (made of cotton)   le coton (en coton)
to cough   tousser
cough syrup   le sirop
country   le pays
countryside   la campagne
of course   bien entendu
cow   la vache
craftsman   l'artisan (m)
crisps   les chips (f)
to criticise   critiquer
cross, angry   fâché(e)
to cross   traverser
cup   la tasse
customer   le client
cycle path   la piste cyclable
cycling   le cyclisme

D

to dance   danser
dangerous   dangereux(-euse)
date   la date

day   le jour, la journée
day nursery   la halte-garderie
D and T   la technologie
dead   mort(e)
death   la mort
December   décembre
to decide   decider
delay   le retard
to deliver   livrer
dentist   le dentiste
departure   le départ
depressed   déprimé(e)
despite   malgré
detached house   la maison individuelle
detective films   les films policiers (m)
diary   le journal intime
dictionary   le dictionnaire
diet   le régime
difficult   difficile
dining room   la salle à manger
dirty   sale
disadvantage   le désavantage
disadvantages   les inconvenients (m)
dish of the day   le plat du jour
dishes   les plats (m)
dishwasher   le lave-vaisselle
district, area   le quartier
divorce   le divorce
to divorce   divorcer
divorced   divorcé(e)
to do   faire
doctor   le médecin
does ...?   est-ce que ...?
dog   le chien
door   la porte
dormitory   le dortoir
down there   là-bas
downstairs   en bas
dress   la robe
drink   la boisson
to drink   boire
to drive   conduire
drug dealer   le dealer
drums   la batterie
dull, boring   barbant(e)
during   pendant
DVD player   le lecteur DVD

E

ear   l'oreille (f)
early   de bonne heure, tôt
to earn   gagner

earring   la boucle d'oreille
east   l'est (m)
Easter   Pâques
easy   facile
to eat a well-balanced diet   manger équilibré
education   l'éducation (f)
Eid   l'Aïd (m)
electrician   l'électricien (m), l'électricienne (f)
electronic messages   les messages électroniques
eleven   onze
employee   l'employé (m)
end   la fin
at the end of   au bout de
engineer   l'ingénieur (m)
English   l'anglais (m)
enough   assez
environment   l'environnement (m)
era, period of time   l'époque (f)
eraser   la gomme
even if   même si
every day   tous les jours
everywhere   partout
exam   l'examen (m)
for example   par exemple
except   sauf
exit pass   la carte de sortie
expensive   cher(-ère)
eye   l'œil (m)
eyes   les yeux (m)

F

factory   l'usine (f)
faithful   fidèle
to fall   tomber
family room   la chambre familiale
fantastic   fantastique
far from   loin de
farmer   le fermier (m), la fermière (f)
fashion   la mode
fashion show   les défilés de mode (m)
fat   gros(se)
father   le père
fatty pork   le porc gras
February   février
to feel   se sentir
to feel well   se sentir bien
festival   la fête
field   le champ
to fill   remplir

finally, at last enfin
to finish finir
firm l'entreprise (f)
first d'abord
fish le poisson
fishing la pêche
to go fishing aller à la pêche
flat l'appartement (m)
flight le vol
floor l'étage (m)
'flu la grippe
flute la flute
to fly voler
fog le brouillard
food la nourriture
on foot à pied
foot le pied
football le football
for pour
to go for a walk (walks) faire une promenade (des promenades)
forbidden interdit(e)
foreign étranger(-ère)
foreigner l'étranger (m)
forest la forêt
to forget oublier
free gratuit(e)
French le français
Friday vendredi
fridge le frigo
friend le copain (m), la copine (f)
friends les copains (m)
from de
full board la pension complète
full of plein de
funny amusant(e), comique, drôle, rigolo, marrant(e)
furniture (item of) le meuble
future l'avenir (m)
in the future à l'avenir, au futur

G

game le jeu
garden le jardin
to garden faire du jardinage
gardening le jardinage
geography la géographie
to get on well with ... s'entendre bien avec ...
to get up se lever
girlfriend la petite amie
gite le gîte
to go aller
to go out sortir

goldfish le poisson rouge
good bien, bon(ne)
good cause la bonne cause
in good shape en bonne forme
grade (school work) la note
gramme le gramme
grandfather le grand-père
grandmother la grand-mère
great chouette, formidable
green vert(e)
green beans les haricots verts (m)
greengrocer's shop l'épicerie (f)
grey gris(e)
ground floor rez-de-chaussée
guided tour la visite guidée
guitar la guitare
gym le gymnase

H

habit l'habitude (f)
hair les cheveux (m)
half demi(e)
half board la demi-pension
half brother le demi-frère
ham le jambon
hand la main
handbag le sac à main
happy birthday! bon anniversaire!
harbour le port
hard dur(e), pénible
hard drugs les drogues dures (f)
hat le chapeau
to have a good time bien s'amuser
to have a lie-in faire la grasse matinée
to have a party faire la fête
to have the right to avoir le droit de
head la tête
health la santé
healthy eating une alimentation saine (f)
heart le cœur
heart disease les maladies cardiaques (f)
to help aider
here ici
by high-speed train en TGV
to go hiking faire des randonnées
hire la location
to hire louer
to hire a gite louer un gîte

historic monuments les monuments historiques (m)
historical historique
history l'histoire (f)
holiday camp la colonie de vacances
holidays les vacances (f)
homeless SDF (sans domicile fixe)
homework les devoirs (m)
to do homework faire les devoirs
horrible affreux(-euse)
horrid moche
horror films les films d'horreur (m)
to go horse riding faire du cheval
horse riding l'équitation (f)
hot chaud(e)
house la maison
housework la ménage
housing le logement
how? comment?
however cependant, pourtant
husband le mari

I

to go ice skating faire du patinage sur glace
ICT l'informatique (f)
ill malade
illness la maladie
immediately tout de suite
in dans
in, to à, en
included compris(e)
including y compris
industrial industriel(le)
information les renseignements (m)
information office le bureau de renseignements
in front of devant
inhabitant, occupant l'habitant (m)
instead of au lieu de
interactive whiteboard le tableau interactif
to be interested in s'intéresser à
interesting intéressant(e)
internet chatrooms les forums sur Internet
is est
Italy l'Italie (f)
IT room la salle d'informatique

J

jacket   la veste
January   janvier
jealous   jaloux(-ouse)
jeans   le jean
jewellery   les bijoux (m)
job   l'emploi (m), le poste, la place
judo   le judo
to do *judo*   faire du judo
July   juillet
jumper   le pull
June   juin

K

to *keep in shape*   garder la forme
keyboard   le clavier
kilo   le kilo
kilometer   le kilomètre
kind   gentil(le)
kitchen   la cuisine
knee   le genou
to *know (a fact)*   savoir

L

laboratory   le laboratoire
language   la langue
laptops   les ordinateurs portables (m)
large   grand(e)
to *last*   durer
late   en retard
later   plus tard
to *laugh*   rire
lazy   paresseux(-euse)
to *learn*   apprendre
leather (made of leather)   le cuir (en cuir)
to *leave*   sortir, quitter
left   à gauche
leg   la jambe
lemon   le citron
lemonade   la limonade
lesson   le cours
level   l'étage (m), le niveau
library   la bibliothèque
lift   l'ascenseur (m)
like   comme
to *listen (to)*   écouter
to *listen to music*   écouter de la musique
litre   le litre
little   petit(e)
a *little (of)*   un peu (de)
to *live*   vivre, loger
lively   animé(e)

liver   le foie
living room   la salle de séjour, le salon
lonely   seul(e)
a *long time*   longtemps
to *look*   regarder
to *lose*   perdre
a *lot*   beaucoup
lots of   beaucoup de, plein de
love   l'amour (m)
low   bas(se)
loyal   fidèle
to be *lucky*   avoir de la chance
lungs   les poumons (m)

M

main course   le plat principal
to *make*   faire, fabriquer
make-up   le maquillage
March   mars
mark (school work)   la note
market   le marché
marriage   le mariage
married   marié(e)
to *marry*   se marier
marvellous   merveilleux(-euse)
maths   les mathématiques (f)
May   mai
meal   le repas
mechanic   le mecanicien (m), la mecanicienne (f)
meat   la viande
to *melt (down)*   fonder
menu   le menu
metre   le mètre
microwave oven   le four à micro-ondes
midday   midi
in the *middle of*   au milieu de
midnight   minuit
minute   la minute
to *miss*   manquer
mobile phone   le (téléphone) portable
modern   moderne
Monday   lundi
month   le mois
once *more*   encore une fois
more (of)   encore (de)
morning   le matin
mother   la mère
motorway   l'autoroute (f)
mountain   la montagne
mountain bike   le VTT (vélo tout terrain)

mountaineering   l'alpinisme (m)
mouth   la bouche
to *move*   se déplacer
mp3 player   le lecteur mp3
museum   le musée
mushroom   le champignon
musician   le musicien
Muslim   musulman(e)

N

naughty   méchant(e)
near (very near)   près (tout près)
near to   près de
negative   negatif(-ive)
neighbour   le voisin
neither … nor   ni … ni
never   jamais
news   les actualités (f)
newspaper   le journal
next   ensuite, prochain(e)
next day   le lendemain
next to   à côté de
nice   gentil(le), sympa
night   la nuit
nightclub   la boîte de nuit
non-smoker   le non-fumeur
normally   d'habitude, généralement, normalement
north   le nord
nose   le nez
notebook   le cahier, le carnet
nothing   rien
November   novembre
now   maintenant
numerous   nombreux(-se)
nurse (m)   l'infirmier (m), l'infirmière (f)

O

obesity   l'obésité (f)
October   octobre
odour   l'odeur (f)
of   de
office   le bureau
often   souvent
old   ancien(ne), vieux/ vieil(le)
older   aîné(e)
old-fashioned   démodé(e)
on   sur
one   un
online   en ligne
in the *open air*   en plein air
in my *opinion*   à mon avis
opposite   en face de

optimistic   optimiste
or   ou
on the   *other side*   de l'autre côté
outside of   en dehors de
own   propre

P

packet   le paquet
parents   les parents (m)
park   le jardin public
to   *park*   stationner
partner   le / la partenaire
party   la fête
passenger   le passager
pasta   les pâtes (f)
pastille, lozenge   la pastille
pavement   le trottoir
to   *pay attention*   faire attention
PE   l'EPS
peaceful   tranquil(le)
peas   les petits pois (m)
pedestrian zone   la zone piétonne
pen   le stylo
pencil   le crayon
pencil case   la trousse
perhaps   peut-être
permit, licence   le permis
petrol   l'essence (f)
pharmacy   la pharmacie
physical activity   l'activité physique (f)
physics   la physique
piano   le piano
picnic   le pique-nique
picturesque   pittoreqsue
piece   le morceau
pink   rose
by   *plane*   en avion
plastic bag   le sac en plastique
to   *play*   jouer
to   *play table-tennis*   jouer au ping-pong
to   *play the clarinet*   jouer de la clarinette
playground   le terrain de jeux
playtime   la récréation
pleasant   agréable, content(e)
plenty   suffisamment
pocket money   l'argent de poche (m)
policeman   le policier
polluted   pollué(e)
poor   pauvre

pork   le porc
pork butcher's shop and delicatessen   la charcuterie
port   le port
positive   positif(-ive)
postcard   la carte postale
postman   le facteur
potato   la pomme de terre
present   le cadeau
the   *press*   la presse écrite
pressure   la pression
prices   les prix (m)
probably   sans doute
problem   le problème
programme (television)   l'émission (f)
to   *protect*   protéger
public transport   les transports en commun (m)
publicity   la publicité
purple   violet(tte)
pyjamas   le pyjama

Q

to   *quarrel*   se disputer
quickly   vite
quite   assez

R

radio   la radio
rain   la pluie
rarely   rarement
to   *read (to some reading)*   lire (faire de la lecture)
reading   la lecture
to   *receive*   recevoir
recently   récemment
recyclable   recyclable
to   *recycle*   recycler
recycling centre   le centre de recyclage
red   rouge
reduced price   le tarif réduit
to   *refuse*   refuser
regularly   régulièrement
relationships   les rapports (m)
to   *relax*   se relaxer, se détendre
to   *remarry*   se remarier
to   *reserve*   réserver
reserved   réservé(e)
responsibility   la responsabilité
return ticket   l'aller retour (m)
to   *revisit*   revisiter
rich   riche
ridiculous   ridicule
right   à droite

ringing of mobile phones   la sonnerie des téléphones portables
river   la rivière
romantic films   les films romantiques (m)
room   la pièce
roundabout   le rond-point
all   *routes*   toutes directions
rubbish   les déchets (m)
rubbish   nul(le)
rugby   le rugby
ruler   la règle
rules, regulations   le règlement
to   *run*   courir

S

sad   triste
safe and sound   sain et sauf
to go   *sailing*   faire de la voile
salary   le salaire
sales   les soldes (m)
satellite television   la télé par satellite
Saturday   samedi
to   *save*   sauver
to   *save up (money)*   faire des économies
school library   le COI
school report book   le carnet de notes
schoolbook   le livre scolaire
science   les sciences (f)
science fiction films   les films de science-fiction (m)
sea   la mer
seaside   le bord de la mer
seasonal work   le travail saisonnier
secondary (upper school)   le lycée
secretary   la secrétaire
selfish   égoïste
to   *sell*   vendre
semi-detached house   la maison jumelée
to   *send*   envoyer
sensational   sensass
sense of humour   le sens de l'humour
separated   séparé(e)
separation   la séparation
September   septembre
series (television)   le feuilleton
serious   grave

service charge (included) le service (compris)

service-station la station-service

to *set up, found* fonder

severe sévère

shampoo le shampooing

shelf l'étagère (f)

shirt la chemise

shoes les chaussures (f)

shop assistant le vendeur (m), la vendeuse (f)

shopping les courses (f)

to go *shopping* faire les magasins

shopping centre le centre commercial

shops les magasins (m)

shorts le short

to *show* montrer

shy réservé(e), timide

sick malade

since, for depuis

to *sing* chanter

singer le chanteur (m), la chanteuse (f)

single ticket, one-way ticket l'aller simple (m)

single-parent family la famille monoparentale

sister la sœur

situated situé(e)

size la pointure, la taille

skateboard le skate

skating rink la patinoire

to go *skiing* faire du ski

skirt la jupe

sleep le sommeil

to *sleep* dormir

sleeping bag le sac de couchage

slice la tranche

small petit(e)

to *smoke* fumer

smoker (f) le fumeur (m), la fumeuse (f)

so alors

soap le savon

soap opera le feuilleton

socks les chaussettes (f)

soft drugs les drogues douces (f)

sometimes parfois, quelquefois

somewhere quelque part

soon bientôt

so-so, ok comme ci comme ça

south le sud

Spain l'Espagne (f)

Spanish l'espagne (m)

specialities of the region les spécialités de la region (f)

to *spend* dépenser

spicy épicé(e)

sports field le terrain de sport

sporty sportif(-ive)

in *spring* au printemps

spring le printemps

stadium le stade

staff room la salle de professeurs

to *stamp* composter

starter l'entrée (f)

stay le séjour

steak le bifteck

stepbrother le demi-frère

stepfather le beau-père

stepmother la belle-mère

still déjà

stomach le ventre

stop l'arrêt (m)

to *stop* arrêter

straight on tout droit

strange bizarre

strawberry la fraise

street la rue

stressful stressant(e)

strict sévère

strong fort(e)

student l'étudiant (m), l'étudiante (f)

to *study* étudier

study period l'heure d'étude (f)

stupid stupide

stylish chic

subject la matière

suburbs la banlieue

to *succeed* réussir

suddenly soudain

sugar le sucre

suitcase la valise

in *summer* en été

summer l'été (m)

sun le soleil

to *sunbathe* bronzer

Sunday dimanche

super superbe

to *surf* surfer

sweatshirt le sweat

sweet sucré(e)

sweet, cute mignon(ne)

to *swim* nager

swimming la natation

to go *swimming* aller à la piscine

swimming costume le maillot de bain

swimming pool la piscine

T

tablet, pill le comprimé

to *take* prendre

to *take (an exam)* passer

to *take drugs* se droguer

to *take photos* prendre des photos

to *talk* parler

tall grand(e)

taste le goût

to *teach* enseigner

teacher le professeur

technician le technicien (m), la technicienne (f)

teeth les dents (f)

tennis le tennis

term le trimester

terrace la terrasse

textbook le livre scolaire

texts les textos (m)

theatre le théâtre

then puis, ensuite

there là

therefore donc

thermal spa la station thermale

thin maigre, mince

to *think* penser

thrilling passionnant(e)

throat la gorge

to *throw* jeter

Thursday jeudi

tie la cravate

tights le collant

on *time* à l'heure

timetable l'emploi du temps (m), l'horaire (m)

tin la boîte

tiresome pénible

to prevent, warn prévenir

tobacco le tabac

today aujourd'hui

together ensemble

toilet les toilettes (f)

tomato la tomate

tomorrow demain

too many people trop de monde

too much trop

tourism le tourisme

tourist touristique

tourist information office
l'office de tourisme (m), le syndicat d'initiative

towards   vers

town   la ville

town centre   le centre-ville

town hall   la mairie, l'hôtel de ville (m)

toys   les jouets (m)

track   la voie

traditional food   les plats traditionnels (m)

traffic   la circulation

traffic lights   les feux rouges

by train   en train

to train   s'entraîner

trainers   les baskets (f)

train station   la gare SNCF

to do training, an apprenticeship (in a firm)   faire un stage (en entreprise)

travel agent   l'agence de voyages (f)

trousers   le pantalon

truth   la vérité

to try   essayer

Tuesday   mardi

to turn   tourner

U

unbelievable   incroyable

under   sous

underground (train)   le métro

by underground   en métro

to understand   comprendre

understanding   compréhensif(-ive)

unemployed   sans travail

unemployment   le chômage

unfortunate   malheureux(-euse)

uniform   l'uniforme (m)

United States   les États-Unis (m)

upstairs   en haut

to use   utiliser

usually   d'habitude, généralement, normalement

V

vanilla ice cream   la glace à la vanille

varied   varié(e)

vegetable   le légume

vegetable soup   la soupe aux légumes

vegetarian   végétarien(ne)

very   très

video game   le jeu vidéo

view (fine view)   la vue (belle vue)

village   le village

viola   l'alto

violin   le violin

to visit   visiter

voluntary   bénévole

W

to wait (for)   attendre

waiter   le serveur

waiting room   la salle d'attente

waitress   la serveuse

to wake up   se réveiller

Wales   le pays de Galles

walk   la promenade

to walk the dog   promener le chien

walks, hikes   les randonnées (f)

war   la guerre

wardrobe   l'armoire (f)

war films   les films de guerre (m)

washing machine   la machine à laver

washing-up   la vaisselle

to watch   regarder

to watch DVDs   regarder des DVD

to watch telly   regarder la télé

water   l'eau (f)

water skiing   le ski nautique

watersports   des sports nautiques (m)

to wear   porter

website (to go to a website)   le site (aller sur un site)

Wednesday   mercredi

week   la semaine

weekend   le week-end

welcome   bienvenue

well-balanced   équilibré(e)

well-being   le bien-être

west   l'ouest (m)

what?   que? quel(le)?

when?   quand?

where?   où?

white   blanc(he)

who?   qui?

why?   pourquoi?

wicked   méchant(e)

wide   large

wife   la femme

wind   le vent

window   la fenêtre

to go windsurfing   faire de la planche à voile

windsurfing   la planche à voile

wine   le vin

in winter   en hiver

winter   l'hiver (m)

winter sports   les sports d'hiver (m)

with   avec

without   sans

woman   la femme

wood (made of wood)   le bois (en bois)

wool (made of wool)   la laine (en laine)

to work   travailler

work   le boulot

Y

year   l'an (m), l'année (f)

in year 7   en sixième

in year 8   en cinquième

in year 9   en quatrième

in year 10   en troisième

in year 11   en seconde

in year 12   en première

in year 13   en terminale

yellow   jaune

yesterday   hier

yoghurt   le yaourt

youth club   le club des jeunes

Acknowledgements

Illustrations:
Kathy Baxendale pp53, 58, 92 (1); Russ Cook pp61, 132, 142, 143; Mark Draisey pp14, 18, 20, 21, 25, 26, 35, 55 (5), 59, 63, 67, 77, 97, 99, 109 (reporter), 122, 127, 137, 139, 141, 144, 145; Mark Duffin p62; Robin Edmonds pp42, 81, 101 (2a A–E), 108, 123 (1a); Tony Forbes pp19, 36, 52 (2a), 75, 90 (2a), 111; Dylan Gibson p92 (2a); Celia Hart pp10, 11, 12, 18, 27, 28, 79, 91; Abel Ippolito pp38, 40, 52 (1a, 2b), 54, 55 (3a), 93, 101 (boy on bed), 103, 109 (2a A–C), 123 (2a), 136; Martin Sanders pp90 (1), 100

The authors and publisher would like to thank the following for permission to reproduce materials

Photographs courtesy of:
p9 © iStockphoto.com / lisegagne; 11 © Dolomiti – Fotolia.com, © Val Thoermer – Fotolia.com; p13 © National Gallery of Art, Washington DC, USA, Photograph by R. Doisneau / Rapho / Eyedea, Camera Press London; p17 (and banner) © iStockphoto.com / P_Wei; p21 © iStockphoto.com / peeterv; p22 © iStockphoto.com / borchee, © iStockphoto.com / ranplett, © Michal Adamczyk/123rf.com; p24 © iStockphoto.com / tomazl, © Studio1One. Image from BigStockPhoto.com; p32 © Bernardo Ertl. Image from BigStockPhoto.com; p34 © monkeybusinessimages – Fotolia.com, © iStockphoto.com / Yuri_Arcurs, © ifong. Image from BigStockPhoto.com, © HONGQI ZHANG/123rf.com; p38 courtesy of Médecins Sans Frontières; p50 © Images of France / Alamy, © Alain Jocard / Stringer / Getty Images; p51 (and banner) © iStockphoto.com / dennysb; p54 © nateperro – Fotolia.com, © paul prescott. Image from BigStockPhoto.com, © iStockphoto.com / jhorrocks; p56 © Ievgeniya Zakharova/123rf.com, © kuhar – Fotolia.com, © Kay. Image from BigStockPhoto.com; p60 © ginaellen. Image from BigStockPhoto.com; p64 © iStockphoto.com / iconogenic; p69 © Beboy – Fotolia.com; p70 © Alexander/ Fotolia, © matt_collingwood. Image from BigStockPhoto.com, © iStockphoto.com / matthewleesdixon, © Marta – Fotolia.com, © iStockphoto.com / fotovoyager; p72 © Ben Goode/123rf.com, © iStockphoto.com / elkor, © Nbina – Fotolia.com; p74 © iStockphoto.com / BettinaRitter, © Chrissie Shepherd/123rf, © iStockphoto.com / diane39, © iStockphoto.com / cgering; p76 © Durand Patrick/ Corbis Sygma, © Ron Hilton. Image from BigStockPhoto.com, © Uolir – Fotolia.com, © iStockphoto.com / Anyka; p78 © Christophe Testi /123rf.com; p79 © dfs – Fotolia.com; p88 © iStockphoto.com / gelyngfjell, © Andrew Fox / Alamy; p89 (and banner) © Justagirl. Image from BigStockPhoto.com; p94 © Oliver Grey; p96 © Kevin Eaves / 123rf.com, © iStockphoto.com / Lighthousebay, © Riviera. Image from BigStockPhoto.com, © Enna Van Duinen /123rf; p98 © cepesh. Image from BigStockPhoto.com, © Elena Elisseeva / 123rf.com; p100 © iStockphoto.com / daaronj, © hassan bensliman – Fotolia.com; p106 © Martin Jenkinson / Alamy; p107 © Sasha Radosavljevic / 123rf.com, © czardases / 123rf.com; p110 © iStockphoto.com / Nancy Nehring; p112 © iStockphoto.com / kreci, © Pat Tuson / Alamy, © Martina Berg – Fotolia.com; p120 © Stockfolio® / Alamy, © maredana. Image from BigStockPhoto.com, © iStockphoto.com / NoDerog; p121 (and banner) © Moodboard/123rf.com; p122 © Tatiana Markow/ Sygma/CORBIS; p124 © Martyn F. Chillmaid; p126 © QueenMother. Image from BigStockPhoto.com; p128 © iStockphoto.com / Tateos; p130 © AFP/Getty Images; p137 © iStockphoto.com / track5; p140 © iStockphoto.com / barsik, © ZanyZeus – Fotolia.com, © sbonk. Image from BigStockPhoto.com, © iStockphoto.com / ArtBoyMB; p152 © ImageState / Alamy, © lisafx. Image from BigStockPhoto.com